TARGET COSTING

The Next Frontier in Strategic Management

THE CAM-I TARGET COST CORE GROUP

SHAHID L. ANSARI
*California State University
Northridge*

JAN E. BELL
*California State University
Northridge*

JAMES H. CYPHER
Chrysler Corporation

PATRICIA H. DEARS
Texas Instruments

JOHN J. DUTTON
Arthur Anderson & Co., LLP

MARK D. FERGUSON
Allied Signal

KEITH HALLIN
*Boeing Commercial Airplane
Group*

CHARLES A. MARX
Arthur Anderson & Co., LLP

CHARLES G. ROSS
Eastman Kodak

PETER A. ZAMPINO
CAM -I/CMS

**Consortium for Advanced
Manufacturing International**

**Consortium for Advanced
Manufacturing International**

©Consortium for Advanced Manufacturing International, 1997

CAM-I
7850 N. Beltine Rd.
Suite 631
Irving, TX 75063 USA
Tel: 972 / 556-8058
Fax: 972 / 556-8009
www.cam-i.org

Library of Congress
ISBN: 1-932301-23-2

ACKNOWLEDGMENTS

Many companies and individuals have contributed to the success of this project. We thank and gratefully acknowledge the help of the following in particular:

Peter Van Hull, Arthur Andersen & Co., shared with us the global best practices survey conducted by his company.

Lynn Thompson shared the material on value engineering being used at Boeing.

Jim Carpenter shared Boeing's target costing experience on the 777 project.

Tom Sexton, presented to the group the target costing system used at Caterpillar Corporation.

Mark Brackon shared the target cost process used for the development of Chrysler Corporation's Neon.

Jim Houghtling presented Eastman-Kodak's supply chain management with respect to target costing.

Steve Turner discussed the target costing efforts at Texas Instruments in connection with the development of the digital micromirror device.

Bill Russo and Kevin Popis of Chrysler Corporation facilitated the sessions at which we developed the process model presented in Appendix A.

George Millush of Chrysler Corporation made many significant contributions to the development of the process model and provided subsequent feedback on draft chapters.

Dr. Judy Hennessey of California State University, Northridge, helped to clarify issues related to the voice of the customer in target costing.

Dr. Hiroshi Okano of Osaka City University identified and provided us with copies of Japanese language papers on target costing not available in the English language. He also presented his research on target costing at Toyota to the Target Cost Interest Group.

Ayako Ishizaki of California State University, Northridge, translated and prepared abstracts of Japanese literature. Her patience in translating highly technical papers has been invaluable for this project.

Dr. Carol Lawrence, University of Richmond; Dr. Patrick Keating, California State University, San Jose; and Roger White, GTE, provided useful ideas on prices, profit margins, and performance measurement that were used in the writing of Chapters 4 and 12.

Betsy Maclean Grosel of Allied Signal Corporation coordinated a summary of key English language articles on target costing.

Lionel Woodcock, CAM-I Europe, shared with us the target costing efforts of that group.

Randolph Holst, Society of Management Accountants of Canada, shared with us the society's publications on target costing, monitoring customer value, and performing competitive analysis.

Andrew Grisin of Eastman-Kodak provided useful feedback on earlier drafts of this book.

F O R E W O R D

The Consortium for Advanced Manufacturing International (CAM-I) is an organization devoted to performing and sharing leading edge research on topics vital to U.S. industry. It is unique in that it brings together industry and academia in collaborative research projects. The research issues are selected by practicing managers and the research is undertaken by leading thinkers in the field. The results of such research are reported for practitioners and represent the best current thinking in the field.

Since its inception in 1987, CAM-I's Cost Management Systems (CMS) program has pushed the frontiers of cost management research. Starting with the book by Brimson and Berliner, *Cost Management for Today's Advanced Manufacturing,* (Harvard Business School Press, Boston, MA, 1988) the CMS program has produced a number of important research articles and monographs on topical subjects such as activity based costing, capacity management, strategy deployment, and capital investment management. The target costing project continues this tradition of excellence in cost management research.

This project was chosen because industry recognized that a robust target costing process is critical for success in today's global economy. The process used to develop the material in this book is unique. It represents a truly collaborative effort between industry and academia in performing the research. Materials were collected and organized by a "core group," which included seven industry representatives and one academic member. The group met every six weeks to discuss, organize, and distill key ideas from research materials collected. Several brainstorming sessions were used to organize these materials.

The research of the core group was augmented by a larger "interest group," whose members undertook tasks such as translating the key articles on target costing from Japanese and examining performance measurement, competitive intelligence, and profit margin issues within the target costing context. The larger group also met with the core group once every quarter to provide guidance and feedback.

The core group's effort has been aided by many organizations, who shared their experiences in the area of target costing: Arthur Andersen, Caterpillar, Chrysler, Boeing, Toyota, Texas Instruments, Eastman-Kodak, and Sandia National Laboratories. The contributions of these organizations to the project has made it possible to present a "native's view" of practice from the perspective of those who have experienced it. Their commitment also reinforces their belief in the new collaborative approach to CAM-I/CMS research.

I thank all the members of the core group for their dedicated effort in producing this book. While every member has made important contributions to this effort, its success is due largely to John Dutton's leadership. As team leader for the interest and core groups, John has been indefatigable. He has organized meetings, identified data sources, coordinated team efforts, and kept the momentum going. As a senior manager with Arthur Anderson & Co., LLP, John has unique insight into industry practice that draws upon Andersen's global best practices data base. He was responsible for obtaining this critical best practice information and making it available to the research team.

The target costing interest group has been ably supported in this work by Dr. Shahid Ansari, who had the unenviable task of converting raw data and the results of brainstorming sessions and discussions into meaningful text. Shahid's ability to organize materials from many different sources, to distill them with clarity, and to add his own teaching, research, and consulting materials have been invaluable for this project.

Last, but not least, Nancy Thomas and Tram Ngyuen provided the critical administrative support to make this project happen and to keep us all on track. I thank them for their dedication.

We hope that you and your organization will reap many benefits by implementing a target costing process using the principles and methods recommended in this book.

> **Peter Zampino**
> **Director of Advanced Management Programs**

CHAIRMAN'S REMARKS

Just as quality emerged as a key competitive issue in the 1980s, cost management will be critical to survival and success into the next millennium. This landmark work by the CAM-I/CMS target costing core group is a synthesis of research, global best practices, and experience. The book describes the scope, framework, process, and tools for implementing a robust and integrated target costing process.

Target costing represents a fundamental shift in enterprise management. As a comprehensive profit planning system, target costing is based on the fundamental principle that cost management starts before a product is produced. It is driven by competitive market prices and shaped and guided by the voice of the customer. Target costing requires the participation of all functions within an organization. Ultimately, it should involve the various members of the value chain, including suppliers, dealers, and recyclers. The process provides a common focus for the enterprise and makes cost management everyone's responsibility.

The two year process used in developing this book was unique. We had frequent core group meetings, in which we shared and generated ideas, explored new concepts, and defined the content of this work. Every team member made important and valuable contributions to this effort. This book is a testament to the persistence and cooperation of the team.

I hope that you find the content of this book stimulating and beneficial on your own journey to excellence.

September, 1996
John J. Dutton
Chairman CAM-I/CMS Target Costing Core and Interest Group
Senior Manager, Advanced Cost Management Leadership Group
Arthur Andersen & Co., LLP

C O N T E N T S

Chapter 4

Establishing Price and Profit Margins   29

Chapter 5

From Allowable to Achievable Target Cost   42

Chapter 8

Target Costing Organization and Participants   98

Chapter 9

Filling the Information Gap   111

APPENDICES

Appendix A

Target Cost Process Map   180

Appendix B

Relations with Other Business Processes   213

Appendix C

Tools and Process Milestones   217

Appendix D

Target Costing and Legacy Costs: An Illustration   224

Appendix E

Sample Deployment Tools   229

CHAPTER

Introduction

TARGET COSTING AT CHRYSLER

The year 1990 was not the best of times at Chrysler Corporation. It culminated a decade in which stiff competition from the Japanese and European auto industry had squeezed profits for all three U.S. automakers. The quality was catching up to its competition's but the years of bad publicity had taken their toll, and the market did not share the perception of increased quality. The competition had kept adding new features and new technology. Despite a strengthening yen, the Japanese auto industry maintained its share of the U.S. market. Chrysler was strapped for cash, profitability was down, and the stock price hit a low of $10 per share. Things looked grim. The only thing going for Chrysler was its immense faith in comebacks. After all, it had been there once before, in the 1970s, and had made a comeback with the K-Car and the Minivan.

This time, however, it needed more than a hit product. It needed to restructure the way it did business. Chrysler management shifted to a focus on process. A key process introduced was target costing. It was applied to all product development efforts in the company, including the Neon, a new small car developed for the lower price range. The Neon program was launched in late 1990, and the company introduced the first models on the road in 1994. The results of using target costing on the Neon were impressive. The Neon:

Concluded

- Met customer requirements for safety and driveability by providing dual airbags and a powerful (132 cc) engine.
- Was named Auto of the Year in 1994.
- Had a relatively short development time, going from product concept to market in 31 months.
- Came in below its projected development and investment budget.
- Was one of the few small cars that earned a positive return.

Chrysler's share price has gone from $10 per share in 1990 to $54 per share in 1995. Since 1990, its revenues have increased by 70 percent and market share in numbers of cars and trucks sold has increased by 2.1 percent. However, its profits and cash flow have increased almost 400 percent since 1990. The firm's profit margin ratio, which was 0.33 percent in 1990, had gone up to 7.1 percent in 1995. This is the best evidence of how well Chrysler's target costing process has managed costs. But this is not all. Chrysler's target costing process has transformed the organization. It has created a culture characterized by effective cross-functional teams, use of simple product/process design rules, engineering decisions based on cost impact, use of productivity enhancing production processes, elimination of expensive and time consuming changes to products, and early customer, supplier, and dealer input into product design.

A target cost is the allowable amount of cost that can be incurred on a product and still earn the required profit from that product. It is a market driven costing system in which cost targets are set by considering customer requirements and competitive offerings. Cost targets are achieved by focusing on product and process design and by making continuous improvements in all support processes.

Exhibit 1–1 provides an overview of how target costing joins a firm's external markets with its internal design efforts.

The Chrysler story shows how a target costing process, when well executed, can improve a firm's competitive position by reducing costs, improving quality, and reducing time to market. Nor is Chrysler the only success story in this respect. Caterpillar has a similar story. It, too, has made an impressive comeback after losing considerable ground to competitors such as Komatsu. Target costing not only made Caterpillar competitive again, it has become a part of their organizational culture—a core competence.

E X H I B I T 1–1

Target Costing—An Overview

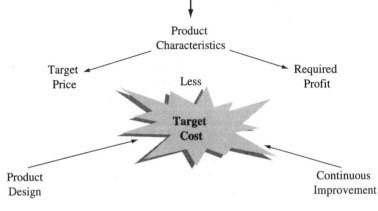

Even in organizations that have not fully implemented target costing, the results have been impressive. Boeing is a good example. While the company is still implementing a fully integrated target costing system, it already has realized significant cost savings on the 777 plane. The use of target costing tools, such as value engineering, has yielded impressive results on other Boeing projects as well. Some sample results are shown in Exhibit 1–2.

What Chrysler and Caterpillar learned after going through hard times, and what Boeing is learning, is a lesson very familiar to Japanese companies. Target costing originated in Japan in the 1960s. As with quality, Japanese industry took a simple American idea called *value engineering*[1] and transformed it into a dynamic cost reduction and profit planning system. This is not to minimize the achievement. As you will appreciate on reading this book, target costing is a system that goes well beyond value engineering and cost reduction. It is a comprehensive system for profit planning that requires a significant investment in information and tools. Today more than 80 percent

---

[1]Value engineering originated at General Electric during World War II as an effort to do more with less when there were shortages of parts. Later it became an organized effort to examine how to provide the needed functions in a product at the lowest cost.

EXHIBIT 1–2

Effect of Target Costing on Various Boeing Projects

Project	Results
737 Flight Deck Valve	90% recurring cost reduction
	79% part count reduction
737/757 Sidewall Panel Assembly	$14,700 savings per airplane
	45% part count reduction
737 #1 Window Replacement	Time reduced from 12 hours to 3 hours
737 Entry Door Operating Force	Improved Door Forces
737-X Stowage Bin Support	56% cost reduction
	12 lbs per ship set savings

of all assembly industries in Japan use target costing.[2] Naturally, some of the best practitioners of target costing are leading Japanese companies such as Toyota, Nissan, Sony, Matsushita, Nippon Denso, Daihatsu, Canon, NEC, Olympus, and Komatsu.

TARGET COST IMPERATIVE

What makes target costing so important today? The answer lies in the nature of the contemporary industrial environment. Today's businesses face a globally competitive environment that changes rapidly and plays by its own set of rules.

Quality through technology leadership, a traditional competitive strategy, no longer provides companies with a lasting competitive edge. For instance, a major U.S. electronics company, a recognized technology leader, often has not made an adequate return on its investment in new products. Competitors who are technology followers but cost leaders have often profited from the firm's innovations.[3] Similarly, defense aerospace firms find that the Pentagon, their prime customer for new technology, no longer can afford to buy on technology alone. Cost plus has been replaced with fixed price contracting. In addition, quality differences between competitors are declining,

---

[2]See, for example, Y. Kato, "Target Costing Support Systems: Lessons from Leading Japanese Companies," *Management Accounting Research,* March 1993, 4, pp. 33–47. Also, see T. Tani, H. Okano, N. Shimizu, Y. Iwabuchi, J. Fukuda, and S. Cooray, "Target Cost Management in Japanese Companies: Current State of the Art," *Management Accounting Research,* 1994, 5, pp. 67–81.

[3]For an excellent discussion of why firms fail to profit from their innovations, see Howard Guile, *Profiting from Innovation.* (Free Press: NY), 1992.

making it difficult to differentiate on that variable. While quality has to be high, cost must be reduced as well. Toyota's management captures this well:

> The lowest-cost producers of the highest-quality products will cope best with the present slump. They soon will start growing and profiting again. Some never stopped . . . Costs, especially, are a decisive factor. Most automakers now are competitive in terms of product quality. But big differentials remain in cost structures . . . **Cost management is going to be for the automobile industry in the 1990s what quality control was in the 1970s and '80s.** (S. Toyoda & T. Toyoda, *Toyota Annual Report,* October 1993, p.1.)

In addition to quality and cost, time has become an important third leg of this new strategic triangle. For example, INTEL maintains its market leadership by providing high quality central processing units (CPUs) for personal computers. It was also the first to introduce a new generation of chips while bringing down the costs of the prior generation of chips. This makes INTEL the market leader in quality, cost, and time.

This changed and more complex and competitive business environment has four major characteristics. It is:

- *Competitive,* because prices are decreasing over time in many key industries and there are new entrants with lower cost structures. As the yen and deutsche mark have become stronger against the dollar, Japanese and German industries have searched for ways to reduce costs in order not to increase prices in the U.S. market. New entrants, especially in Asia, who enjoy structural cost advantages, have also put a downward pressure on prices. In many of these countries, environmental regulations are less stringent, skilled labor is relatively inexpensive, technology is sophisticated, and government regulations are fewer. This lowers their cost of doing business and increases the downward pressure on prices.

- *Rapidly changing,* because the dissemination of technology and knowledge has accelerated considerably. New markets, new technologies, and new competitors such as Eastern Europe and the former Soviet republics are constantly challenging the competitive advantage of industrialized nations while simultaneously opening new markets.

- *Unforgiving of mistakes or delays,* because shorter product lives have increased the rate at which new products have to be introduced. At the same time, there is less time to respond to changes in the marketplace or to make mistakes. Product, profit, and cost planning are necessary to manage these shorter product cycles.

■ *Demanding* because sophisticated consumers are demanding better quality products with more features at an affordable price. Decreasing quality or increasing prices is not a viable long-term strategy.

How does a firm respond to this changed environment? It needs processes that:

■ *Anticipate and react* to environmental changes before a firm is affected by them. This means avoiding problems before they occur rather than correcting them after they happen.

■ *Continually improve* the operations and not merely seek a temporary equilibrium.

■ *Externally focus* on customer requirements and competitive threats. Customer requirements drive the organization. Knowledge of rivals' competitive strategies and product offerings influence all product and profit plans.

■ *Systematically relate* all elements, internal and external, so problems are solved holistically rather than incrementally. Internally, this requires cross-functional integration so the problem is viewed and solved as a whole. Externally, it means building long-term relations with the suppliers and other members of the extended enterprise to bring a common perspective to problem solving.

Does a traditional approach to profit planning and cost management do this? The answer is no. Traditional cost systems were designed in an era of benign environments, when product life cycles were long, Japan made toys, and Singapore and Korea were countries referred to as *underdeveloped*. Traditional approaches are inappropriate for today's environment because they attempt to control costs and quality after production, try to search for a temporary equilibrium, are internally focused on efficiency, and solve problems incrementally rather than holistically.

A target costing process is better suited to meet the needs of the environment we face today. As we will show you in this book, a well-designed target costing system integrates all three elements of the strategic triangle: quality, cost, and time. It is a system of profit planning and cost reduction that manages costs before they are incurred, is committed to continual improvement in product and process designs, is externally focused on customers and competition, and systematically relates the complex web of value-chain and cross-functional relationships into a cohesive and integrated planning and execution system. We will demonstrate that target costing will improve profits and returns dramatically for a business committed to effectively executing the process.

WHY THIS BOOK

As we said earlier, target costing has been successfully used as a strategic weapon by many Japanese companies for nearly two decades. However, it is relatively new and generally not applied well by most American and European companies. Even companies that are adopting target costing have run into difficulties in employing it successfully. There are several reasons for this:

- Many companies mistake some elements of target costing systems, such as affordable design criteria, design to cost, or design for manufacturability, for target costing. They fail to appreciate the breadth of target costing as a process for integrating strategic planning with profit and cost planning. This lulls many companies into thinking that they have arrived when they only have begun the journey.

- Target costing is a relatively new and largely undocumented technique in the English-language literature. The writing that exists fails to convey the strategic significance of target costing as a competitive weapon for today's global marketplace.

- The basic ideas of target costing are so simple and so intuitive that there is a tendency to underestimate their power or scope. Many companies often view target costing as another cost estimation or a reduction method like budgeting, regression analysis, or learning curve applications.

- Target costing requires cross-functional teams to take ownership and responsibility for costs. This key attribute typically is not part of today's engineering and marketing culture. Most engineers and salespeople regard cost management to be a finance function. Finance, for its part, must provide cost data that can support the type of analysis that target cost systems require.

OVERVIEW OF THIS BOOK

This book is the result of more than two years of research by the CAM-I Target Costing Core Group. The group consists of managers from companies that have recently installed or are in the process of installing target costing systems and academics and consultants who have or currently are working with companies on target costing. We have drawn upon a number of data sources for writing this book.

First, recognizing that Japan is a leader in the area, we set about to learn from the Japanese experience. It quickly became apparent to us that simply reviewing the English-language literature on target costing was not sufficient.

Therefore, we read and translated more than 80 major articles on target costing written in Japanese. This provided us with valuable insights about some of the details of the process missing in the English-language literature on the subject.

Second, Arthur Andersen & Co., LLP, shared with us some valuable data on global best practices of Japanese, U.S., and European companies in the area of product development and target costing. It also shared training materials, lessons from client engagements, and leading edge developments in target costing.

Finally, many U.S. companies shared their own experiences with full or partial implementation of target costing. Boeing, Chrysler, Eastman-Kodak, and Texas Instruments have all actively participated in this research. In addition, Caterpillar, Rockwell, and Sandia National Laboratories have also shared with us their efforts in this area.

This book is meant for managers and companies interested in strengthening their strategic and competitive advantage in the marketplace. It is written for all managers: marketing, engineering, finance, support, and logistics. We hope that those in each function will see how they participate and contribute to a firm's target costing efforts.

The organization of this book reflects our view of target costing as a strategic process that brings a different philosophy to profit and cost management. Target costing requires changes in an organization's internal and external relationships, necessitates investment in new information and tools, and requires a deployment plan.

Chapter 2 provides a formal definition of target costing, describes its intellectual foundations and key principles, and introduces some of the terminology and acronyms used in the following chapters. Our purpose is to show that target costing is based on foundations and principles very different from traditional cost management systems. Chapter 3 and Appendix A present details of the target costing process. An important motivation is to show that the target costing process requires both a "top-down" perspective of establishing target costs and a "bottom-up" perspective of attaining these costs. It also shows that the target costing process requires support from many other critical processes within a company. Chapter 4 deals with the establishment of target costs. It looks at how to set prices and profit margins. Chapter 5 and Appendix D discuss steps in attaining target costs. They illustrate how costs are analyzed, targets decomposed, estimates made, and costs reduced.

Chapters 6 through 9 deal with the organizational relationships that enable target costing to function effectively. The first one is the relationship with the customer. Chapter 6 addresses how to bring the voice of the customer into target costing. Chapter 7 links target costing with the economic value chain of suppliers, dealers, and recyclers. It deals with the role and participation of the extended enterprise in target costing. Finally, Chapter 8 shows the role of cross-functional teams in target costing. It discusses the composition of teams that participate at each stage of target costing as well as the roles of the process owner and top management.

Chapters 9 and 10 deal with the technical enablers of target costing. Chapter 9 outlines the type of information that needs to be collected and how to collect it, organize it, and share it with cross-functional teams. Chapter 10 and Appendixes B and C deal with the support processes and tools for target costing. They describe how target costing relates to other business processes. Also, they discuss what support tools are used, when they are used, where in the organization to find the functional expertise, and how much investment might be needed to acquire various tools.

Chapter 11 pulls together the entire process in a simple to follow example that integrates the discussions from all the previous chapters. Chapter 12 ends this book with a discussion of how to deploy target costing in an organization. Practical suggestions and advice on how to proceed with deployment are covered in this chapter and in Appendix E.

This book, because of its comprehensive coverage of the subject matter, may create an impression that target costing is a daunting task. This is not our intention. While we want to emphasize that full benefits from target costing can come only from a complete implementation, we can reap many of the benefits of target costing as we are getting there. It may be a long journey but it is also one that provides rewarding travel as well as a rewarding destination. Our message is simple and can be summed up in the ancient Chinese proverb: A thousand mile journey begins with the first step.

2
CHAPTER

Foundations of Target Costing

This chapter provides a formal definition of *target costing,* describes its fundamental principles, and traces these principles to their intellectual roots. We compare the ideas and concepts underlying target costing with those that form the foundations of traditional approaches to cost management. Our discussion is designed to help firms assess the extent to which they have embraced the key concepts of target costing. We also introduce terminology that is necessary to understand the discussion in later chapters of this book. There are three key messages in this chapter.

KEY MESSAGES

- Target costing is a strategic profit and cost management process. Six key principles within it represent a way of thinking about cost management that is quite different from traditional approaches to cost management and profit planning. They are:

    Price led costing

    Customer focus

    Focus on design of products and processes

    Cross-functional teams

> Life cycle cost reduction
>
> Value chain involvement

- The intellectual roots of target costing are in open systems theory, a body of knowledge that recognizes that it is better to proactively manage systems before they deviate from their intended paths than take corrective action after they have deviated.
- Successful target costing requires being faithful to both its intellectual roots and its key principles. The ideas and principles need to be adopted as a whole. Picking and choosing among them is likely to be suboptimal.

TARGET COSTING—DEFINITION AND KEY PRINCIPLES

The basic idea of a target cost is fairly simple and straightforward. It is the allowable cost of a product that yields the required rate of return. The target costing process, however, is complex and multifaceted. We define it thus:

> The target costing process is a system of profit planning and cost management that is price led, customer focused, design centered, and cross functional. Target costing initiates cost management at the earliest stages of product development and applies it throughout the product life cycle by actively involving the entire value chain.

The purpose of target costing is to ensure adequate profits by undertaking simultaneous profit and cost planning. Our definition contains six key fundamental ideas or principles that provide the conceptual foundations for target costing. These six principles are explained next.

Principle 1. Price Led Costing

A target costing system sets cost targets by subtracting the *required profit margin* from the *competitive market price*. (Chapter 4 describes this process in detail.) This is summarized in the equation

$$C = P - \pi$$

where C = target cost
P = competitive market price
π = target profit

Price is typically controlled by the situation in the marketplace, and target profit is determined by the financial requirements of a firm and its industry. For example, if the competitive market price for a product is \$100, and a company needs a 15 percent profit margin to remain financially viable in its industry, then the target cost for this product is $85 (100 – 15). Price led costing has two important subprinciples.

    1a. Market prices define *product and profit plans*. These plans are analyzed frequently so that a firm's product portfolio provides resources only to products that produce consistent and reliable profit margins.

    1b. The target costing process is driven by active *competitive intelligence and analysis*. An understanding of what is behind market prices is used for meeting or pre-empting competitive threats and challenges.

Principle 2. Focus on Customers

Target costing systems are market driven. The voice of the customer is paramount and represented continuously throughout the process. Customer requirements for quality, cost, and time are simultaneously incorporated in product and process decisions and guide cost analysis. It is essential to understand what customers want and what the firm's competition is currently doing or might do to meet customer needs. A target cost cannot be attained by sacrificing the features customers want, lowering the performance or reliability of a product, or by delaying its introduction in the marketplace.

    A focus on customers drives engineering development activities. The demands of the marketplace shape engineering requirements. Product development is not a hobby shop for technologists. Product feature and function enhancements take place only if: (1) they meet customer expectations, (2) customers are willing to pay for them, and (3) the additions enhance market share or sales volume.

Principle 3. Focus on Design

Target costing systems consider the design of products and processes key to cost management. They spend more time at the design stage and reduce time to market by eliminating expensive and time consuming changes needed later. By contrast, traditional cost reduction methods focus on economies of scale, learning curves, waste reduction, and yield improvement to manage costs. Four subprinciples capture the implications of this design orientation.

    3a. Target costing systems manage costs before they are incurred rather than afterward. Exhibit 2–1 shows the typical relationship between committed and incurred product costs. As depicted, the

E X H I B I T   2–1

Comparison of Committed and Incurred Costs

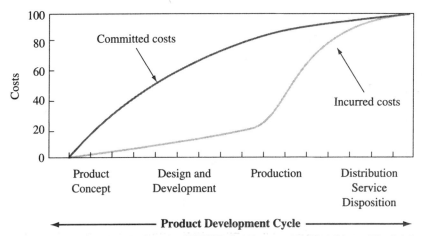

Source: Adapted from the life cycle costing discussion, CAM-I/CMS, *Cost Management for Today's Advanced Manufacturing System* (Arlington, Texas: CAM-I/CMS, 1991), p. 140.

majority of the costs are committed at the design stage while most of the costs are incurred at the production stage. This is why the target costing process focuses on design; that is, when costs are committed. It looks at the impact of design on all costs, from R&D to disposition, which allows cost reduction over the entire life cycle of a product.

3b. Target costing systems challenge engineers to look at the cost impact of product, technology, and process designs. All engineering decisions are filtered through a relative customer value impact assessment before being incorporated into the design. As one Danish manufacturer phrased it, it is design driven by "state of the market" rather than "state of the art" technology.

3c. Target costing systems encourage all participating functions of the firm to examine designs, so product or engineering changes are made before the product goes into production. In traditional cost systems, many of these changes occur well after production commences. Exhibit 2–2 compares this timing difference between the two approaches. World class practitioners of target costing have very few engineering changes after production starts while companies not using target costing typically have a significant number of design changes well after production starts.

EXHIBIT 2–2

Comparison of Engineering Changes

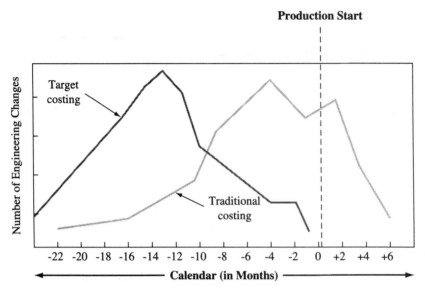

Source: Adapted from a Boeing Company manual.

3d. Target costing systems encourage simultaneous engineering of products and processes rather than sequential engineering. This reduces development time and cost by allowing problems to be solved earlier in the process.

Principle 4. Cross-Functional Involvement

Target costing uses product and process teams, with members representing design and manufacturing engineering, production, sales and marketing, materials procurement, cost accounting, service, and support. These cross-functional teams also include outside participants, such as suppliers, customers, dealers, distributors, service providers, and recyclers. The teams are responsible for a product from initial concept through production. Downstream functions are part of product development and help to avoid problems that might occur later. For example, problems with shipping or possible environmental costs can be avoided if these functional areas participate before a product or process design is final. Cross-functional participation also cuts the time to market by reducing design reviews and engineering changes. The time to market is closely related to cost reductions and quality increases, since problems are caught and fixed early in the development cycle.

A cross-functional team is not a set of specialists who contribute their expertise and leave; they are responsible for the entire product. A good example is Chrysler's Neon. During the development of the car, the accountants assigned to the team traveled to Nova Scotia in the winter to observe "crash testing." This was done to help make them understand how the product works, take ownership of the product, and appreciate the impact of their recommendations on a product's performance.

Principle 5. Life Cycle Orientation

Target costing considers all the costs of owning a product over its life, such as purchase price, operating costs, maintenance and repairs, and disposition costs. Its goal is to minimize the life cycle costs for both the customer and the producer. For example, a customer who owns a refrigerator pays more than the initial purchase price. The customer must pay for electricity (operating cost), repairs, and any final disposition cost of removing the refrigerator at the end of its useful life.[1] From a producer's point of view, life cycle costing means minimizing all costs from birth (R&D) to death (disposition or recycling costs). In the case of the refrigerator, a design that reduces weight, locates parts for easy access during repairs, and uses remanufacturable materials will decrease the delivery, installation, repair, and disposition costs of the refrigerator. Two subprinciples are embedded in this principle.

5a. From a customer's viewpoint, a life cycle focus means minimizing the cost of ownership of the product. This means lowering the costs of operating, using, repairing and disposing of the product.

5b. From the producer's viewpoint, a life cycle focus means minimizing development, production, marketing, distribution, support, service, and disposition costs.

Principle 6. Value-Chain Involvement

Target costing involves all members of the value chain, such as suppliers, dealers, distributors, and service providers, in the target costing process. It diffuses cost reduction efforts throughout the value chain by developing a collaborative relationship with all members of the "extended enterprise." A target costing

---

[1]The costs of disposition can be very significant for products that have an adverse environmental impact.

system is based on long-term and mutually beneficial relationships with suppliers and other members of the value chain such as distributors and recyclers.

TARGET COSTING VERSUS TRADITIONAL COST MANAGEMENT

These six features distinguish target costing from traditional approaches to profit and cost planning. The traditional approach to profit planning used by many companies is a *cost plus* approach. This approach typically estimates costs of production first, then adds a profit margin to obtain a market price. If the market is unwilling to pay the price, then the firm tries to find cost reductions. Target costing starts with a market price and a planned profit margin for a product and establishes an *allowable cost* for the product. Product and process design is used thereafter to reduce product cost so it is equal to this allowable cost. Exhibit 2–3 provides a comparison of the traditional cost plus approach with the target costing approach.

INTELLECTUAL FOUNDATIONS OF TARGET COSTING

The differences between traditional and target costing approaches to profit and cost planning reflect the different intellectual foundations on which each is built. These foundations have their origins in systems theory, from which

EXHIBIT 2–3

Comparison of Target Costing And Cost-Plus Approaches

Cost Plus	Target Costing
Market considerations not part of cost planning.	Competitive market considerations drive cost planning.
Costs determine price.	Prices determine costs.
Waste and inefficiency is the focus of cost reduction.	Design is key to cost reduction.
Cost reduction is not customer driven.	Customer input guides cost reduction.
Cost accountants are responsible for cost reduction.	Cross-functional teams manage costs.
Suppliers are involved after product is designed.	Suppliers are involved early.
Minimizes initial price paid by customer.	Minimizes cost of ownership to customer.
Little or no involvement of value chain in cost planning.	Involves the value chain in cost planning.

many of our contemporary ideas about management and control have emerged. A traditional cost plus approach represents a "closed systems" approach. This approach ignores the interaction between an organization and its environment, considers very few variables in explaining system behavior, takes corrective action after observing actual results, and attempts to conform to a predetermined standard. Target costing represents an "open systems" approach. This approach recognizes the importance of an organization's adaptation to its environment, considers a more complex set of interactions in explaining system behavior, takes corrective action before actual outcomes occur, and recognizes the importance of the need to move to higher standards over time.

Exhibit 2–4 summarizes these four key differences between traditional cost management and target costing. Traditional cost systems are focused on internal cost efficiency rather than external market demands. In addition, cost management efforts are restricted to a firm's boundaries and not across the value chain. Postproduction variances play a key role in cost reduction instead of product and process planning. Finally, costs

E X H I B I T 2–4

Intellectual Foundations of Cost Management Approaches Compared

Systems Theory Concept	Traditional Cost Management (Closed Systems)	Target Costing (Open Systems)
Relations with external environment	Ignores external environment; cost system focuses on internal measures of efficiency.	Interacts with external environment to respond to customer needs and competitive threats.
Number of variables considered	No consideration of cross-functional or extra-organizational impact of cost system.	Considers many complex relationships among functions and across the value chain.
Form of regulation	After the fact, based on cost incurred and correction of error using variance information.	Before the fact, by anticipating and designing costs out of a product before production.
Purpose of regulation or control	Keep costs to a prespecified limit set by standards or budgets.	Continuous improvement of cost for both customers and producers over a product's life.

are kept within some prespecified level of standard costs, and no effort is made to improve standards over time. Since closed systems theory is designed for stable and predictable environments, it is inappropriate for today's dynamically changing and highly unpredictable business environments.

IMPLICATIONS FOR PRACTICE

The influence of open systems thinking is quickly apparent if we examine the six fundamental principles of target costing discussed earlier in this chapter. The intellectual origins of these principles have two implications for practice.

First, *target costing is a business tool as well as a holistic way of managing business*. Holism demands that we embrace the whole and not just adopt components piecemeal. For example, it is insufficient to institute one element of target costing such as concurrent engineering or design to cost and conclude that a target costing system is in place.

Second, to use target costing effectively, we must be *faithful to both the intellectual concepts it is built upon,* open systems theory, *and its fundamental principles,* which are rooted in practice. It is not enough to have one without the other. Unfortunately, many firms or managers pick and choose principles they like or find easy to implement and say "we are doing target costing." Unless you are willing to ultimately adopt all principles, you are unlikely to get the full benefits of target costing. If supplier partnerships are problematic, do not expect cost reductions or improvement ideas to percolate freely from them. If you are not serious about focusing on customers, you are highly unlikely to have an effective target costing system.

SUMMARY

This chapter has explored the intellectual and practical foundations of target costing systems. We compared the intellectual foundations and fundamental principles of target costing with those that underlie traditional cost management systems. These latter were designed as closed systems that strive to keep costs within acceptable limits. The closed systems approach ignores the environment and therefore does not orient an organization toward changing markets, processes, and technologies. It also does not anticipate cost problems or move the organization down a continuous path of improvement and customer responsiveness. Target costing uses an open systems approach that is externally focused. It is responsive to customer needs and competitive threats. Profits are planned and costs are managed when committed and not when incurred.

Many companies adhere to one or more principles of target costing and mistakenly assume they have adopted the entire process. This is a mistake. Successful target costing means being faithful to the intellectual and practical principles of target costing. A pick and choose approach to these principles is unlikely to lead to effective target costing.

3

CHAPTER

The Target Costing Process

This chapter provides an overview of the target costing process. The description contains technical terms that may be unfamiliar. You may wish to consult the Glossary at the end of the book now or as you come across these terms. The Glossary provides a simple explanation of these technical terms.

Target costing, by nature, is a strategic process. It has two major phases and requires the support of many other key organizational processes. A step by step description of the subprocesses, inputs, outputs, tools, and participants involved in target costing is detailed in Appendix A. We want to communicate five key messages in this chapter.

KEY MESSAGES

- Target costing takes place within the strategic planning and product development cycles of a firm. Product design goes through this development cycle in a recursive, rather than linear, fashion.
- The first phase of target costing is the establishment phase. The focus here is on defining a product concept and setting allowable cost targets for products or a family of products.
- The second phase of target costing is the attainment phase. This phase transforms the allowable target costs into achievable target costs.

- The establishment and attainment phases of target costing occur at different points in the product development cycle. Different organizational processes play primary and secondary roles in these two phases.

- Target costing is supported by many other business processes. The success of target costing depends on these other processes being performed effectively within an organization.

THE CONTEXT OF TARGET COSTING

Target costing is intimately linked to an organization's competitive strategy and its product development cycle.

Competitive strategy defines the *goals* that an organization must attain to satisfy market demands and remain profitable. Target costing provides the *means* by which the organization achieves these goals. It does so by integrating the strategic variables of market trends, customer needs, technology advances, and quality requirements into a product definition that meets a customer's price, quality, and time expectations. Target costing is the simultaneous planning of how to satisfy customers, capture market share, generate profits, and plan and manage costs. Without a target costing system, meeting competitive prices and generating acceptable returns on a consistent basis is difficult, if not impossible, in today's environment.

The product development cycle provides the other context for target costing. Target costing manages costs at the design stage when costs are being committed. The opportunity to use design as a vehicle for cost management typically applies only to new products. This is why target costing and new product development are intimately linked. While target costing can be used for existing products, this is possible only if these products or their manufacturing processes are being radically redesigned.

The typical product development cycle has four stages:

1. Product Strategy and Profit Planning. The product development cycle starts with enterprise level strategic planning. The result is a business, product, and profit plan that spells out the particular market segments a firm intends to sell in and the products it intends to produce for this chosen niche. The plans typically spell out the planned market shares and required profit margins from the various products.

2. Product Concept and Feasibility. The next step in the product development cycle is to translate product and profit plans into specific product concepts. Product concepts are developed using

customer input and competitive intelligence. Product feasibility is determined by making preliminary life cycle cost estimates, evaluating the technology needed, computing the required investment, and estimating the available capacity.

3. **Product Design and Development.** Once a product concept is accepted and its feasibility tested, it goes into full-fledged design and development. Detailed specifications for manufacture and assembly are developed at this step. Manufacturing processes are concurrently designed and suppliers are called in to provide design and process improvement ideas.

4. **Production and Logistics.** The start of full-fledged production and distribution marks the culmination of the product development cycle. Service and support plans are activated. Market results and customer responses are monitored to provide information for continuous improvement or redesign of the existing or next generation products.

Exhibit 3–1 locates the target costing process within the twin contexts of competitive strategy and the new product development cycle. It shows that competitve strategy is the product of research on customers and competition. This research also is used for product planning, which gives a concrete shape to a firm's competitve strategy. Product planning is the first step in the product development cycle. Target costing plays a key role during the product planning, concept, and design stages of this cycle. Once production begins, target costing assumes a backseat and continuous improvement (also referred to as *kaizen costing*) takes over the cost management role.

Exhibit 3–1 depicts competitive strategy and product development cycles as sequential processes. A product, however, does not necessarily go through these steps sequentially. Products with longer development periods may go through iterations of this cycle numerous times. A strategy based on a particular market and technology may start the product development cycle. Markets and technologies, however, are dynamic and may change before a design is final. With new market conditions and technologies, a product may have to be recycled through the concept and feasibility steps.

A good example is Texas Instruments' development of the Digital Micromirror Device™ (DMD) microchip. Designed for high-resolution display, this chip marries traditional complementary metal oxide semiconductor (CMOS) technology with precision mirror technology. The original development of this product was aimed at large size and high definition TV

The Organizational Context of Target Costing

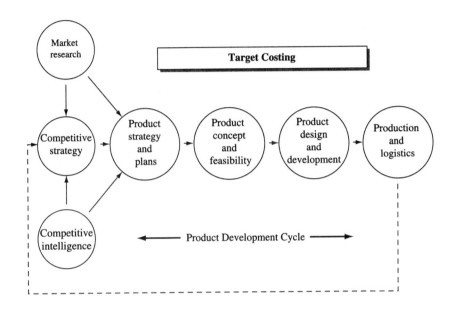

displays to replace the traditional cathode ray tube technology.[1] The product has since been repositioned for high-end large screen projection displays for business, home, and entertainment as well as future applications for color printing. The repositioning is the result of iterative internal technology planning that opens new opportunities and closes others as they become nonviable.

PHASES IN THE TARGET COSTING PROCESS

Target costing occurs in two phases that correspond, roughly, to the first and second halves of the product development cycle. We call them the *establishment* phase and the *attainment* phase of target costing. The establishment phase occurs during product planning and concept development stages of the product development cycle and involves setting a target cost. The attainment phase occurs during the design development and production stages of

---

[1]See "The Big Picture," *Popular Science,* November 1994, for a description of the product and its intended market applications.

Target Costing and the Product Development Cycle

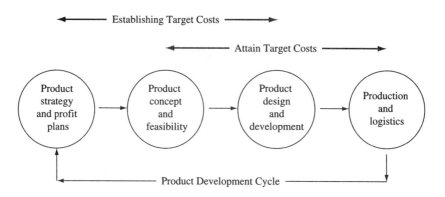

target costing and involves achieving that target cost. The two phases of the target costing process in relation to the product development cycle are shown in Exhibit 3–2.

ESTABLISHING TARGET COSTS

Target costs are established within the parameters defined by a firm's product strategy and long-term profit plans. These plans specify the markets, customers, and products that a firm intends to develop. New products can be developed by applying new technology or combining existing technologies. The original fax machine is an example of a product created from the application of new technology. Products that combine a fax machine, printer, copier, and a scanner in one box are examples of new products created by combining existing technologies. Products aimed at specific markets or customers are tested for feasibility and then *allowable* target costs are set for feasible products. Exhibit 3–3 provides an overview of how this allowable target cost is established.

As shown in Exhibit 3–3, *seven major activities* occur in establishing target costs. These activities are described next.

Market research provides information about the unrecognized needs and wants of customers. The research is used to define the market or product niche a company plans to exploit. Typically, a market niche is a broad definition of a class of customers such as "health conscious eaters" or "computer power users."

Competitive analysis determines what competitors' products are currently available to the target customers, how the customers evaluate these other

EXHIBIT 3–3

The Establishment Phase of Target Costing

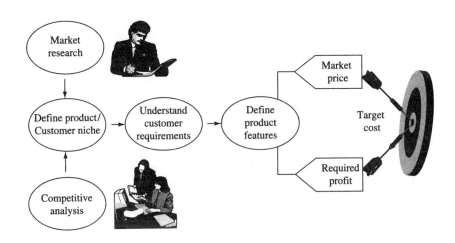

products, and how competitors might react to our company's new product introductions.

Customer or market niche determination involves analyzing market and competitor information to decide what particular customer segment to target. A customer or market niche is a more specific definition of customers, such as "young, upwardly mobile professional, two-income families between the ages 30 and 45."

Customer requirements involve specific product-related information from customers. The initial product concept is used for determining preliminary requirements. Continuous input from customers is solicited, and the product design is refined until it meets their requirements.

Product features involves setting specific requirements about the features a product will have and the levels of performance of each feature. The latter captures traditional quality variables such as reliability, dependability, and frequency and ease of repair.

Market price establishes a price that is acceptable to customers and capable of withstanding competition. Market prices can be established in many different ways, which will be discussed in the next chapter.

Required profit target is the profit a product must yield. It is typically expressed as return on sales (ROS) ratio. This ROS must take into account the long-term profit plans and the financial return on assets (ROA) a company must earn in its industry.

ATTAINING TARGET COSTS

While the establishment phase focuses on macro planning processes, the attainment phase deals with technical cost planning and engineering needed to attain target costs. This phase focuses on how to make the *allowable* target cost *achievable*. Activities designed to attain target costs occur primarily during a product's concept development, feasibility testing, and design development stages. All three stages precede the release of a product design for manufacturing. Once a design has been released, the focus of cost reduction shifts to continuous improvement efforts.

Attaining target costs is a three step process:

1. Compute cost gap.
2. Design costs out of a product.
3. Release design for manufacturing and perform continuous improvement.

These three steps are shown in Exhibit 3–4.

Computing the gap between the allowable cost and the current cost is the first step in attaining target costs. *Note that this is total product cost and*

EXHIBIT 3–4

The Attainment Phase of Target Costing

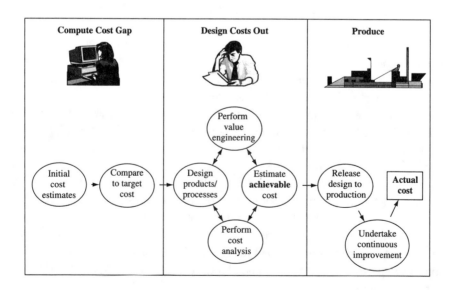

not just manufacturing cost. The current cost is the initial "as-is" estimate of the cost of producing a product based on current cost factors or models. The overall gap between allowable and current cost must be decomposed by life cycle and value chain. A life cycle decomposition assigns total product cost into birth to death categories of research, manufacturing, distribution, service, general support, and disposal. Value chain analysis breaks down the cost by whether it is incurred by the firm or one of its value chain members such as suppliers, dealers, or recyclers.

Designing costs out is the most critical step in attaining target costs. The key to cost reduction is to ask one simple question: How does the design of this product affect all costs associated with the product from its inception to its final disposal? To include all costs, and not just manufacturing costs, may appear farfetched at first. However, many "downstream" costs such as distribution, selling, service, warehousing, support, maintenance, and recycling can be greatly affected by product design.

Consider a product such as a convection oven. The weight of the oven and the complexity of its control panel are two elements affected by design. The design of these elements, in turn, affects both manufacturing and other downstream costs. A heavy machine will increase loading costs, transportation costs, and installation costs, since two people instead of one may be needed to handle the machine. A complex electronic control panel will increase the time salespeople may have to devote explaining to customers how the oven works. It may also increase product support and repair costs as electronic components may fail more rapidly than mechanical components. Finally, the material used to manufacture and give it the extra weight may result in a significant disposal cost. All these factors add to a product's life cycle cost. Many of these costs can be reduced if they are anticipated and explicitly considered by product and process designers.

Cost reduction through design requires recursive problem solving using four key activities: product design, cost (and value) analysis, value engineering, and cost estimation. (These four activities are explained in greater detail later in this book.) The activities recur until the product design goes from an initial concept to a design ready for manufacturing. A design is released for manufacturing only when a product's projected actual cost is equal to its allowable target cost. This recursive problem solving is a characteristic of target costing. Its purpose is to generate cost effective designs. Unlike traditional cost management, recursion avoids later manufacturing problems by eliminating the need to correct design errors after manufacturing starts.

Production and continuous improvement represent the last stage in attaining target costs. These activities focus on product and process improvements that reduce costs beyond that possible through design alone. This stage includes steps such as eliminating waste, improving production yields (such as getting more production from raw materials), and other efficiency enhancing measures. Japanese companies refer to these activities as *kaizen costing*. Some U.S. companies refer to it as *value analysis,* others refer to it as *continuous improvement.* It is after production starts that actual costs can be compared against targets and lessons learned passed on to the next generation of products developed.

SUMMARY

Target costing occurs in two phases: an establishment phase that sets an allowable cost target and an attainment phase that makes the allowable cost achievable. These phases occur within the four-stage new product development cycle. New products offer the best opportunity for target costing, because 70–90 percent of all costs are typically committed at the development stage of a product. This does not mean that existing products cannot benefit from target costing—they can. The benefits, however, are limited to the extent that design options have been locked in.

4

CHAPTER

Establishing Price and Profit Margins

Target costs represent the difference between market determined prices and a firm's required profit margin. This chapter discusses the technical issues relating to establishing prices and profit margins for target costing. It recognizes that prices are market driven and not controllable by management. Market prices shift and are dynamic. The target costing process does not set prices, it models them.

This chapter contains several key messages:

KEY MESSAGES

- Traditional pricing methods, including cost plus, marginal, volume, and premium pricing, are inappropriate or of limited usefulness in a target costing environment.
- In target costing, product strategy and long-term profit planning establish a product's target profit and also help to fine tune product prices within a product family.
- Product prices in target costing are determined by the physical and aesthetic properties of a product as well as customers' acceptable prices, competitors' product offerings, and the market share goal of a firm.
- Setting target profit requires combining product mix information and required return on sales, from the business level plan, with

29

Establishing the Allowable Target Cost

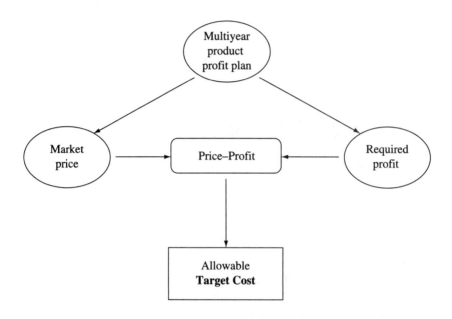

projected sales volume (assuming market size, share, and price), from the product level plan.

ESTABLISHMENT PHASE OF THE TARGET COST PROCESS

As depicted in Exhibit 4–1, the establishment phase needs a product price and a required profit to determine the allowable target cost of a product. In this phase, product strategy and the long-term profit plan determine a product's price and its required target profit. The difference between price and the required profit margin is the allowable target cost. The allowable target cost is the initial target that guides product development efforts.

SETTING PRODUCT PRICES

Price, as used here, refers to the realized price net of discounts, payment terms, and any other off-invoice adjustments. We use it in the traditional sense of what a customer pays at the time of purchase. However, the reader should remember that a target cost system aims to minimize the cost of ownership and not just the price a customer pays at the time of purchase.

The costs associated with the cost of ownership must be considered at the time the initial purchase price is set for a product. Cost of ownership includes invoice cost plus transportation, repair and maintenance, service and support, and disposal costs.

Traditional Pricing Methods

The economic literature and industry practice offer several methods for product pricing. Some of the major ones, along with their rationale, are briefly discussed next:

- *Cost plus pricing* is a very popular method of pricing used by many companies. It is unsuited for target costing environments, however. As we said in Chapter 2, prices lead costing in target costing situations because of the competitive nature of markets. Use of cost plus pricing in competitive environments negates the entire rationale for the use of target costing. In fact, being wedded to cost for product pricing is an impediment to the successful adoption of target costing.

- *Marginal cost based pricing* is a short-term capacity utilization strategy and not very useful for long-range pricing decisions of the type required for target costing. Furthermore, indiscriminate use of marginal pricing can seriously hurt profit margins and lead to improper capacity utilization decisions.

- *Volume based pricing* uses learning curves and economies of scale to predict prices at different levels of output. It is a one-dimensional pricing method, which determines product cost based on expected volume, and does not consider customer tastes and methods for product differentiation. It may be appropriate for products where little or no product differentiation exists. Since most products today compete on the basis of quality, service, time, support, and other factors, the role of volume based pricing is limited.

- *Skimming or premium pricing* is a method that takes advantage of temporary monopolistic market conditions. While it may be an appropriate strategy for exploiting temporary monopoly, it has limited usefulness in the type of competitive environment in which target costing is used. As long as substantial barriers to entry exist, premium pricing can be used to fund new product development.

Setting Prices in a Target Cost Environment

All these traditional methods for pricing are either inappropriate or have limited usefulness for pricing products in a target costing environment. Target costing typically occurs in a competitive environment, in which firms differentiate their products on the basis of quality, service, time to market, support, product functions, and features. In this environment, customer needs, wants and tastes, coupled with their ability to pay, are central in determining product prices. The product price becomes a statistic that summarizes the market's judgment on the particular package of quality, service, support, time, functions, and features bundled into a product. Prices, therefore, are determined by the physical and aesthetic properties of the product. Japanese companies refer to these as the *hard* and *soft* functionalities of a product.

Japanese companies use four key determinants in setting a product's price in a target cost environment:

- *Consumer needs/wants/tastes* related to physical features and aesthetic functions in a product are a key input in setting prices. These requirements are turned into tangible product features and functions.

- *Acceptable price* is the price that customers are willing to pay for desired functions and features. An acceptable price turns a customer wish list into a marketable product feature. Only affordable features and functions are included in a product, and the price is adjusted for these feature and function additions.

- *Competitive analysis* of product features, aesthetic functions, and prices offered by the competition influence a firm's own prices. Head to head product comparisons are performed, customers are surveyed, and teardowns or reverse engineering techniques are used to determine what features the competition is offering and how much it may cost to provide these features. Another important input is the customers' evaluation of competitor offerings.

- *Market share goal* for the product is a fundamental pricing strategy Japanese companies often employ. They estimate what price will capture their desired market share. Using that information, they set their price to obtain that share. An aggressive pricing approach may also be used to deter competitors from entering the market. For example, Fanack, a Japanese company, uses a simple pricing rule: Prices are set at a

EXHIBIT 4–2

Setting Prices in Target Costing

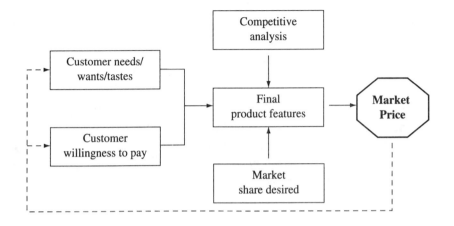

level that gives them a five year price lead over their competitors.[1]

Exhibit 4–2 graphically depicts the role of these four determinants in setting target prices. It suggests a recursive relationship between these determinants, the product's physical and aesthetic features, and the final market price. Several iterations and revisions may be needed before a final product price is set. Also the process varies by whether the prices are being set for brand new products or new versions of existing products.

Setting Prices for New Products

The process depicted in Exhibit 4–2 is well suited for pricing products that are based on or are new versions of existing products. Products that are new to a marketplace or new to a company pose a more difficult challenge. While the process shown in Exhibit 4–2 can be used to price new products, the weight assigned to the four determinants of price (customer requirements, acceptable price, competitive offerings, and desired market share) will vary by the "newness" of a product.

---

[1]K. Inaba, "Target Cost Management and Industrial Engineering," *Industrial Engineering Review* 32, no. 2 (May 1991) [in Japanese]. (For the English abstract, see "Japanese Language Literature on Target Costing: An Abstract of Key Ideas," CAM-I, December 1995.)

Eliciting customer requirements, determining acceptable prices, and doing competitive analysis are easier for products that are new to a company but have a market history. Determining customer requirements in these situations goes hand in hand with finding a competitive market niche that justifies entry of the company into this market. An example is "light" beer. Here the market niche was determined by finding customer needs unsatisfied by existing beers, such health consciousness of drinkers or a desire for a lighter taste. Also, existing prices for beers provided an easy reference point for pricing light beers.

Products that have no history in the marketplace typically are more challenging to price. There is no prior base from which to gauge customer requirements or evaluate competitive offerings. An example of this is the Sony Walkman. When it was first introduced, the Walkman was an unfamiliar product. This makes it difficult for Sony to evaluate features customers desire or determine the price they might be willing to pay for those features. Strategic and competitive factors, rather than customer requirements, play a larger role in pricing new products.

Setting Prices for Existing Products

Existing products typically provide an initial starting point in the form of the current selling price, a customer use history, and an existing package of physical attributes, features, and functions. The typical pricing formula is to adjust the current selling price for the added functions and features. Three methods are used in practice. Which of these three methods is, or should be, followed depends on the nature of the industry and the type of product being considered. The three methods are described next.

A *function based adjustment* method sets prices by adding or subtracting the value of functions added or deleted from an existing product. Toyota's pricing of new car models is a good example of a formula used by many Japanese companies. Takao Tanaka describes Toyota's system as starting with the price of the current year's model and augmenting it by the value of added functions and features.[2] A function or feature in Toyota's context might be air bags, multichanger CD systems in the trunk, a hands-free telephone, and so on. Toyota's pricing formula is

$$P^n = P^c + (f_1 + f_2 + f_3 + \ldots f_n)$$

where P^n = new market price;
P^c = current price;

[2]T. Tanaka, "Target Costing at Toyota," in M. S. Young, *Readings in Management Accounting* (Englewood Cliffs, N.J.: Prentice-Hall, 1995).

f_n = value placed by market on a function.

While Toyota's formula implies that price is an additive function of incremental features, this is not universally true. For many products, such as computer peripherals, cameras, or personal electronics, the price of an existing product drops as technology moves to a higher level. The price point is fairly well fixed for these products, and features added are a function of that price point. The computer industry is a good example of this phenomena. New features (faster drives, CD-ROM, accelerated video) have to be added at a cost that is equivalent to the planned target price reduction on the older model. For instance, assume a fully loaded Pentium PC sells for an introductory price of $2,500. Two years later, the price will drop to $1,500. The next generation of PCs must add features to make up the $1,000 difference between the old and the new models. The price setting formula is

$$P^n = P^o$$

if and only if $(f_1 + f_2 + f_3 + \ldots f_n) = P^o - P^c$

> where P^n = new market price;
> P^o = price of older model at introduction;
> P^c = current price of older model;
> f_n = value placed by market on an additional function of the new product.

Physical attributes-based adjustment method sets prices with reference to the physical attributes of a product, such as weight, torque ratio, horsepower, and so on. Functionality is embedded in these physical attributes. This pricing model is used in situations in which functionality changes slowly and physical attributes embody a customer's requirement. The attributes are used to set prices in a manner analogous to the use of functions. Caterpillar and Komatsu provide good examples of this formula:

$$P^n = P^c + (a_1 + a_2 + a_3 + \ldots a_n)$$

> where P^n = new market price;
> P^c = current price;
> a_n = measure of physical attributes of the product.

Competitor based adjustment method sets prices with reference to competitors' products or attributes. The formulas are based on estimating the differential value that a market places on a competitor's products, based on the functions or attributes of that product. A typical formula may be as follows:

$$P^c = P^o \times (X_c/X_o)^n$$

where P^c = competitor's market price;
      P^o = our product's price;
      X_c = measure of attribute of competitor's product;
      X_o = measure of attribute of our product.

To illustrate this formula, assume that competition offers a 2.0 horsepower (X_c) lawn mower for \$510 (P^c). Assume that our company has a lawn mower that is 1.75 hp (X_o) at a price of \$470. Since the ratio of the two prices (P_c/P_o) is equal to the ratio of the two horsepower ratings raised to nth power, $(X_c/X_o)^n$, we can estimate the coefficient n. In the example, this coefficient is equal to 0.6. It relates price to horsepower ratings. Conversely, if 0.6 were a stable industrywide coefficient for horsepower differentials between power tools, then we could use that to predict the selling price of our product, which has a 1.75 hp rating.

This price estimation method is suited only for products in which one dominant characteristic explains price differences. It is not suited for complex products, such as automobiles, where many dimensions capture price differences. The method, however, can be used for preliminary price estimates if one characteristic can be used as a surrogate for product differences.

SETTING TARGET PROFIT MARGINS

Setting target profits is a function of bringing together (macro) business level plans with (micro) product level plans. At the business level, target profit is determined by considering the profit requirements for the business as a whole. This is done by taking into account the product mix the firm intends to produce and establishing a required profit from this product mix. The product mix comes from a firm's multiyear product plan and the profit comes from applying a target return on sales (ROS) percent to the sales revenue from the product mix. The ROS ratio, in turn, is determined by the financial returns, typically measured by the return on assets (ROA), return on equity (ROE), or economic value added (EVA) that a firm must earn to remain viable. The required target profit is the result of profit simulations and represents an assignment of profit needed from all products in a firm's product line.

This macro plan is combined with individual micro profit plans for each product. These plans represent a product manager's expectations for his or her product. The product manager considers the projected market size, targeted market share, and the competitive market price to develop a projected sales volume. Applying the return on sales targets from the

EXHIBIT 4–3

Setting Target Profit

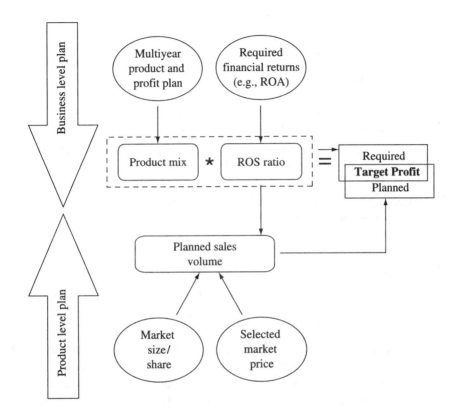

profit plan to this projected sales level yields the planned profit at the product level. The two profits, required and planned, are compared to set a final target profit for the product. Exhibit 4–3 summarizes these relationships.

Four things are noteworthy about Exhibit 4–3:

- The required profit is a business level profit projection while the planned profit is a product level action plan.
- The required profit and the planned profit are based on estimates of lifetime sales from the product.
- The profit targets may change as the product goes through its development cycle, and the final target may vary over the product's life cycle.
- Individual product profit plans may include subsidies from products that may command a monopoly share of their markets.

The key elements that determine target profits, shown in Exhibit 4–3, are explained next.

Multiyear Product and Profit Plan

Each product has its own profit plan. The multiyear product and profit plan shows all the products (or services) to be developed and introduced over the time horizon of the long-range business plan. Product strategies are defined for multiple business groups. These strategies describe product goals and opportunities and competitive threats for product lines and particular products. A key consideration in the plan are the lengths of product life cycle for both existing and new products. The other element of the plan is to couple product introductions and deletions with projected sales and profit margins from these products over their lives. The final output is an annual product mix that shows aggregate profits by year and over the life of a product.

Financial Returns

The target profit rate is usually determined by the financial rates of return required by a company. These parameters are linked to the return on sales ratio.

A common practice in Japanese industry for setting a required ROS is to use a weighting scheme that combines information about a company with industry information. The scheme combines a firm's past ROS and the industry's past ROS with the firm' future five year target ROS to yield a required ROS for a product. The following formula reflects this practice:[3]

$$\text{ROS(new)} = w_1 \times (\text{firm's past ROS}) + w_2 \times (\text{industry's past ROS}) + w_3 \times (\text{firm's next 5 year ROS target})$$

where w = weighting factor;
$w_1 + w_2 + w_3 = 1$;
and, over time, $w_3 = 1$.

This formula combines firm and industry past ROS experience with future target ROS to yield a current ROS. As time passes, the weights assigned to past experience decrease to zero.

ROS is a critical input to another popular financial metric, the return on assets (ROA). ROA is the product of asset turnover and profit margin. It is expressed as

---

[3]Y. Monden, *Target Costing and Kaizen Costing* (Portland, OR: Productivity Press, 1995), p. 40.

$$ROA = (sales/assets) \times (profit/sales).$$

The first part of the formula is the asset turnover; the second part is the ROS ratio. If assets are stable, the turnover ratio can be treated as fixed, and we can solve for the profit margin ratio required to get the target ROA. A numerical example can be used to illustrate this. Assume that a company has $250 million in assets and the multiyear profit plan projects the following sales from its three products:

Product A	$200 million
Product B	100 million
Product C	200 million
Total sales	$500 million

The asset turnover ratio, therefore, is 2 (500/250). Assume further that the company is expected to produce a ROA of 20 percent. Dividing this required ROA of 20 percent by the asset turnover of 2 yields a profit margin ratio of 10 percent or a target profit of $50 million.

Product Mix Analysis

The overall target profit of $50 million must be allocated to the three products in the product mix. Two possibilities exist.

- In an *equal assignment,* all three products are expected to produce a 10 percent profit. The target of $50 million will become $20 million, $10 million, and $20 million, respectively, for Products A, B, and C. This method has the advantage of being simple and easy to communicate to product managers. Like the weighted average cost of capital, it becomes a corporatewide hurdle rate for new products. It is particularly suited for business level and product family level analyses, since it allows individual managers to redistribute this average to individual products within the family. However, it ignores the strategic reasons for a product mix and does not account for the market realities facing individual products. The business planning team needs to take these factors into account. If strategic reasons exist for varying rates, then uniform hurdle rates should be used solely to establish an internal benchmark.

■ *Differential assignments* can be done using profit simulations on a product by product basis. The projected profit is computed by using the life cycle volumes for each product and applying to them historical cost ratios or industry averages. This type of simulation recognizes the differential profit capabilities of each product. It is particularly well suited for existing products that have a stable market history, such as automobiles. However, it can be complex and also opens the door for individual product managers to request a profit margin rate less than the average for the company or the business unit. Assume that, based on profit simulations, a target ROS of 15 percent is assigned to Product A, 8 percent to Product B, and 6 percent to Product C. Then the required target profit for the products becomes

Product A	$30 million
Product B	8 million
Product C	12 million

Product Level Profit Plans

While the required profit typically is based on macro assumptions at the business unit and the product line levels, a profit plan is a product manager's action plan for achieving a particular volume, price, and profit. The final assignment of the target profit therefore is a match between the required profit and the planned profit. To the extent that the multiyear product plan and profit simulations are accurate, the required and planned profit will match. However, if demand forecasts are in error, *the required profit still remains the final target.*

We can illustrate this by assuming that, in our example, the sales forecast for Product C is only $150 million instead of $200 million. The required profit target remains the original $12 million and is not revised downward to $9 million (6 percent of $150 million), which effectively increases the margin requirement to 8 percent. This is done because a profit plan represents a product manager's *commitment* and is also the basis for getting commitments from manufacturing and suppliers. It is imperative that there be no slippage in this plan. Since the profit plan has been revisited several times during the product development cycle, margins must be maintained even when volume is off. Making the profit target a commitment forces serious product and profit planning in the early stages of the product development cycle.

Margin over a Product's Life

The required profit of $12 million in our example is a lifetime target profit. Two things must be kept in mind.

- First, the target has been refined throughout the product development cycle. As the product concept takes shape and the features and functions are designed into the product, target profit margins must be revisited.
- Second, the target margin can change over the product's life cycle. As market conditions change or as continuous cost reductions are achieved, target margins may be increased. This is particularly true for cases in which a lower introductory margin is used to increase market share and establish a product.

The profit margin, therefore, needs to be strategically apportioned over a product's life.

SUMMARY

In this chapter we have examined the issues related to setting prices and profit margins in target costing. Traditional methods for setting prices are not well suited for target cost environments. Pricing is dynamic; it is an art form too complex to capture for every scenario. While other approaches to pricing exist in practice, we present the most commonly documented methods used by Japanese firms.

Typical formulas used in target cost situations adjust a base price for the value a customer places on the product differentiation factors. These formulas use functions, features, or physical attributes as differentiating variables. Price differentials also are computed using competitors' product features. The target profit margin results from bringing together the long-range product and profit plan with the required financial rates of return for a business. The target profit is computed over a product's life and apportioned to individual products based on a company's required market share goals and business strategy.

5

C H A P T E R

From Allowable to Achievable Target Cost

This chapter deals with the second part of the target costing process—turning an allowable target cost into an achievable target cost. Three critical elements help to accomplish this goal: cost analysis and estimation, value engineering, and continuous improvement. Cost analysis is closely intertwined with value engineering and continuous improvement efforts. In this chapter we describe the cost analysis and engineering efforts undertaken simultaneously within a company and its value chain. Chapter 10 deals with value engineering and other core target costing tools that help close the gap between allowable and achievable target costs. We want to leave you with six key messages in this chapter.

KEY MESSAGES

- The purpose of cost analysis is to focus cost reduction and design efforts so that product costs are aligned with customer values.
- Cost planning requires a cost system that is "kaleidoscopic" in nature and permits many different views of the allowable target cost.
- Cost elements to be included in product cost must be consistent with existing cost definitions so that an organization can communicate and evaluate actual costs against target costs.

- Cost reduction targets must be decomposed so that they can be assigned to product function and product design teams.
- All costs, including legacy costs, must be addressed by target costing so that there is no undue pressure on product designers to come up with all cost reductions.
- Target costing requires a good cost estimation system that provides increasing levels of accuracy as a product goes from a concept to a design ready for manufacturing.
- Guidelines must be established that allow for flexibility in dealing with unattainable functional cost targets. These guidelines should communicate that product or subsystem cost targets are commitments to be taken seriously.

COST ANALYSIS—AN OVERVIEW

Attaining target costs requires cost planning, which has two key steps: computing the cost gap between attainable and current costs and analyzing this cost gap so value engineering and continuous improvement efforts can be fo-

E X H I B I T   5–1

Cost Planning in Target Costing—an Overview

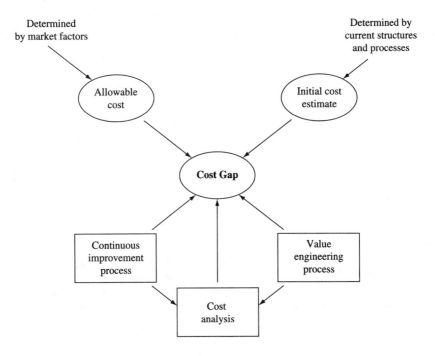

cused on closing the gap. This two step cost planning process is depicted in Exhibit 5–1.

The top half of Exhibit 5–1 shows the cost gap. This is the difference between the allowable cost and the current or initial estimated cost. As described in the previous chapter, the allowable cost is determined by market forces. The initial cost is the preliminary estimate of a product's cost, assuming existing work structures, technology, and processes. No change in production technology, methods, or distribution channels is assumed. The current cost simply asks the question, "What will it cost to produce this new product design with the existing production, capacity utilization levels, and distribution methods?" Some Japanese authors refer to the current cost as a *drifting* cost, because it drifts toward the allowable cost through successive design iterations.

It is important to remember that the cost planning process is dynamic and iterative. At each stage of the product development cycle, the cost reduction target is continually refined until the "allowable" and "achievable" costs merge.

The cost planning process has five steps. These are shown in Exhibit 5–2 and discussed in greater detail in the remainder of this chapter.

COMPUTE OVERALL COST GAP

The first step in cost analysis is to compute the gap between the allowable cost and the initial estimated cost. This requires specifying the cost elements to be included in the comparison. The definition of allowable and initial costs should be based on full product life cycle costs and must include components that are consistent with existing cost object definitions.

Full product costs should be used because profit planning and customer prices are at the total product level. This means that the allowable cost must include R&D, manufacturing, sales, distribution, service, support, and disposal costs. Because of the emphasis on product design, many companies, in our opinion, place undue emphasis on the costs of manufacturing and purchased parts in

EXHIBIT 5–2

Steps in the Cost Planning Process

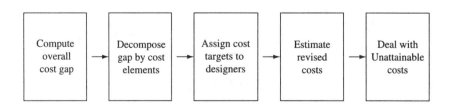

target costing. This tends to place too heavy a burden for cost reduction on engineering design while other support costs escape scrutiny. By setting cost targets at the total product level, we focus on all costs and not just manufacturing ones. Further, the same design orientation used to address product costs can be used to plan and reduce support process costs. Activity based management (ABM) and business process reengineering (BPR) are valuable tools for doing this.

Life cycle costs are important to consider from both the producer's and the customer's perspectives. Costs of operating, repairing, warranty, support, and disposal are some elements that should be part of the initial cost estimate. All of these are part of a customer's cost of ownership. They should be predicted, even if some elements are difficult to predict at the time of product design. Similarly, a producer's cost from R&D to abandonment must be considered in cost estimates as well.

Consistency with existing definitions is important for both communication and evaluation of performance against targets. If the allowable cost includes definitions that are not part of a company's existing accounting system, then the cost is liable to create confusion and cause the targets to become less credible. A good example is depreciation. While profit and cost targets should provide for recouping replacement cost depreciation, most firms typically use historical cost based depreciation methods. Use of replacement cost depreciation will create an anomaly, because target costs will be stated in terms of replacement cost while the actual product cost will be computed using historical cost. As a result, comparisons between target costs and actual costs will be invalid, unless reconciled.

DECOMPOSING ALLOWABLE COST

To assign cost reduction targets, we must decompose the overall product cost into discrete elements. This requires understanding the various components of product cost. It is analogous to viewing costs through a kaleidoscope. Cost elements are like the little pieces of glass in the kaleidoscope, and with each turn they reassemble themselves into a different pattern.[1] Each pattern provides us a unique insight. Some useful views of costs for target costing purposes are

Value chain (organizational) perspective

Life cycle (time) perspective

Customer (value) perspective

---

[1]The concept of costs as elements of kaleidoscope is borrowed from the work of S. Ansari, J. Bell, T. Klammer, and C. Lawrence, *Management Accounting: A Strategic Focus.* (Burr Ridge, Ill.: Irwin, 1996).

EXHIBIT 5-3

Multiple Views of Allowable Cost

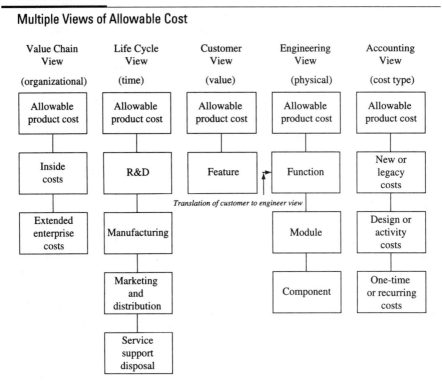

Engineering (design) perspective

Accounting (cost type) perspective

Exhibit 5–3 depicts each of these views of the allowable product cost.

The *value chain* view arranges costs by where in the extended enterprise they are incurred. This helps a firm to focus cost reduction efforts both within and outside its own boundaries. For example, in assembly industries, purchased parts and subassemblies account for as much 60–80 percent of manufacturing costs. In these industries, therefore, cost reduction must have an external (supplier) focus. Similarly, in many industries, service and support costs typically are incurred by downstream organizations. An inward focus on costs, therefore, is not likely to yield significant dividends. Efforts must be focused on diffusing target costing throughout the extended enterprise.

The *life cycle* view arranges costs by time when they are incurred. Some costs are early in the product cycle (R&D) and some are incurred many years later (disposal and environmental costs). This time based view allows a firm to focus not only on today's costs but also on future costs committed by today's decisions. It also encourages a long-term perspective on costs that considers both a producer's and a customer's life cycle costs.

The *customer* view arranges costs by product features. A *feature* is defined as an attribute of the product, physical or aesthetic, desired by a customer. The main purpose of decomposing a target cost by product features is to view these costs from the customer's perspective. This requires taking the total allowable cost and assigning it to each feature in proportion to the importance customers place on that feature. The decomposition of cost by features determines the maximum allowable amount that should be spent on providing a particular feature. Consider some of the features customers may desire in a personal computer (PC):

- Software executes rapidly
- Ample disk storage space
- Allows multitasking
- Screen refresh rate is fast
- Appearance (sleek vs. clunky)
- Sufficient memory to run graphics applications

Customers will be asked to indicate how important these features are in their decision to buy a PC. (How to obtain this information is the subject of the next chapter.) Assume that customer responses indicate that speed of software operations represents 50 percent of total importance for all features. This means that half of the allowable cost for this PC should be assigned to this feature. Later we will show how this feature cost can be decomposed into functional cost targets for subassemblies, components, and parts.

The *engineering* view is a functional view of the product. A *function* is defined as a major subsystem, subassembly, component, or performance dimension that has its own unique design and manufacturing team, department, or specialty. A functional view is the perspective from which design engineers view a product. For instance, car companies typically define functions by engineering specialties such as engine, chassis, body, brakes, and so on. Aircraft manufacturers, such as Boeing, typically use a work breakdown structure to define functions. Their functions are represented by wing, ailerons, door, rudder, tail, and so on. Each of these major elements, such as an engine or the door, typically is broken further into subfunctions. The engineering view decomposes the allowable cost into what can be spent on each function and then decomposes this functional cost target into subsystems, components, and parts. It thus provides a manufacturing view as well because the final decomposition is based on the "bill of materials" for the product.

The *accounting* view arrays costs by three main subcategories. The first category, one time or recurring costs, differentiates costs by whether they continue annually or occur only one time. The second category, new or legacy costs, focuses on whether the cost is related to the new product or is part of the legacy costs inherited by that product. The last category, design or activity driven costs, focuses on what drives the cost. It differentiates between costs that are driven by product and process design and those that are driven by work activities.

- *One time costs* typically include product development and capital costs related to a new product. Often these costs benefit more than one product or benefit a family of products. Assigning them to a single product penalizes the lead product unfairly and is inconsistent with the capital investment analysis used to justify such investments. One time costs should be treated for both capital investment analysis and target costing in a consistent manner. When investments are justified based on multiple products, their costs should be assigned to these multiple products on the basis of projected benefits. The focal product should not bear the full cost of one time investments meant for multiple products or product families.

- *New costs* are created by the decision to launch a new product. They typically include incremental materials, labor, equipment, marketing, and promotion. *Legacy costs* are amounts expended as a result of past decisions. New products, however, benefit from these past costs and are required to pay their fair share of them. These costs typically include administrative, distribution, and business support costs. Legacy costs sometimes can be influenced by new product designs. In addition, they can be addressed by other cost management tools. Appendix C discusses how to deal with legacy costs in target costing.

- *Design driven costs* are all costs affected by changes in product design, regardless of where in the value chain they are incurred. While design is a major cost driver for manufacturing costs, many other costs such as distribution, service, support, and recycling are affected by product design also. For example, the length, width, or diameter of a product can have an impact on the quantity of packaging materials required and the shipping space needed. This in turn affects shipping costs by determining the mode of shipment to be used (trucks, trains, or ship). Service costs are affected by the robustness of quality designed into a product. Support costs, such as field training and installation, are affected by the ease of operating or installing a product. Recycling costs are affected by the degree to which materials used can be remanufactured. The quantity of waste products generated can create environmental hazards (costs). Finally, even some general business support costs may be affected by product design. In the toy industry, designing products with many small pieces that may be swallowed by children can increase the chance of product liability litigation.

Exhibit 5–4 provides a sample checklist incorporating the life cycle, value chain, and accounting views of some of the typical cost elements included in the allowable target cost. It breaks down recurring and nonrecurring costs, costs driven by design, and costs driven by activities. Finally, the in-house column of the value chain separates the costs that are new to this product from those inherited by the product. We have not shown the breakdown of activity costs by recurring or nonrecurring since they are not the prime focus of design efforts. However, they are addressed by other cost management tools. Costs incurred in this category typically include sales commissions, advertising, product managers' salaries, and allocated common general overhead costs. These costs are neither directly traceable to a product nor affected by product design decisions.

COST TARGETS FOR DESIGN AND BUILD TEAMS

The third step in cost planning is to assign cost reduction targets to various design and build teams and to various organizational units. The kaleidoscopic view of costs, shown in Exhibits 5–3 and 5–4, helps to do this by highlighting cost reduction areas and the appropriate cost management tools to use. Internal and external design and build teams are assigned responsibility for *design driven costs*. Their primary tools are value engineering and continuous cost improvement. *Activity driven costs* are addressed by activity based cost management tools and continuous improvement efforts. Together these efforts allow a firm to turn the allowable cost into an achievable target cost.

While cost reduction is an iterative activity that begins at the product concept stage, there is a difference in the way in which cost targets are set at the various stages of the product development cycle. The initial cost reduction target, identified at the product concept stage, is usually at the total product level and not decomposed by functions or teams. It is used for analyzing "affordability," "quality," and "value trade-offs." These analyses allow determination of the market price early in the product development cycle and establish the level of quality that can be provided at that price.

E X H I B I T   5–4

Multiple Views of Typical Elements of Allowable Target Cost

	In-House				
	New	**Legacy**	**Suppliers**	**Dealers**	**Recyclers**
Design-Driven Recurring Cost					
Manufacturing					
Raw Material					
Purchased Parts					
Processing Costs					
Material Handling					
Quality Assurance					
Sales and Marketing					
Sales Training					
Additional Sales Salaries					
Distribution					
Packaging Materials					
Shipping and Handling Costs					
Service and Support					
Warranty Repairs					
Customer Training					
Recycling					
Waste Disposal					
Clean-up Costs					
Design Driven One Time Cost					
Product Development Costs					
Research, Development and Testing					
Test Marketing					
Capital Costs					
Machinery, Equipment, Tools and Dyes					
Special Training					
Allocated Activity Driven Costs					
Manufacturing					
General Purchase Support					
Grounds and Parking Lot					
General Property Taxes					
Sales and Marketing					
Sales Management Salaries					

(continued)

General Advertising and Promotion				
Distribution				
Transportation				
Shipping Clerk Salaries				
Service and Support				
Salaries				
Supplies and Travel				
General Overhead				
Divisional Salaries				
Corporate Overhead Allocations				
Total Allowable Target Cost				

Consider again our PC example. Assume that customers want their PCs to have a telephone answering capability and want to pay no more than $75 for this feature. An initial cost estimate for this feature allows a PC manufacturer to determine whether the cost reduction target is too large relative to what the customer is willing to pay. If it will cost $150 for a telephone application to be bundled with a PC, then the manufacturer may decide that the cost reduction target is unattainable and may drop this feature.

Cost targets assigned to design and build teams are based on a functional decomposition of the allowable cost. Functional decomposition is usually done after a product concept has been approved and the design is being developed. Functional cost targets, therefore, incorporate changes in market price and product features that occur during the product development cycle. They are commitments to reduce cost.

The process of assigning cost targets to design and build teams has five key elements:

1. Customer features are translated into functional cost targets.
2. Seasoned judgment is applied to translate features into product functions. This process is difficult and inexact.
3. Indirect methods for assigning functional targets often are used when a direct feature–function mapping is not possible.
4. Functional cost targets are decomposed into cost targets for major components and parts.
5. Cost targets are assigned to design teams throughout the value chain.

Each of these elements is discussed next.

Translating Features into Functional Cost Targets

The key step in assigning cost reduction targets to design and build subteams is to convert the allowable "feature" costs into allowable "functional" cost targets. In the PC example, we stated that customers valued "speed of software operations" to be one half of the total importance for the entire product. Assume that the total allowable cost for that PC is $1,000. Then, the allowable cost for the feature "speed of software operations" is $500. The $500, however, has to be converted into functional targets that engineers can use to design the physical parts and components of the PC.

To convert the $500 into functional cost targets, we must determine how each function of the PC contributes to this feature. That is, we must determine which subsystems or components of the PC (microprocessor, power supply, case, memory, hard disk, and bus) contributes to speed of software operations. Further, if more than one subsystem or component contributes to "speed," we must determine their relative contributions to this feature. This requires mapping features to functions and assigning each function a relative weight that can be used as a basis for assigning the allowable cost. The mapping represents a reconciliation of the customer's view with the engineering view of a product. It is typically captured in a quality function deployment (QFD) matrix. This tool is described in more detail in Chapter 10.

A sample feature to function mapping for our PC example is depicted in Exhibit 5–5. It shows that the feature speed of software is provided by three functions: microprocessor, memory, and bus. Assume that, in the judgment of the design team, the microprocessor contributes twice as much to speed as the other two. Then the importance weighting will be 2/4, 1/4, and 1/4. Since a customer derives 50 percent of the value from speed, the manufacturing cost target will be will be assigned as follows: 25 percent to the microprocessor (2/4 × 50%) and (1/4 × 50%) or 12.5 percent each to the memory and bus.

Difficulties in Functional Analysis

The translation of customer features into functions is not easy to capture for design and build teams. As Exhibit 5–5 shows, often these relationships are indirect or are many to one or one to many.

- The feature may have an *indirect relationship* to functions. A customer feature, such as "a sleek, attractive and modern looking PC," is difficult to map to particular functions. However, it must be tied to specific functions, and a cost target has to be attached to

E X H I B I T 5–5

Feature to Function Mapping—An Example

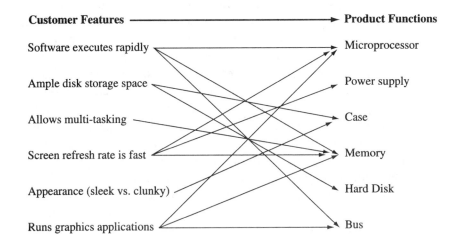

each of these functions. Without this, the designers have no direction for proceeding. The firm, therefore, must find measurable quality characteristics that correlate with features. In this example, "sleek, attractive and modern looking" may translate into the characteristics of length, width, height, or color for the case.

■ Features may have *many to one relationships.* Customers may want a PC that "executes software rapidly" and "refreshes screens fast." Both features are affected by one function, the microprocessor. The cost target for these two features must be assigned to the microprocessor to establish its allowable cost target.

■ Features may have *one to many relationships.* Often one single feature, "fast screen refresh rates," is served by three functions, the microprocessor, memory, and the bus size. In this case, a one to many relationship can make it difficult to determine the importance of a function. This in turn affects a function's allowable cost.

Indirect Methods of Functional Analysis

Because of these practical difficulties firms often employ other methods for setting functional cost targets. Three of the most common ones are anchored ratings, comparison against other products, and plotting cost/performance data.

- The *anchored ratings* method uses the design or product team's pooled judgment of relative importance of functions. Pooled judgment is particularly useful when there are many to many relationships, making a mapping difficult. The method typically starts with the function that is easiest to evaluate and assigns that function an anchor value. Other functions are then assigned a value relative to that base function. In the PC example, assume that the computer case is the easiest and assigned a value of 5. The next easiest function is the power supply, which the product team judges to be three times as important as the case in satisfying customer requirements. The power supply is assigned a value of 15. Other functions are evaluated in a similar fashion relative to the case and assigned values. The final total is used to derive percentage weights for each function. Costs are assigned using these percentages. A sample cost assignment using this method is shown in Exhibit 5–6. Since the case is 1.9 percent of the total importance ranking, it will get 1.9 percent of the total cost target. It is important to remember that these importance ratings are for *setting cost targets only.* Clearly, it is not meaningful to say that a microprocessor is twice as important as memory, since we cannot produce a PC without both. It is acceptable to say, however, that the cost of a microprocessor should be no more than twice the cost of memory.

- *Comparison against other products* requires looking at the cost at which the same function is performed in other products. For

EXHIBIT 5–6

Functional Cost Analysis: A Sample Using Anchored Weights

	Anchored Value	Importance in Percentage
Case	5	1.9
Power supply	15	5.7
Hard disk	20	7.7
Bus	40	15.4
Memory	60	23.1
Microprocessor	120	46.2
Totals	260	100.0

example, a power supply is used in a wide variety of products. The cost of providing this function in the other products can be used as a benchmark for assigning target cost to power supplies. The main problem with this method is finding a relevant comparison. While power supplies may be easy, it is much harder to find relevant comparisons for microprocessors, since other products typically do not have PC type microprocessors.

■ *Plotting cost/performance data* requires plotting the cost to performance ratio for a function. In the case of a PC's power supply, it means plotting the performance in terms of stable voltage output against cost. This ratio allows us to predict what it should cost for a power supply with desired performance characteristics. This can be used to assign an allowable cost for power supplies. The use of this method requires a large amount of data on a function. It may be easier to use for power supplies, which have narrow performance characteristics and wide usage, than for microprocessors, which have a narrower use and a larger number of performance variables.

Components and Part Level Cost Targets

After allowable target costs have been established for each major function or subassembly of the product, they can be further decomposed into major components and parts. At this level, it becomes much harder to assign targets based on customer features. The three methods discussed in the preceding section are particularly useful for decomposing costs at the component and part level. Costs can be assigned to each component using one of these procedures. For the PC example, the microprocessor may be broken into its components, such as arithmetic logic unit, memory registers, data bus, and so on. Based on the functional importance of each, the cost target for the microprocessor can be decomposed to its various components. Each component may be served by several parts. For example, the memory registers may be broken into substrate, transistors, clock timer, and the like. Exhibit 5–7 shows the hierarchical decomposition of the allowable target cost for the PC example.

Assigning Cost Reduction Targets to Teams

After a functional cost breakdown has been done, cost reduction targets are assigned to various participants simultaneously. The in-house breakdown of cost elements is assigned to the relevant organizational units and design and

EXHIBIT 5-7

Breakdown of Allowable Target Cost

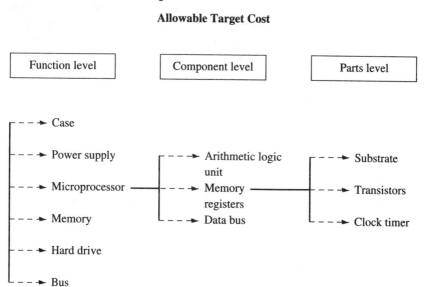

build subteams. Purchased parts are assigned to supplier teams. Chapter 7 discusses how these relations are managed.

The product team has the overall responsibility for coordinating the accomplishment of these decomposed targets. The primary responsibility for attaining targets is with the design and build subteams. In most organizations, departments are responsible for function level costs, teams are responsible for component level costs, and designers are responsible for individual parts. The units, teams, and individuals are responsible and committed to meeting their assigned cost target. Exhibit 5–8 shows the simultaneous decomposition of costs by functions (work breakdown structure) and the departments involved. The top part of the matrix shows the work breakdown structure and the left side lists the cost elements used.

COST ESTIMATION

The fourth step in cost planning is cost estimation. As teams and individuals strive to meet target costs, they must continually estimate costs to determine their progress toward the allowable cost. Many cost estimating methods are used by companies. Each firm develops models for cost estimation that meet its needs. A PC manufacturer has to deal with relatively few components in cost estimation. Its cost model is likely to be simpler

EXHIBIT 5–8

Simultaneous Assessment of Costs at Boeing

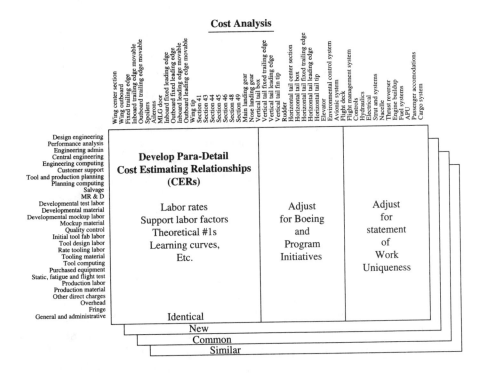

than that of a company such as Boeing that typically deals with hundreds of thousands of parts in an airplane. In both cases, however, the variables used for cost estimation and the level of accuracy required change with the different stages of the product development cycle.

Variables Used for Cost Estimation

The variables used in cost estimation models for target costing must be related to the physical attributes of the product or the process. Since attributes are the focus of design, cost estimation models tell designers how changes in these attributes affect a product's cost. In general, cost models are either parametric or detailed.

A *parametric* cost estimation model uses a few salient physical attributes of a product as independent variables. Parametric models are used primarily at the product concept and early design stages. Since detailed specifications for a product have not been developed, only a few key parameters of the product are available. A simple regression model often is used. The purpose is to get system level or product level cost estimates. For example, a simple regression model using wing weight and lift may be used to estimate an airplane's cost at the concept stage. As the design progresses, more parameters may be added or the model may be applied to individual components. In the case of building construction, square-footage is often used to estimate the initial overall cost of construction. Later contractors use more specific design parameters such as number of electrical outlets to estimate wiring cost, bathrooms to estimate plumbing costs, and so on. The method is the same in both cases.

The output of parametric estimation models is used to simulate the impact of design on cost. These simulation models are referred to as *manufacturing and design evaluation* (MADE) tool.[2] Many MADE tools are available from commercial software vendors, and it is beyond the scope of this chapter to describe them. When linked with good parametric cost estimation models, they show how costs respond to alternative product designs.

A *detailed* cost estimation model is used at the final stage of the product development cycle before the product design is released for manufacturing. A detailed bill of materials is used for this purpose. Internal process costs are estimated for all "make" items, and purchased parts costs are estimated for all "buy" items as well. This step requires detailed cost buildups from parts to components to subsystems to the final product. Each type of material is listed and its cost identified. Setups, labor hours, and other costs of each manufacturing process is determined. In building construction, a detailed cost buildup will list all construction materials and the labor hours for all operations to estimate the final cost for the project.

Accuracy of Cost Estimates

It is unrealistic to expect the same level of cost estimation accuracy at each stage of the product development cycle. Nor is this necessary. Initial parametric cost estimates are designed to assist in deciding whether a product concept is feasible. Later cost estimates, however, are cost commitments and need to be more accurate. As the product concept becomes better defined, and processes and parts are finalized, the accuracy of cost estimates should

---

[2]For more information about MADE tools, see S. R. Hedberg, "Design of a Lifetime," *Byte* (October 1994), pp. 103–105.

improve. The level of accuracy expected will vary in each line of business, depending on the cost and design factors and their rate of change. An example from practice is Kubota Tekko, a Japanese steel company.[3] The company requires the following levels of accuracy in its cost estimates at the various stages of the product life cycle:

Product concept stage	Within ±12%
Design stage	±8%
Prototyping stage	±5%
Premanufacturing stage	±2%
Manufacturing drawing stage	±1.5%

The required accuracy at each stage reflects the accuracy acceptable for the decisions to be made at that stage. It is extremely important that estimates fall within the band of acceptable accuracy at each stage. Even when the accuracy is not extremely high, as in the product concept stage, the cost estimates are very important in guiding design and cost reduction efforts. The integrity of the entire target costing process relies on the estimates staying within a relatively narrow tolerable band. Exhibit 5–9 presents both the type of cost estimation method and the band of accuracy required for it at the various stages of the product development cycle.

DEALING WITH UNATTAINABLE COSTS

What happens if product teams or design and build teams are unable to attain their cost targets? Nonattainment of targets at the product team level means the product will not meet its target cost. Failure of a design or build subteam means that a function, component, or part will not meet its assigned target cost. It is important to remember that allowable costs and target profits are meant to be realistic and achievable. They are commitments that should not be taken lightly. Nonattainment, therefore, is a serious problem that needs to be carefully thought out and policies to deal with it should be put into place.

At the overall *product level,* nonattainment of a target cost can be addressed in several ways:

---

[3]See T. Iwahashi, "Target Costing and a Cost Table in the Development Stage of Kubota Tekko" [Kaihatsu Sekkei Dankai ni okeru Genka kikaku Katsudo to Cost Table], *Management Practice [Keiei Jitsumu],* no. 426 (October 1989), p. 13.

EXHIBIT 5-9

Type and Accuracy of Cost Estimates

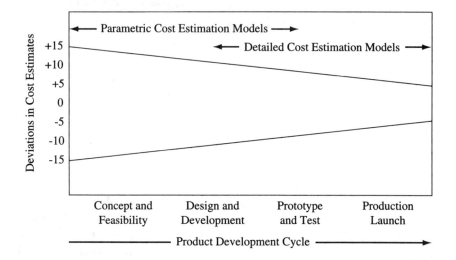

- Evaluate the possibility that targets can be met with kaizen or continuous improvement. If this is a realistic expectation, the product design can be released for production. Obviously, a firm must have confidence in its kaizen costing process.
- Keep the target costs in place and reduce the features offered. This should be done after ascertaining that the features being reduced have no adverse impact on the market price used for setting target costs.
- Postpone launching the product until target costs have been met. This should be used only when time to market is not a critical variable and delaying the launch will not hurt profits from the project significantly. Since this is rarely the case, postponement should be considered only after all efforts to meet the target costs have been exhausted.
- Raise the target cost. This should be done only in rare cases and only when it makes strategic sense. If it is done carelessly, it will break down the discipline and commitment needed to attain target costs.
- Abandon the product. This should be a choice of last resort, since considerable development effort has gone into the project.

However, a nonviable product should be discontinued if target profits cannot be achieved.

At the *function, component, or parts level,* nonattainment poses a slightly different problem. It is possible for a product to meet its overall target because some components may be below allowable cost offsetting those that are above allowable costs. Clearly, the product should proceed forward, since target costs can be met. However, for purposes of internal performance evaluation and cost discipline, we need to recognize that a problem exists. There are three ways to deal with this issue:

- Transfer savings from other components and products to meet the shortfall in components that do not attain target costs. The advantage is that it fosters a team approach to attaining targets and ensures that the product is a success. The risk is that cost discipline may be undermined because people will come to expect these subsidies.
- Transfer savings but attach a stigma to subsidies. Problem solving teams should be assigned to understand and solve the problem for future products.
- Do not transfer savings from one component to another. This approach will reinforce cost discipline. The risk is that it may be perceived as too rigid and may lower employee morale.

SUMMARY

This chapter describes the cost planning and analysis needed to move from an allowable to an achievable target cost. Cost planning and analysis proceeds in five steps.

The first step is to compute the cost gap between allowable and current costs. The gap should include all product costs defined on a life cycle basis. Cost elements included in the allowable cost should be defined in the same way as they are in the accounting system. This makes it easier to communicate cost targets and evaluate performance against these targets.

The second step is to decompose costs into their various elements. The decomposition is designed to allow a view of costs from different vantage points. Some of the more important ones are value chain, life cycle, customer, engineering, and accounting.

The third step is use the decomposed costs to assign cost reduction targets. Only design driven costs are assigned to design and build teams. Other costs are addressed by cost management tools such as ABM or BPR.

Design driven costs are further decomposed into functions, components, and parts and assigned to units, teams, and individuals. The functional analysis should be driven by customer requirements. However, in many cases this becomes difficult, and other methods are used to assign cost targets to functions.

The fourth step is to track progress toward the target cost through cost estimation. Models for cost estimation should use physical attributes of a product in the early stages and detailed cost buildups in the later stages of the product development cycle. Further, different stages of the product life cycle require different levels of accuracy in cost estimates.

The final step is to develop guidelines for dealing with unattainable cost targets. In general, target costs should be treated as commitments. Targets should be relaxed at the product level only after careful thought. Nonattainment of the target at the function or component level presents a different problem. The effects on morale and teamwork should be assessed before using savings from one component to subsidize other components.

6

C H A P T E R

Incorporating Customer Input in Target Costing

This chapter provides an overview of how to incorporate the voice of the customer in the target costing process. It explains what is meant by customer voice, introduces common methods of getting information about what customers want, and discusses the shortcomings of the various data collection methods. It concludes with a matrix presentation of how the customer's voice is introduced into each of the four stages in the product development cycle. The chapter contains five key messages.

KEY MESSAGES

- Target cost systems are market driven. They must incorporate customers' wants, desires, and needs.
- Customer input is used in all four stages of the product development cycle.
- All customer levels, intermediate and ultimate, must have a voice in the target costing process.
- Customer focused firms have several common traits. These firms

  Use state of the market technology.

  Conduct open-minded inquiry into customer needs, wants, and complaints.

Systematically distribute customer and market information throughout the organization.

Whenever appropriate, share information through teams.

Make underlying assumptions about data collection methods explicit.

Challenge all assertions or assumptions about customer needs.

- Many data collection and analysis techniques are available. The technique used should be tailored to fit a firm's needs and used only after considering benefits and shortcomings.

CUSTOMER VOICE AND THE PRODUCT DEVELOPMENT CYCLE

Target cost systems are market driven. Achieving target costs would be trivial if no customer constraints were placed on the quality and functionality of the products. The challenge for product and process designers and cost analysts is to meet or exceed customer requirements at an acceptable price without hurting profit margins. Customer input, therefore, is central to the target costing process. The voice of the customer is needed throughout the product development cycle as an input to set prices and profit targets, to guide design decisions, and to make function and feature trade-offs.

The model presented in Chapter 4 shows that the voice of the customer is a key input to all four stages of the product development cycle. Learning about customers, their needs, delight factors, and market segmentation is a continuous process that pervades all steps of the target cost process. If customer input is sought only at an early stage and the management team becomes immersed in technical development, prototype testing, regulatory issues, and budget approval, the conclusions from the initial customer input will be outdated. In addition, the type of customer input changes as the product development cycle unfolds. Therefore, there must be continuous input from customers, and management assumptions about their needs and wants must be ceaselessly tested.

Exhibit 6–1 is a graphical depiction of customer input in target costing. It shows that customer input is needed at all stages of the product development cycle and the sample input that customers provide at various stages of this cycle. At the product planning stage, customer input is used to identify proposed product features. The production and logistics phase, on the other hand, requires data on actual customer experience with the product. Aircraft manufacturers, such as Boeing, need data on the seats, fuel consumption, and range of its planes at the product planning stage. Actual repair and maintenance input comes at the production and logistics stage. This changing nature of customer input and the methods for collecting this input are discussed in the following pages.

Customer Voice and the Product Development Cycle

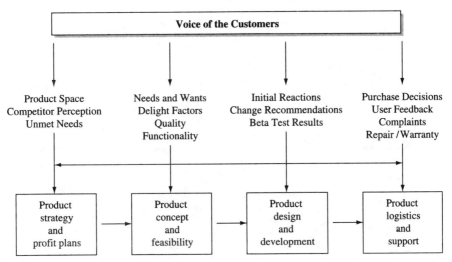

The focus of this chapter is on current customer requirements. It does not address the issue of changing use patterns and lifestyles of customers over time. Such changes may ultimately result in overall decreased demand for products of the type being produced. These changes are sometimes referred to as *criteria shifts*. Criteria shifts can be missed if the only customer input to an organization is micro customer data of the type discussed in this chapter.

The process of collecting information for criteria shifts involves scanning for changes in the macro environment. Data on groups of customers' usage patterns, preferences, trends, cultural norms, and lifestyles are important inputs to this process. Criteria shifts are considered as input to the multiyear product planning process. Chapter 10 provides coverage of multiyear product planning and its critical components. Certainly customer input is important to that process and can help in interpreting the macro data collected.

UNDERSTANDING CUSTOMER REQUIREMENTS

Companies may have more than one level of customers to satisfy. We refer to these as "ultimate" versus "intermediate" customers. For example, a car parts or aircraft parts manufacturer may have two or more intermediate customers and one ultimate customer. The intermediate customers are the assembly plant and the car dealer. The ultimate customer is the user or purchaser. An aircraft manufacturer must please both the airline (intermediate customer)

EXHIBIT 6-2

Customer Ideas in the Boeing 777

Some of the Great Ideas From Our Customers

and the passenger (ultimate customer). Time must be taken to identify and solicit input from all customer groups. When done properly, listening to customers not only is a good way to meet their needs, it also can result in
generating some good improvement ideas. Exhibit 6–2 shows some of the
ideas that Boeing's customers provided for the design of the 777 airliner.

To understand customer requirements we must understand what is
meant by customer value and customer focus. We must also understand the
types of customer inputs available.

Value to the Customer

If a company truly understands what is valued by customers, designers may
add features that add cost without significantly adding value in the customers' eyes. So what does *value to the customer*[1] actually mean?

---
[1] For an extended discussion of customer value and its components, see Society of Management Accountants of Canada, *Draft Management Guideline,* "Monitoring Customer Value," (Ontario,
Canada) 1995.

Value is the difference between the benefits received and the costs incurred by customers in getting those benefits. Benefits received include each customer's selective perception and opinion of the utility derived from physical and aesthetic attributes of a product and the way the product fits his or her needs and demands. The attributes of a car include both the physical features of the product (weight, size, power) and its aesthetic properties (sexy, youthful, fun to drive). The costs include the price paid and related immediate outlays for transportation, installation or training as well as life cycle costs such as maintenance, repairs, and disposition. Another element of the cost is the risk associated with life cycle costs. In general, products with longer lives have greater risk and therefore higher perceived costs. Exhibit 6–3 depicts the two dimensions of customer value.

What Does Customer Focus Mean?

Every organization claims to be customer focused. How does an organization that is truly listening to its customers behave? Learning what the customer wants is difficult. It involves more than just taking in information. The process of monitoring the voice of the customer includes asking the right questions, absorbing the answers into a proper mental model of the market, communicating that information to other members of the management team, and then acting on it. As this process becomes refined, management broadly shares market information as well as perceptions of what the customer thinks of its products against those offered by the competition.

Market oriented firms follow a similar sequence of activities to acquire, communicate, interpret, and remember knowledge. Their systems, procedures,

EXHIBIT 6–3

Dimensions of Customer Value

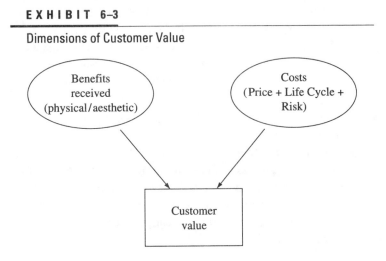

routines, files, and data banks are designed to aid the process. More important, their managers share the same mental decision rules to accept or reject information and interpret data. Further, they make analogous simplifying assumptions about how the market will respond to actions they take based on their information.

A market focused firm exhibits the following traits:

- It uses *state of the market technology* in products. That is, technology is introduced into products because customers want it and not because engineers think it makes for a great product. Compaq decided to delay Pentium shipments for a while and concentrate on deliveries of faster 486 based machines. This paid off handsomely for the firm. Perhaps it correctly read customers' needs and provided them with the technology they wanted.

- It conducts *open-minded inquiries*. Managers agree that market information is what drives an enterprise. There is an openness to trends and events that present market opportunities. Service people do not get upset because their schedule is thrown off by a customer request for modification; front line people must hear complaints and requests for service as opportunities not nuisances to be avoided. All levels of the company must avoid arrogance, "we know what's wanted because it's our product that's selling," and complacency, "we grew sales in the past doing business this way, don't fix what's not broken."

- It has a coherent and systematic way to make *customer and market information available throughout the organization*. Feedback data such as sales and cost have always been accessible to managers. On the other hand, forward looking information on customers needs and wants has not been widely distributed across the company. Often employees do not know if the information exists or, if it does, who has it and how to gain access to it. A market focused company has a coherent strategy to make information available organization-wide. All data are entered into a central repository and easily accessed.

- It *shares information through teams*. Working in teams is important in understanding customer input and developing shared mental decision rules and perceptions of market responses. Teams should be cross-functional as well as global, if feasible. Each team member brings a unique way of viewing the product, its performance, its technical functions, its target customers, and its feeling and image. Broad based team membership reduces interpretation bias.

EXHIBIT 6–4

Accommodating Conflicting Views of Customer Requirements

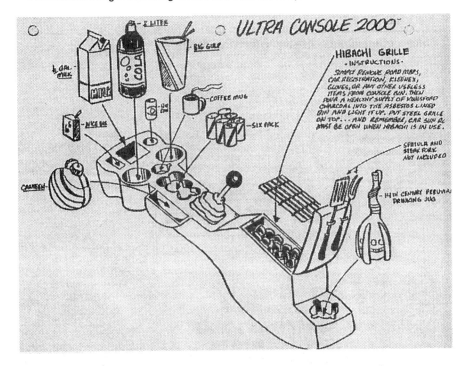

- It *challenges all assumptions.* Lively debate and frequent interaction should be encouraged of teams members so that mind-sets and implicit assumptions are not left unchallenged. If a member has an unchallenged assumption about what will happen, it may become a self-fulfilling prophecy.

- It makes *underlying data assumptions explicit.* All models of understanding customer and market information are simplifications. Pitfalls with using simplifications arise when the models and their assumptions are not stated explicitly for users. Models for understanding and analyzing information need to be made explicit so that they can be scrutinized and challenged. The divergent views of the product coming from team members must be examined, and a convergent view must emerge to make critical design choices. Exhibit 6–4 is a designer's humorous representation of what might happen if all views of customer requirements related to a car's console were taken literally and accommodated.

E X H I B I T 6–5

Traits for Organizational Learning from Customers

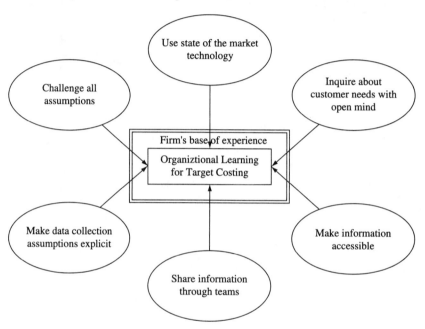

A market focused organization that acquires the traits just listed is well geared to learning what it needs to know for target costing. Exhibit 6–5 shows how these traits help to build an organization's base of experience. This base, in turn, creates the foundation for faster and more rapid organizational learning about customer needs and for becoming market focused. Both are essential for making intelligent trade-offs in the target costing process.

Types of Customer Input Available

Understanding customer requirements also means knowing the types of customer input to collect and when to collect them. Customer input takes two forms. It is either forward looking data about what the customer perceives he or she wants or it is feedback data that reflect actual choices made by customers. The emphasis today in the literature on survey design seems to suggest that organizations should be acting almost *exclusively* on forward looking information. Feedforward information is critically important but no more important than feedback information. Feedforward information elicits customers' attitudes. Attitudes reflect what customers think they want and would be willing to pay for. Feedback information encompasses actual decision and action data: purchases, returns, complaints, and product failures. Results of attitudinal research indicate that actions do not always follow expressed attitudes. Therefore, it is important to combine both forward looking and feedback information in the target costing process.

Feedforward information is most useful in the profit strategy/profit planning and product concept and feasibility stages of the product development cycle. It declines in importance in the product design and development and production and logistics stages, in which an abundance of feedback information is available. Note, however, that both feedforward and feedback information are used throughout all four stages of the product development cycle. This is depicted in Exhibit 6–6.

Regardless of whether the information is feedforward or feedback in nature, management should be proactive in data collection. Proactive customer contact is initiated by the organization and includes cross-functional employee participation. For example, it could involve senior executives from different functions visiting with customers or talking to them by phone, customer panels meeting regularly with design engineers and finance people to suggest improvements to products and services, or using select customers as beta sites to test new products before widespread market release.

TECHNIQUES FOR SOLICITING THE VOICE OF THE CUSTOMER

Techniques for gathering data about customers abound.[2] They include focus groups, surveys, customer service records, and sales feedback. New ways of arraying this data in matrices also exist. This section presents some of the more recognized methods of collecting and arraying data. It will also discuss some shortcomings of the methods.

Data Collection Methods

Several methods are used for collecting data about customer requirements. Some of the common ones are briefly described next.

- *Customer panels* are formal groups that meet regularly to suggest improvements to products and services. The organization's employees ask questions of the panel, and minutes are kept of the

---

[2] This section draws on "Monitoring Customer Value," *Management Accounting Guideline* (Hamilton, Ont.: Society of Management Accountants of Canada, 1995).

EXHIBIT 6–6

Types of Customer Information in Product Development Stages

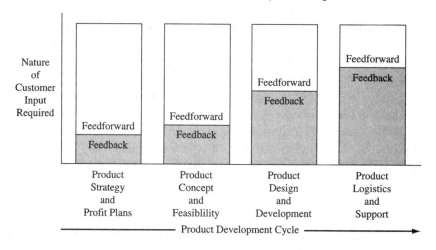

suggestions. The insights gained usually come from the interactions among the panel members. Panels usually cover topics that are not too complex and can be discussed in a group setting comfortably. Boeing uses a variant of this method and includes intermediate customers on design and build teams. Pilots, attendants, and maintenance personnel have directly participated on such teams.

- *Focus groups* include customers or potential customers who are given dimensions of value developed from internal data and one on one interviews. These groups are used iteratively to narrow down the value dimensions of the product or service to 10 to 25 attributes to use in survey research. Often focus group sessions are videotaped.

- *Beta sites* involve the use of targeted customers to test new products or services. Feedback from the beta sites allows modification of the product or service before the final market release. Software companies typically use this method for refining software code and features.

- *Customer value surveys* are conducted after the organization has tentatively identified the key dimensions of customer value through internal and external sources. Internal sources include front line salespeople, customer representatives, and customer service records. External sources include individual customer discussions or focus groups. Customer value surveys are usually conducted by telephone or through the mail or some combination of the two. The data collected through value surveys must tell us:

- The most important factors in purchase decisions.
- The weight of various quality attributes in decisions.
- Features that are needed (will cause dissatisfaction if not present), exciting and unexpected (will "delight" the customer if present), or wanted (will give customers exactly what they ask for).
- The rank of each competitor's product on each quality attribute.
- The factors that affect customer's perceptions of a product's cost.
- How the various cost factors are weighted in their decisions.
- The rank of each competing product on each of the price attributes.
- *Face-to-face interview* with customers during site visits, golf, or other social settings is another way of learning about customers' requirements and their evaluation of the firm's product and price versus the competitors.
- *Trade journals* contain articles that provide information about the changing needs of customers and new product innovations.
- *Warranty claims or customer complaints or follow-up calls* provide information about any problems customers face with the product.
- *Market Statistics* about sales, market share trends, customer retention rates, allowances granted, or products returned typically are available in an organization's information system. These statistics provide feedback information about the market's acceptance of a product.

Data Collection Problems

All data collection methods pose some problems and have some shortcomings. To get valid data, we must execute these methods carefully. The most commonly used method for data collection is the customer survey. No generic survey can be used or modified to fit all circumstances. To design an effective survey, the objective of the survey must be clear and the research design must be well thought out so that it is reliable, valid, free of bias, useful, and precise. The target population must be considered as well. The sample must be representative of diverse population segments and cover wide geographical areas. Careful attention must be paid to select a proper rating scale to measure either micro or macro shifts in responses.

Another data collection problem involves capturing information from open-ended discussions when using customer panels, focus groups, and face to face interviews. To capture the essence of the conversation and have it shared across the organization, a standardized form needs to be devised to record information. The completed data form constitutes a record in a centralized data base. It is important that one data location in the form includes the customer's words or key phrases. The remaining data locations will contain inferences the listener makes from the conversation. Those inferences depend on the nature of the communication but may include information such as customer demands (both physical attributes and aesthetic properties) and quality characteristics or features of the product that respond to the demands, new technology, new concepts, product failures, parts or subsystems, mechanisms, and the like. These inferences are biased by the functional expertise of the listener. Ideally, the customer's words and phrases allow alternate interpretations and examination of the inferences made by different functional experts in the organization.

Both surveys and personal data collection methods will be biased by the process or the interpretation of observed data. Recognizing these biases and making an effort to deal with them explicitly will increase the chances of using valid customer input in target costing. Product teams can overcome these biases, one hopes, because they bring alternative experience, technical expertise, and worldviews to the process. Another way is to use external market research firms to foster greater objectivity in data collection.

Data Analysis

The purpose of data analysis is to separate what customers must have from what they expect to get and from what they want but do not expect—the delight features. It is also critically important to understand the relationship between the features valued by customers and the characteristics or functions of the product that deliver those features to the customers. Therefore, the voice of the customer must be reconciled with the voice of engineers in analyzing data to understand which features are under the control of the company. Typical ways of arraying and understanding data include the following:

- *Matrix data analysis for market segmentation* is a two-dimensional view of the product. It involves using two important attributes of the product or service that can occur in high and low levels and showing them on different axes of a graph. We can illustrate the process using a study of California State University students. The study captures the perceptions of various brand names with status (high or low) on one dimension and the amount of traditional or conservative appeal (high or low) on the other dimension. The results are shown in Exhibit 6-7. The matrix shows brand grouping across products on the prestige dimension. The same analysis can

E X H I B I T   6–7

Perceptions of Brands

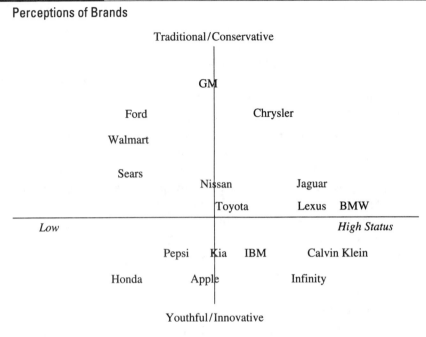

Traditional/Conservative

GM

Ford   Chrysler

Walmart

Sears
              Nissan   Jaguar
              Toyota   Lexus   BMW

Low   *High Status*

          Pepsi   Kia   IBM   Calvin Klein

    Honda   Apple   Infinity

Youthful/Innovative

Youthful/Innovative

Source: Amy Evans, H. Bruce Lammers, and Students of Marketing Research, "Lifestyles, Values, Interests, and Opinions of CSUN Students," a study funded by a grant from Ford Motor Corporation. Results are available from Dr. Bruce Lammers, CSUN, Marketing Department, 18111 Nordhoff St., Northridge, CA 91330–8245.

be used to compare specific products. Information from customers could be used to place each competitor's product on the graph. This kind of analysis, combined with information on the market share of the products, tells a great deal about market segmentation.

■ A *quality table* is a matrix presentation of customer's demanded features on one dimension and the functions of the product that relate to those features on the other. It typically is used to better define individual products or major upgrades of existing products. The information about how strongly the product characteristics correlate with the customers' valued attributes is obtained from the engineering department. It also includes information about how important each attribute is to customers, how the company is rated on each attribute presently, and how its competitors are rated. The data typically are arranged in what is called a *quality function deployment* (QFD) matrix. The matrix is discussed more fully in Chapter 10.

- A *quality profile* is an attempt to compare the organization's product or service with that of competitors. It is done numerically by dividing the organization's score for each product attribute by the average score for all competitors. This number can be weighted by the importance assigned each attribute.

- A *price profile* is an analysis very similar to the quality profile. It compares a product's cost to customers with that of competitors.

- A *customer value map* illustrates how a customer chooses between alternative product offerings. It is a 2 × 2 matrix with relative price (higher and lower) on one dimension and relative performance or quality (higher and lower) on the other. It has four cells: high price/low performance, low price/low performance, high price/high performance, and low price/high performance. Customer's perceptions of each competing product is assigned to one of these four cells, as illustrated in Exhibit 6–8.

- A *won/lost analysis* is typically used in competitive bidding situations. It analyzes bids won and lost. The purpose is to isolate which product and service attributes were present and at what relative prices, when bids were won and lost.

- A *head to head chart of customer value* compares the performance of the organization's product or service on each attribute with that of its most important competitor(s). It is similar to a QFD type analysis except that it is competitor based and not customer based.

- A *Pareto chart of complaints* shows the most frequent cause of customer complaints against the firm's products.

EXHIBIT 6–8

Customer Value Map for Luxury Cars

Performance		
Relative Price	**Higher**	**Lower**
Higher	Lexus 400	Mercedes Benz 400
Lower	Cadillac STS	Lincoln Towncar

■ A *time plot of market share* trends tracks progress in sales over time versus that of competitors.

■ A *plot of customer retention rates* over time shows how well the firm has satisfied customers over time.

These are only some of the methods possible for analyzing data collected. There is no generic way or best way of analyzing and arraying data. To design the best data display, the objectives of data collection must be clear and the method best suited for that objective should be used. Exhibit 6–9 attempts to summarize the data collection and analysis at each stage of the product development cycle. It shows the type of data that is collected, who is best suited to collect that data, the method used for data collection, the analysis to be done, and the limitations of the data. Chapter 9 discusses methods of disseminating this information throughout the organization.

EXHIBIT 6–9

Customer Data in the Product Development Cycle

Product Development Cycle	What Data?	How Collected?	What Analysis?	Limitations
Product strategy and profit planning	Market segmentation data, customer need survey competitor product profile	Focus groups, ethnographic interviews, surveys	Segmentation matrix, repeat feedback from focus groups, head to head comparisons	Hard to define unfilled spaces for new products that have no history
Product Concept Feasibility	Needs, wants, delight factors	Surveys, focus groups, direct participation	Value quality map, value quality matrix, price map on teams	Customers often do not state a need but are dissatisfied if it is not provided
Product concept and feasibility, continued	Quality characteristics	Brainstorming by team members, direct customer participation on teams, from customers' own evaluation	Correlation between product characteristics needs, and wants, and delight factors; value quality	

Product design and development	Feedback data from test user groups.	Interviews, participant/ observer data, beta tests, customer previews, prototype testing	Value profile, price profile, quality profile	Customer input may not be completely indicative of purchase preferences
Production and logistics	Feedback data on actual decisions or purchase returns, complaints, warranty repairs, post purchase satisfaction	Data on returns, warranties, complaints; follow-up interviews; customer analysis	Progress charts, warranty repair costs, defect rates, product recalls	Usually too late for existing products

SUMMARY

In this chapter we have shown that effective target costing requires customer input throughout the product development cycle. An organization must clearly understand who its customers are and what they mean by *value*. We have identified six traits that we believe are hallmarks of a "listening" organization. No matter how attuned an organization is to its customer, the task of getting customer input poses several technical challenges. These include selecting an appropriate data collection method, arraying the data in comprehensible ways, and making sense of the data through sound data analysis.

7

CHAPTER

Target Costing in the Extended Enterprise

For target costing to be effective, it must be diffused throughout the value chain. Beginning with research and development and continuing through manufacturing, delivery, servicing, and disposing of a product, today, the steps in the value chain are performed by a number of different firms. Products are seldom completely made by a single firm or sold to customers by the firm whose brand it bears. A substantial portion of parts and components (and sometimes even research) is procured from outside suppliers, and many sales activities are carried out by dealers. A typical good is produced, sold, serviced, and recycled by a network of firms, referred to here as the *extended enterprise*. This network of firms has joint control of cost and quality, and each firm has unique information about customers' desires. How to effectively involve the extended enterprise in target costing is the subject of this chapter. We want to communicate five key messages.

KEY MESSAGES

- The key to total cost reduction is to reduce costs in the entire value chain.
- Passing on cost reductions to suppliers, dealers, and recyclers is not target costing. To maintain their viability, these firms must maintain their profit margins.

- Value chain members must be involved in each of the four stages of the product development cycle.
- Involving value chain members in target costing provides many benefits to both parties. Products are more durable and reliable, they better meet customer requirements, and they are made using more efficient production processes.
- A key element of managing the extended enterprise is managing suppliers. Optimizing the supply chain by using CAM-I's strategic supply chain management principles can greatly increase the effectiveness of target costing.

THE EXTENDED ENTERPRISE

Exhibit 7–1 depicts the extended enterprise graphically. It shows that the market maker, the firm that develops the concept for the product,[1] is supported by suppliers and is linked to customers through distributors. Customers have a backward link with the service and support providers while the product is in use and with recyclers when the product is to be disposed of.

EXHIBIT 7-1

A Typical Extended Enterprise

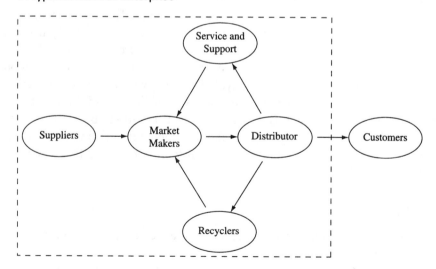

---

[1] There are other ways the term *market maker* is used in the literature. For example, an inventor may develop a product and may consider another company with brand name recognition to be the market maker for its product.

These may be part of the market maker organization, or they may be separate organizations. When separate, service providers and recyclers have a link back to the market maker through service and remanufacturing relationships. These links, which will vary by organization, are referred to as a *value chain.* Each step or each organization adds value to the product.

VALUE CHAIN PARTICIPANTS IN TARGET COSTING

To get the most out of target costing, a firm must identify and then locate itself in the value chain. This helps to clarify the role the firm performs in the product/customer interface. It also determines the scope and expected contribution of each member of the value chain to the cost reduction process. For example, Texas Instruments is a supplier of memory chips to PC manufacturers. Texas Instruments must understand that the relative price range for PCs in the market will determine the ultimate price it can charge for any improved memory chip. It also must understand that customers desire new features in PCs, along with high quality and low cost. Texas Instruments has to provide PC manufacturers memory chips that not only provide good value at the time of purchase but also are cost effectively integrated into the end product.

The sharing of experience and technical expertise by value chain members pervades all stages of the target costing process. The nature of the participation and the contributions of value chain members change over the four stages of the product development process. This is depicted by Exhibit 7–2.

In the *product strategy and profit planning stage,* value chain members contribute information about technology and its capabilities, changing use patterns for products, changes in lifestyle that affect demand for services, and cultural changes like environmental awareness. An example of the impact of this on product strategy is found in the development of new types of sound systems in cars. Children listen to their Walkman while parents use the car's sound system. GM Hughes Electronics, as a supplier to GM, has aimed technology developed for aircraft to redesign sound systems for cars so each passenger can control his or her own music selection. Another example is the timing of new generations of microprocessors. It does no good to introduce a faster microprocessor until the technology of the other supplier components can match the output capability of the new microprocessor.

In the *product concept and feasibility stage,* the value chain's contribution is critical. Without good input the market maker may end up with a product concept that is not feasible. This may be because suppliers cannot produce it or distributors cannot distribute it or scrap buyers cannot recycle it. Design feasibility is the ability of every member in the value chain to perform to the

EXHIBIT 7-2

Contributions of Value Chain to Target Costing

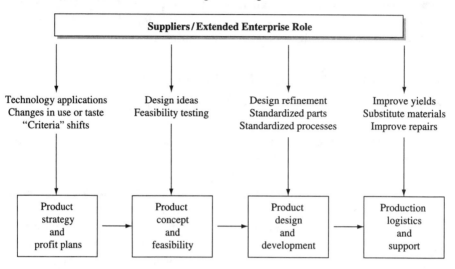

required specifications. It is ineffective to design an earthquake-safe foundation that has shock absorbers if the concrete, masonry, electric, and plumbing trades lack the ability to design their products to work with these "flexible" foundation designs.

During the *product design and development stage,* value chain members are active in coordinating their products and services so they fit together to yield the product desired by customers. As an example of input during this phase, consider Chrysler's design of a car dashboard. All parts manufacturers must be involved so that each component, such as the speedometer, will fit into the space allowed and maximize the design features of the dashboard. The use of alternative materials may be considered, so processes are simplified and environmental costs are avoided.

In the *production logistics and support stage,* ideas from value chain members can lead to continuous improvement in product and processes. Value chain members work together on developing processes and methods that improve yields and quality. For example, suppliers may discover better ways of attaching or combining parts, alternate materials, or other innovations after the product has gone into production. Service and support providers may identify problems in parts or design that make them hard to repair. Recyclers may point out the environmental costs of disposition as they gain experience with the product.

Diffusing target costing throughout the value chain involves creating nontraditional relationships among the participants of the value chain. Teams composed of members of the value chain must manage cost and quality. Organizational boundaries have to become permeable, and an extended enterprise must be created. Each member of this enterprise can bring unique experience and functional expertise to the target costing process. Based on the Japanese experience with teams of suppliers, a team approach outperforms both the vertically integrated organization and arms-length transaction specific relationships with those in the value chain.

To get members of the extended enterprise to contribute at all stages of the product development cycle, two questions must be carefully answered: What do we need from participants in the value chain? How do we manage the extended enterprise to get what we need? The rest of this chapter focuses on these two questions. We place a greater emphasis on suppliers because they typically control a large portion of costs in most industries. However, most of the information is equally relevant to distributors and recyclers as well. In some industries, these participants are as important as the supplier. Consider, for example, the software industry. A large part of the product cost in this industry is for service and support. In the software industry, inclusion of service and support organizations in target costing is as important as the inclusion of suppliers.

EXPECTED CONTRIBUTIONS FROM THE VALUE CHAIN

The key to total cost reduction is to bring the costs down in the entire value chain. Simply passing on costs to suppliers, dealers, or recyclers is not target costing. All members of the value chain must understand that target costing is a process of life cycle and value chain cost reduction. Further, they must understand that, depending on their position in the value chain, each member brings a different level of contribution to the target costing process. Some of the more important contributions expected of value chain members are discussed next.

Provide Better Focus on Customer Requirements

Suppliers, dealers, service and support providers, and recyclers can supply a wealth of information about customer requirements. Each member brings a unique customer perspective based on its own function. For example, a seat manufacturer may have a better idea of what a customer wants than the automobile manufacturer. The target costing process should meld these different perspectives into a cohesive view of customer requirements.

Enhance Technology

All participants should be willing to increase the level of technology in a product. Each member may bring expertise on a certain technological frontier. In particular, suppliers are better equipped to bring specialized technology not available to the market maker. For example, Accustar provides state of the art electronic components for Chrysler while Hughes and Delco do the same for General Motors. Often this increased level of technology reduces new product development time, increases product quality, and decreases cost. Ideas on technology and its uses should be shared by all members of a value chain to maximize the use of technology.

Provide Input and Ideas Early in the Concept Formation Stage

Each member of the chain needs to provide input and ideas early in the concept formulation stage. The ideas can be tested, refined, and incorporated into the product specifications or the manufacturing process with minimum cost and improved innovation cycle time. Further, participation in the target costing process must be followed with a commitment to implement changes to reduce costs and cycle time.

Eliminate Non-Value Added Activities

To effect the cost reductions required of each member in the chain, processes must be studied and non-value added activities eliminated. By sharing ideas and process information, new win-win solutions can be devised. Consider a bakery that consumes large quantities of eggs. The egg suppliers go to great trouble and expense to pack eggs such that they do not break in delivery to the bakery. The bakery spends a great deal of time and money breaking eggs and disposing of the shells. Together the two can address the problem and devise a win-win solution. The supplier can break the eggs and send them in containers and sell the shells. The bakery can use the desired quantity with less cost and effort. Reduction of non-value added activities also reduces the amount of time it takes to design, produce, and deliver products.

Eliminate Unnecessary Features and Reduce Parts

An important belief that needs to be instilled in all value chain participants is that by eliminating unnecessary features and reducing parts, costs will decrease and quality will increase. This is not obvious to all. Sharing information on the costs (administrative, manufacturing, and support) that occur when parts proliferate should help impart the message. Further, flexibility can increase if the mushroom concept is used by all. Develop a basic product with the same parts and features up to a break off where changes transform it into multiple products at little extra cost. Value chain members can brainstorm about how to minimize parts and features and develop products as break offs from a mushroom platform.

Evaluate Alternative Materials

To reduce costs over the long run, participants need to be aware and give thought to alternative materials. Some of the ideas may relate to controlling environmental costs. The full costs of using materials must be considered. The process difficulty of handling complex, polluting materials, the potential costs of cleanup, bad publicity, and negative impact from the "green" community on product sales are some elements that need to be taken into account. In addition, alternative materials should be evaluated based on their functionality and cost by all participants from their value chain perspective.

Pursue Standardization

Standardization increases quality and reduces costs. Value chain members should work together on standardizing processes, products, and parts as much as possible.

Improve Durability and Reliability

Value engineering by teams should focus on improving the durability and reliability of the product. These ideas should be worked into the product design and not discovered on the manufacturing floor or by service personnel after the fact. These factors are very important to customer satisfaction. Input on these factors comes from service organizations and dealers as well as suppliers.

Improve Yields

All members of the value chain need to improve their own yields, as well as the yield of the market maker. This requires coordination between members firms' manufacturing and design efforts, within and with each other, so that all components and parts work together without problem solving in final assembly.

Reduce Paperwork

As members of the value chain work with one another, they should think about how to reduce paperwork. Transaction processes should be re-engineered so business is conducted with a minimum of paperwork and unnecessary administrative steps. This reduces cost and allows administrative time to be devoted to more productive activities.

Allow for Continuous Improvement

To be an effective member of the value chain, each member needs to have a commitment to continuous improvement. All of them need to participate actively in managing costs and improving quality throughout the chain.

MANAGING THE SUPPLY CHAIN

For a market maker, the most critical relationship, aside from that with customers, is with the supply chain. An optimized supply chain is one of the most critical elements in attaining target costs. CAM-I has identified several axioms that can be used as a guide for determining if an optimum supply chain is in place.[2] These axioms follow:

- There is a shared specific focus on satisfying the common end customer.
- There is an alignment of vision.
- There is a fundamental level of cooperation and performance to commitment (trust).
- There is open and effective communication.
- Decisions are made by maximizing the use of the competencies and knowledge within the supply chain.
- All stakeholders are committed to generate long-term mutual benefits.
- There is a common view of how success is measured.
- All members are committed to continuous improvement and breakthrough advancements.
- Whatever competitive pressures exist in the environment are allowed to exist within the extended enterprise.

---

[2] These principles have been developed by P. Zampino, B. Boykin, M. Doyle, and R. Parker as part of a working document for the CAM-I Strategic Supply Chain Management Program., CAM-I (Arlington, TX), 1996.

To attain the nine principles of an optimal supply chain, we need to manage the supply chain proactively in that direction. Effective management of the supply chain requires executing the steps described next.

Characterize the Supply Chain

Understanding the nature and number of suppliers and rationalizing the supply chain is critical for managing the extended enterprise. This requires classifying suppliers by how far they are in the supply chain and by the extent to which they perform design work for the project.

- Distance from the Market Maker. Asanuma[3] states that historically the number of suppliers used by U.S. firms has been much greater than the number used by Japanese firms because U.S. firms bought subcomponents from a number of suppliers and assembled them in-house. For example, in 1983 GM used 800 suppliers for one assembly plant compared to Toyota's use of 125. The difference occurs because Japanese firms tend to buy components from suppliers organized into tiers. Suppliers who sell directly to a market maker are referred to as *tier one* firms. These suppliers have numerous other firms from whom they buy parts or subcomponents. These other firms are referred to as *tier two* firms. Again, tier two firms buy from numerous others, tier three organizations. For the target costing process to be effective, it must be passed down the many levels in the supply chain from tier one firms to all lower tier firms. In fact, one of the criteria to evaluate a supplier may be the way it manages, trains, and involves its suppliers in managing cost, quality, and time. Exhibit 7–3 depicts this relationship.

- Nature of Design Work Done by Supplier. The second criteria for classifying suppliers is the extent to which they participate in product and process design. Exhibit 7–4 shows various supplier relationships that have been documented. These relationships vary from the supplier offering assembly facilities with no input into the design of the product or manufacturing process (a design provided supplier) to complete control of both product and process design (a design approved supplier). In Exhibit 7–4 the term *core firm* is used to denote the firm to whom the supplier is providing goods. Note that this could be the market maker, a tier one or tier $n - 1$ supplier.

---

[3] B. Asanuma, "Japanese Manufacturer-Supplier Relationships in International Perspective: The Automobile Case," Working Paper No. 8, Faculty of Economics, Kyoto University, 1988.

EXHIBIT 7-3

Understanding the Supply Chain

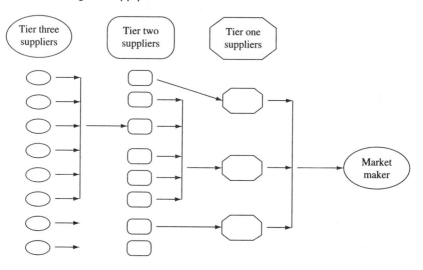

Kodak has a variant of this classification scheme which they use for classifying and managing their suppliers. Its scheme is shown in Exhibit 7–5. The terms *HV* and *LR* refer to high value and low risk, respectively. These categories capture the extent to which Kodak is dependent upon a supplier or vice versa.

Kodak's Type I category is similar to categories *b* and *c* in Exhibit 7–4. There is strong interdependence between Kodak and this category of supplier, the two have high trust in each other and have formed an alliance; they work together to achieve objectives and share failure and successes. The Type II category is similar to category *d* in Exhibit 7–4. Kodak is dependent on its Type II suppliers. These suppliers possess key technology that makes them capable of delivering components Kodak needs, components that, often, no other firm can supply. Type III suppliers are dependent on Kodak. They work with Kodak to find continuous improvements in products and processes and retain their supplier relationship by their contributions in those areas. This is similar to the relationship described for category *a* suppliers in Exhibit 7–4. Finally, Type IV suppliers and Kodak are mutually independent of one another. Kodak relies on the market to determine where to buy these commodity type items. This is similar to category *e* in Exhibit 7–4.

Rationalize the Supply Chain

The supply chain can be made more effective by developing long-term relationships with a more concentrated supply base. In addition, efficiencies are

E X H I B I T   7–4

Types of Supplier Relationships

Type of Supplier	Control of Design	Supplier Role	Description
a Customized goods supplier	CAD drawings and manufacturing process specified by market maker	Details controlled by core firm	Core firm provides detailed instruction and guidelines for manufacturing
b Ordered custom goods—design provided suppliers	CAD drawings supplied by market maker	Manufacturing process designed by supplier	Core firm approves process
c Ordered custom goods—design approved suppliers	Rough drawings supplied by the market maker	Supplier does CAD drawings and designs manufacturing process	Core firm approval, black box process
d Ordered goods—design approved suppliers	Specification issued by market maker	Supplier designs product and process	Core firm approval, black box
e Commodity	Selection from	Supplier	Supplier has many

gained by increasing reliance on suppliers who participate in the design process. Market makers must have a strategy of reducing tiers of end item suppliers. This reduces the internal costs of procurement management. Working with a large number of suppliers causes inconsistencies in input, congestion in production, and difficult administrative procedures. Companies such as Caterpillar, Chrysler, and Kodak develop their suppliers by organizing joint workshops, sharing any savings resulting from teamwork, and working with longer term contracts.

Involve Suppliers in Design

In the United States, firms have traditionally focused on supplier relationships types *a* and *e* in Exhibit 7–4. The market maker either provides a detailed drawing and manufacturing process specifications and firms bid annually to do the manufacturing or commodity products are bought on the open market. Japan's cost leadership has been attributed partially to its tradition of developing relationships with type *b, c,* and *d* suppliers. In recent years, U.S. firms have begun to develop more category *b, c,* and *d*

EXHIBIT 7–5

Kodak's Supplier Relationship Management Models

Low ◄ – – – – – – – – **Kodak Dependence on Supplier** – – – – – – – – ► High

High ▲ Supplier Dependence on Kodak Low ▼	

Type III: HV/LR Multiple Source

$$\mathrm{L^{ow}_K} \big/ \mathrm{H^{igh}_S}$$

- Kodak independence
- Supplier drives relationship
  (continuous improvement)
- Relationship Value >= commercial
  transactions
- Low switching cost
- Competition drives excellence

Type I: IIV/HR and/or Single Source

$$\mathrm{H^{igh}_K} \big/ \mathrm{H^{igh}_S}$$

- Strong interdependence
- Both drive relationship
  (e.g. continuous improvement)
- Relationship Value >> commercial
  transactions for both parties
- High switching cost
- High levels of trust
- Synergistic relationship (1+1>2)
- Overarching mutual objective
- High cost of failure
- Large reward for success

Type IV: LV/LR Convenience HSSource

$$\mathrm{L^{ow}_K} \big/ \mathrm{L^{ow}_S}$$

- Mutual independence
- Value = commercial transactions
- Low switching cost

Type II: LV/HR and/or Sole Source

$$\mathrm{H^{igh}_K} \big/ \mathrm{L^{ow}_S}$$

- Kodak dependence/supplier
  independence
- Kodak drive relationship
- Relationship Value >> commercial
  transaction value for Kodak
- High switching cost
- May be the only game in town
  (time dependent)

type supplier relationships because of the synergies that can be gained from them. In particular, the greater involvement of suppliers in product design has led to more value engineering going into a product. This has reduced lead times, provided process improvements, and led to significant cost reductions for market makers.

Maintain Profit Margins

A key concern of suppliers is that cost reduction will erode their profit margins. Product managers should study margins and the relative value contributions of each member of the supply chain. Cost reduction targets should be assigned based on these value and margin assessments and in a way that does not erode suppliers' profit margins.[4] Suppliers should be treated as partners. Hold them responsible for meeting all objectives, not just cost. However, when cost savings result, share the rewards with suppliers who offer suggestions that save costs. Each class of supplier requires a different approach to profit margin maintenance.

- For *commodity type products,* profit margins are usually unknown and firms are given targeted percentage price reductions for a certain time span. How these reductions are achieved by suppliers is not known to the market maker. The market maker simply uses achieved price reductions to determine whether a supplier is cooperating. The only weapon that can be used is to give the business to competitors.

- For *design provided suppliers,* an invitation to quote is issued from the market maker. This invitation requests a price quote that meets the market maker's quality and time targets for the product. The supplier typically designs the manufacturing process in response to the drawings supplied. It may also conduct value engineering to reduce prospective manufacturing costs by proposing improvements to product design. A limited amount of information about profit margins may have to be shared in these situations.

- For *design approved firms,* the scope of activities undertaken is much broader. These firms must successfully develop a part in response to general specifications issued by the core firm within a limited time frame. This means that they must have the ability and equipment to design, manufacture, test trial parts, and understand and adapt to the needs of the core firm. They also need to be able to offer suggestions on improving the specifications in early development. Since they may have to do special tooling and design work, design approved suppliers often work on an "open book system," in which they share cost and margin data with the core firm and share in cost savings.

---

[4] For additional information on managing profit and cost throughout the value chain, see John Shank and Vijay Govindarajan, *Strategic Cost Management* (Free Press: New York), 1995.

Involve Suppliers (Other Value Chain Members) Early in the Process

Suppliers must be involved early in the product development cycle. They can provide valuable input while the product is still in a concept stage. The make or buy policies of a firm, which determine what products to produce internally and which ones to procure outside, are critical to make early involvement work.[5] These policies determine which suppliers get involved early in the process.

Traditionally, simplistic microeconomic models have been used to determine which products to make internally. The lowest bidder, internal or external, is typically awarded a contract. When excess capacity exists, goods are made internally if they can be produced at a "marginal" cost less than the external bid. These decision rules treat the make or buy issue as a one time short-term problem. With suppliers scattered all over the globe and components becoming increasingly sophisticated, this old way of handling the make or buy decision will not get early supplier involvement.[6] Firms need a more strategic make or buy process.

A strategic approach to this decision requires classifying the products and components a firm needs into three categories: core competency products, key products, and commodity products. Core competency products represent items that draw on a company's areas of strength. These strengths can be possessing a superior technology, organizational skills, accumulated experience, or better production processes. Items tied to an organization's core competency should be made internally only. Key items are those that are technologically difficult to design and manufacture. Key items require special skills and customization. They should be outsourced and supplied by selected strategic suppliers. Finally, commodity products are available on the open market from a variety of sources. They should be outsourced, and there is no reason to produce them internally if the full cost is above the external price.

In Japan, the make or buy decision is done about 36 months prior to production beginning. It comes as an output of process planning. Process planning, handled by the production technology department, determines how to produce and assemble individual parts. This process also addresses whether to produce these items inside or to outsource them. Namely, firms

---

[5] Another important issue is how to organize the procurement function. That is, whether to handle it through a centralized procurement organization or to let target cost teams do their own procurement. Both approaches have merit. It is beyond the scope of this chapter to discuss this issue in detail. Regardless of which approach is pursued, however, a clear centralized make or buy policy is essential.

[6] Boeing's 777 is a good example. This plane has a very international and complex acquisition pattern for its components.

decide how to apportion various processes between company plants and out-side suppliers. About 26.5 percent of components are sourced internally in Japan, 30.5 percent purchased in the market (commodity parts), and 43 per-cent are ordered goods with some participation in the planning process.[7]

In general a good make or buy decision process should eliminate the need for specifying minute details of products and manufacturing processes. It should reduce the number of commodity product vendors, work with tiered vendors, and allow those in the higher tiers to control the lower tiers. Mar-ginal quality vendors should be in the first tier only if uncertainty is high on product sales volumes. In general, the process should protect the volume of high-quality vendors in downturns.

Early involvement of suppliers makes it easier to use simultaneous or concurrent engineering. Simultaneous engineering is a collaborative design process that strives to integrate and balance product development from initi-ation of the concept to customer feedback. Its purpose is to reduce time to market, and it involves all players on the product team. Everyone receives the same information at the same time, so all team members can work together toward a common goal of "doing it right the first time." Supplier concurrent engineering cuts the total lead time for development. Exhibit 7–6 graphically shows the reduction in lead time that results from simultaneous engineering with suppliers.[8]

Other benefits from early supplier involvement are reduction in the number of parts, reduction of non-value added activities, improved qual-ity, and easier assembly and manufacturability. Early involvement also ap-plies to other members of the value chain. Getting dealers, service and support providers, and disposers or recyclers on board early can be very beneficial.

Dealers and distributors solicit information from customers and also provide firsthand contact and service to customers. This information needs to be brought into the target costing process. In addition, product design can have an impact on distribution as well as the cost and quality of products. Without dealer involvement, a product may be designed that does not fit effi-ciently into standard shipment containers, thereby increasing costs. Also, dealers and distributors can provide information about how design elements affect distribution costs and hence profitability. For instance, a manufacturer

---

[7] Asanuma, "Japanese Manufacturer-Supplier Relationships in International Perspective." Working Paper #8, Faculty of Economics, Kyoto University, Japan.

[8] Studies indicate that simultaneous engineering can reduce development time anywhere from 30 to 70 percent, reduce the number of engineering changes from by 65 to 90 percent, improve overall quality by 200 to 600 percent, and increase return on assets by 20 to 120 percent.

EXHIBIT 7–6

Reduction in Lead Time from Concurrent Supplier Engineering

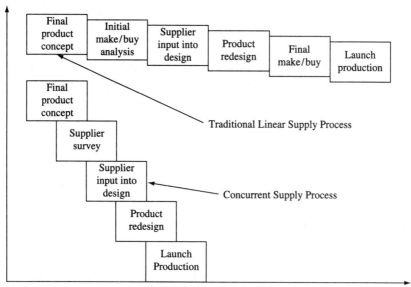

Elapsed Time After Product Strategy

of alarm clock radios might have to change the size, shape, or weight of the product depending on how it decides to distribute the product. Direct mail distribution will have different physical requirements for cost effective delivery than a discount office supply store. Distribution costs can be minimized by designing a product for the selected channel.

Recyclers are likely to have information on "green" issues, suggesting material substitutions and discussing regulatory issues depending on where the product is used. Environmental costs may be driven by decisions made by suppliers and customers, not the market maker. Some of the greatest opportunities for pollution prevention and toxic use reduction may become apparent through value chain analysis. Recyclers provide all other value chain members insight into the product's impact on the environment. Such impacts may cause increases in current operating costs due to measures designed to minimize adverse environmental impact and avoid future remediation costs.

It is important, therefore, to involve all value chain members in target costing *early*. It is too late to discover distribution, service problems, or recycling problems after a product has been designed. Seeking the active participation of these downstream value chain members early provides better information for product design. Typical improvements resulting from early involvement of value chain members are improved distribution, reduced pollution, increased flexibility, and reduced cost.

Develop Cooperative Financial Arrangements

One way to cement a relationship with suppliers is to create joint financial stakes. These may take the form of joint efforts or equity participation in the suppliers' firms. Equity investments allow policy control of suppliers. It ensures that the directorates are interlinked and that the strategic interests of the partners are safeguarded. The Japanese keiretsu system is built on this type of interlocking relationships.

Another method is to create joint venture partnerships with suppliers or other value chain members. A joint venture is a tactical or strategic cooperative alliance between two or more corporate entities, characterized by

Shared risk,

Shared revenue,

A well-defined work agreement,

A product or R&D orientation,

Operational independence,

Contractual agreement.

These arrangements are particularly useful for undertaking joint research and development for new products. Joint ventures have grown in popularity in recent years. They have been particularly popular in Europe. When joint ventures are not possible due to a lack of reliable strategic value chain members, firms often invest in development programs. These programs involve joint training sessions, joint investment programs, and the establishment of proactive planning programs with suppliers.

Encourage Investment in New Technology

Manufacturers face a trade-off between the short-term benefit of price reductions and the long-term benefit of having healthy value chain members who are capable of improvement and innovation. If cost reductions come from their profit margins, suppliers will be unable to invest in technology and stay healthy. The market maker must not take away all cost savings but instead leave some and encourage value chain members' investment into technology enhancement. Without needed capital improvement, the chain is unlikely to be healthy.

Develop Long-Term Relationships

To expect value chain members to participate fully in the target costing process, they must have a feeling of sharing the future with other companies in the chain. They must subscribe to the belief that offering suggestions that cause another in the group to benefit ultimately benefits all in the group. This belief stems from trust developed in long-term relationships with others in the chain.

To protect chain members from fluctuations in the market, a strategy of using multiple suppliers is often pursued. The suppliers are ranked by the market maker into categories based on their long-term performance. When the market is high, marginal suppliers are often used to provide the additional output needed to meet demands. When downturns occur, however, marginal firms are eliminated and only the high-performing firms remain. This protects the long-term nature of the relationships with those rated as excellent suppliers.

Develop Cooperative Relations

Use a cooperative rather than an antagonistic model for dealing with suppliers and other value chain members. An antagonistic model has the following characteristics: tough negotiations are held annually, price is the central topic of discussion, short-term contracts are awarded, multiple alternative suppliers are part of the bidding process, discipline is enforced by threats of eliminating members, and other forms of short-term tactics are used. The antagonistic model does not allow companies to innovate quickly and increase quality and reliability. To do this, all value chain members must cooperate. A cooperative communication model includes ongoing interaction and communication, a focus on quality and competence, and long-term, close relationships. All Kodak suppliers must share information with Kodak as a condition of being part of the value chain.

Exhibit 7–7 shows how an increase in the complexity of customer's needs and requirements coupled with complex interactions among value chain members require a move away from the use of an antagonistic model of communication to a more cooperative model. Since target costing environments are characterized by high complexity of customer needs and complex interactions with the value chain, it requires a cooperative model of information sharing.

Use the Value Chain to Buttress Manufacturing Capability

A firm can increase its own manufacturing capability by proactively involving suppliers and others in the value chain. This can be done in several ways. The firm can use more supplier developed products or components. It can redistribute prototype responsibility to Tier I suppliers. In addition to suppli-

Information Sharing Needs and Target Costing

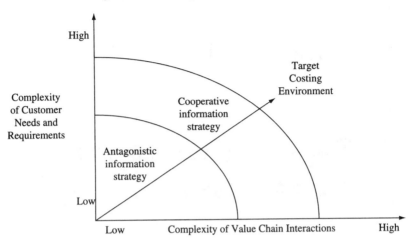

ers, a firm can use distributors to provide customer information for testing product concept feasibility and for product design. Service and support organizations can be used to understand the features customers want and value. Recyclers can suggest the use of alternate and environmentally friendly materials. All these free up the market making organization to focus on its core business and to manage the target costing process.

SUMMARY

This chapter has presented a number of contributions that members of a value chain can make to the target costing effort. It also has suggested ways in which to manage the value chain so that such contributions are readily forthcoming. For target costing to be effective in today's complex environment, it must be extended to all members of the value chain. Suppliers are one of the most critical elements in this value chain. Managing suppliers is a key determinant of the effectiveness of target costing. Sound supplier management creates relations that are marked by trust and openness, a common customer focus, belief in identifying issues before they become problems, honest and fair dealings, commitment to teamwork, mutual respect for each other's financial well being, and effective communication. Through long-term relationships with value chain members, these attributes should be promoted in the supplier organizations as well as the market making firm.

8
CHAPTER

Target Costing Organization and Participants

This chapter describes the membership, roles, responsibilities, and coordination of the various cross-functional teams and other organizational participants involved in target costing. It also discusses how to create an effective cross-functional organization, which maintains the target costing process and the role of top management in the process. We want to communicate five key messages in this chapter.

KEY MESSAGES

- Target costing process is carried out primarily by cross-functional teams.
- Target costing requires spelling out what is expected of team members.
- Target costing needs a strong program manager to effectively coordinate teams during the product development cycle.
- Target costing requires a cross-functional organization that has deep functional roots.
- Target costing must have an active process owner and active top management support.

TARGET COSTING PARTICIPANTS—AN OVERVIEW

Exhibit 8–1 provides an overview of all the organizational participants in the target cost process. The target costing process is carried out by four major and several minor cross-functional teams. In addition, many design and build subteams execute the product and process design and development activities. These design and build subteams are coordinated by the main product team and the design team. Similarly, the manufacturing team coordinates the work of several process subteams responsible for individual manufacturing processes. The four major teams are the business planning team, the product team, the design team, and the product manufacturing team.

The major functional specialties or departments, such as engineering, marketing, accounting, procurement, and manufacturing, are represented

E X H I B I T   8–1

Composition and Output of Teams

Team	Membership	Major Team Output
Business planning team	Senior executives from all major functions including program managers	Long-term strategic plan, core competencies and key technologies, product strategy and plans, deployment plan
Product team	Product team program manager, sales and marketing (including international), product planning, manufacturing; cost analyst, procurement, key suppliers	Product level profit plans, product concept, product feasibility, value engineering (VE), cost targets, capacity and investments plan
Design team	Design engineering, prototype development, product planning, manufacturing, cost analyst, procurement, key suppliers, service and support, sales/marketing/distribution, recycling	Product concept, VE, detailed product and process design, validated product and process
Product manufacturing team	Design engineering, plant manufacturing, quality control, cost analysis, procurement, key suppliers, service and support, sales/marketing/distribution	Production plan, capacity requirements, final make/buy decisions, training on new processes, supplier management, continuous improvement

on these teams. The teams are typically supervised by a program manager, who has senior management standing. Many Japanese companies also have a department that owns and maintains the process and integrates the efforts of the product teams. The unit is typically labeled a *target cost office* or *cost kaizen unit*. It is located both at the corporate level and the business unit level. The entire process has active top management support.

Composition and Output of Teams

The four target costing teams overlap as the product goes from planning and concept to actual production. No firm rule specifies how many teams to use or the maximum number of members on a team. The actual number varies by company and industry. However, the roles and responsibilities of team members remain the same. Also, the names of functional departments from which members are drawn will vary by organization. Two guiding principles govern team composition:

- At each stage of the product development cycle, teams should include *all* functional specialties including downstream functions such as distribution and recycling.
- There must be continuity from team to team so that no task in the product development cycle is left undone.

The composition and output expected from each of the four teams is summarized in Exhibit 8–1. It is important to remember that each functional area may have different representatives on each team. Some organizations feel that continuity is fostered by having the same individual participate on multiple teams. For example the use of the same cost analyst throughout all teams assures analytical continuity. A functional area also may have more than one representative on a team. For example, manufacturing is often represented by engineers from key processes involved, such as casting, cutting, or lathing. Similarly, design engineering may be represented by material engineers who may specialize by engine, wings, body, and the like.

EXPECTATIONS FROM TEAM MEMBERS

Target costing systems must spell out what is expected of team members. This is necessary for the teams to function as teams and not as functional specialists. Certain types of behavior, both general and specific, are expected of all team members. General roles are required of all team members

EXHIBIT 8–2

Chrysler Corporation—General Behavior Required of All
Team Members

Leave functional hats at the door.
Use communication skills that speak the language of other functions.
Commit the time required for the project.
Provide concepts and alternatives for product design and development.
Help negotiate trade-offs based on customer requirements.
Facilitate transfer of knowledge to suppliers and other team members.
Identify roadblocks and improve company and supplier processes.
Work with suppliers to institute continuous improvement.
Document historical data for future reference.
Use benchmarking data to identify improvement opportunities.
Become expert advisers to the team.
Meet all schedules and deadlines.
Think ahead of the process.
Interpret competitive information for the team.

---

regardless of functional affiliation. Specific types of behavior are relevant
only to particular functional team members. An example of a general requirement is that all team members meet deadlines and the project schedule. A specific requirement may be that marketing provide clear and
unbiased data on customer needs.

Exhibits 8–2 and 8–3 is an example taken from behaviors expected of
team members at Chrysler Corporation. Exhibit 8–2 describes the general
behaviors expected of all team members, while Exhibit 8–3 describes the
specific behaviors expected from a cost analyst on a target cost team.

COORDINATING TEAMS

Different teams play primary or support roles at the various stages of the
target costing process. While there is some overlap, team interaction is
akin to a relay race. Each following team must pick up the baton passed on
by the prior team and continue. Clearly, there is a need for continuity and
coordination of activities across teams. Continuity is often achieved by
having the same members continue with following teams. For instance, it
is not unusual to find the same cost analyst or marketing representative to
continue from product team to design team.

EXHIBIT 8–3

Chrysler Corporation—Behavior Required of a Value
and Financial Analyst

Be a business partner and not a policeman.

Provide sound cost estimates.

Provide cost leadership.

Assist in development of cost drivers.

Keep cost history and update financial model.

Learn and utilize value engineering skills.

Participate in shop floor[1] exercises.

Define detailed parts, functions, and feature costs.

Develop good cost models.

Perform financial teardowns.

Meet with suppliers and help perform supplier cost analysis.

Identify risks and opportunities.

Coordination of teams is the role of the program or product manager. He or she is critical to the success of target costing on a particular project or product. The program manager is not responsible for the target costing process, only for the teams that have to attain the target cost on a specific product or program.

Because a program or product manager has to step in and stabilize the process as needed, he or she must have senior management standing and broad range of authority. Arthur Andersen's study of target costing best practices identifies the following characteristics for a program or product manager in best practice companies:

- Broad range of responsibilities.
- Senior rank within the organization, often at the same rank as functional department heads.
- Linkage to a functional discipline, such as engineering, physics, or chemistry.
- No line authority, so unencumbered with large staffs.
- Power source is derived from process management and not from controlling resources.

---

[1] In Chrysler, this term is used to describe exercises to increase operating efficiency and reduce waste.

- Can serve as a strong champion of the product concept.

The Arthur Andersen study also lists the following desired traits in the person selected as a program or product manager:

- Ability to understand and interpret customer needs.
- Skill to translate soft functions into hard functions that engineers can understand.
- Influence and willingness to maintain product concept integrity.
- Desire to have continual direct contact with all functional communities.
- Ability to bridge gaps between functions.

DEVELOPING A CROSS-FUNCTIONAL ORGANIZATION

Target costing requires a cross-functional organization that is supported by strong functional organizations. The functional specialties play important roles and must be effectively integrated to support cross-functional teams. A note of caution, members of cross-functional teams lose their functional identity as they are assimilated into a cross-functional team. This may make it difficult for them to stay in touch with their "home base" and may diminish their effectiveness in garnering resources for cross-functional efforts. This is an issue that must be addressed in deploying target costing (see Chapter 12).

Role of Functional Organization

The functional organization has three important support roles:

1. It accumulates and maintains technical information and expertise that can be used to assist the core teams in their work. The functional departments maintain cost tables, supplier data, customer requirements, material analyses, teardown data, value engineering case studies, cost estimation models, and other target costing information.

2. It provides state of the art functional competence by keeping up with the most recent developments and improvements in the functional area.

3. It develops knowledge-based rules that facilitate planning, design, and problem solving for future product development and target costing efforts.

EXHIBIT 8–4

Integrating by Products—Chrysler's Platform Concept

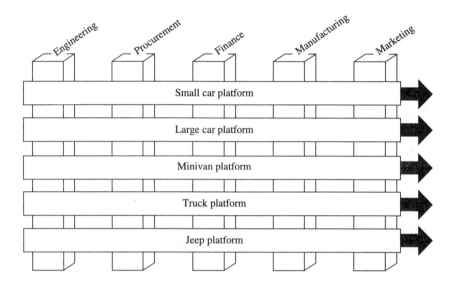

Integrating Functions

Functions can be integrated into a cohesive cross-functional organization in three ways: organize by product, organize by customers, or adopt process management.

1. A *product based* organization provides a common focus for all functions. A good example of this type of integration is Chrysler Corporation's "platform concept" shown in Exhibit 8–4. A platform has all functional areas such as engineering, design, procurement, accounting, organized around the five basic product types (platforms) that Chrysler produces: small car, large car, minivan, truck, and jeep. Chrysler Corporation's platform concept is reflected even in the building architecture of the new Chrysler Technology Center in Detroit. This building is designed in a way such that all functions for a platform are located within the same horizontal quadrant of the building. The vertical coordinates of the building are grouped functionally reflecting the architecture depicted in Exhibit 8–4. While we do not recommend spending several million dollars to rebuild buildings, the physical proximity of the various functional specialists is important. This may be

accomplished by relocating offices within existing buildings or encouraging frequent cross-functional meetings and committees and teams at all levels of the organization.

2. *Customer focus* is a second way to integrate and reorient functional organizations. A good example of using customer focus is the worldwide professional services firm of Arthur Andersen. A key principle of the firm is that a client of *any* office is a client of *every* office of the firm around the world. Services are provided to clients through a single client service partner, who is supported by industry teams, competency centers, and a global best practice knowledge exchange. These services cut across traditional geographic boundaries.

3. *Process management* is the third way to achieve a cross-functional organization. This requires focusing on an organization's work or activities as they flow across vertical units. ABM is a good example of process focus. Process management encourages understanding and managing the linkages and interdependencies within the organization and discourages working in isolated specialist functional or departmental silos. The organization focuses on what it does rather than on who does what. Even if a firm is organized by products or customers, managing the links and interdependencies within the organization is still necessary.

Attributes of an Effective Cross-Functional Organization

No matter which one of the three methods is used to achieve effective functional integration, Arthur Andersen's survey of best practices identifies three key attributes that distinguish a good cross-functional organization. A good cross functional organization has *common processes* that lay down the rules, procedures, and process steps each functional organization has to perform during the target costing process. For example, many Japanese companies use hoshin planning or policy deployment as a means of connecting daily activities to strategic goals. As part of the deployment, each functional organization is encouraged to ask how its daily activities link with quality, cost, and time goals in general and target costing in particular.

Cross-functional organizations have *strong program management leaders*. These leaders have formal, informal, and frequent contact with engineers, marketing, manufacturing, cost planning, procurement, and other key functional specialties.

Effective cross-functional organizations have *frequent contacts and inter-actions between functional managers* at all levels. This is accomplished primarily through service on management committees. It is important that these teams interact at all levels of the organization. Simply collocating design teams, as has occurred with some integrated product development efforts in the United States, is not enough.

PROCESS OWNER AND TOP MANAGEMENT ROLES

While a program manager manages a specific product, someone has to provide the infrastructure to maintain and support the overall target costing process. This is the role of a process "owner" and of the top management.

Process Owner

Our review of best practices shows that it is common for many Japanese companies to use an organizational unit called the *target costing office* or *cost kaizen unit* to oversee the deployment of the target costing process. This unit owns the process within Japanese organizations and provides the structure to support it. The unit is often located at corporate headquarters with corresponding offices in each business unit. The target costing office is responsible for deploying and promoting target costing throughout the organization. It is also responsible for coordinating with the strategy deployment unit so the focus stays on the overall strategy and profit plans of the organization. The target cost unit is headed by a strong leader, preferably a senior executive with program level experience. It is well staffed and has offices at headquarters with counterpart offices within the different business units. The key roles of the target cost office are

- Coordinate target costing efforts at the business unit level.
- Maintain manuals and distribute information about "best practices" and "value engineering successes."
- Maintain cost estimation models and cost tables.
- Monitor progress toward targets.
- Help address problems in the process.
- Maintain and distribute improvement ideas.
- Promote the target costing activities companywide.
- Provide cost estimation and modeling.

Nippon Denso is a good example of how a typical Japanese organization manages the target costing process. As Exhibit 8–5 shows, the cost kaizen unit in Nippon Denso is located at corporate headquarters. The unit is responsible for

EXHIBIT 8–5

Target Cost Process Management at Nippon Denso Corporation

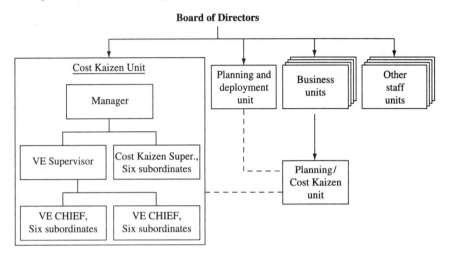

Source: This chart has been adapted from information contained in Fumio Nishiguchi, "Target Cost Deployment at Nippon Denso," *Management Practice (Keiei Jitsumu)*, October 1989, pp. 20–43.

managing the target cost process. It coordinates its activities with both the central planning and policy deployment units as well as the target cost offices within each business unit. Even though Nippon Denso calls its target costing unit the *cost kaizen unit,* the reader should remember that the two processes are different and should not be confused with each other. Cost kaizen takes over at the manufacturing stage, while target costing begins at the product concept phase. Both are driven by the voice of the customer and the needs of the marketplace.

The business units in Nippon Denso have primary responsibility for meeting cost targets. The cost kaizen unit's role is to support these efforts by promoting value engineering ideas, providing training, and maintaining cost tables. The cost kaizen unit has separate supervisors for cost kaizen and for value engineering (VE). The value engineering supervisor has two VE chiefs who, in turn, supervise six subordinates. The cost kaizen supervisor also has six subordinates. The entire cost kaizen unit, therefore, is well staffed.

The use of a formal target cost office is by no means a universal practice. There is definitely a need for a process owner, however. A formal process owner is necessary if the target costing process is to take hold and be effective. Process ownership is often lacking in U.S. companies. In some companies,design engineering owns the process, while at others, it is the responsibility of cost planning groups. It is fair to say that U.S. companies have not yet realized the importance of a process owner for the target costing process.

It is important that the process owner be an organizational unit outside functional departments. This will reinforce the point that target costing is not a finance or engineering or marketing function but an organizational function. A formal target costing office is useful because it can reinforce this cross-functional perspective. Without this perspective, the effort is often limited to design to cost types of engineering efforts. These efforts, no matter how sophisticated, are incomplete.

In addition to coordination, a major function of the target costing office is to coordinate and disseminate design improvement ideas across the organization so other products can take advantage of these solutions. For example, if a body subteam designs a better quality and longer lasting trim for small cars at Chrysler, then this information needs to be shared with other car platforms as well. The same will be true for process innovations that improve quality, cost, and time. This second type of coordination function of the target cost office is depicted in Exhibit 8–6, which uses a hypothetical platform organization as an example.

EXHIBIT 8–6

Coordinating Design Solutions across the Organization

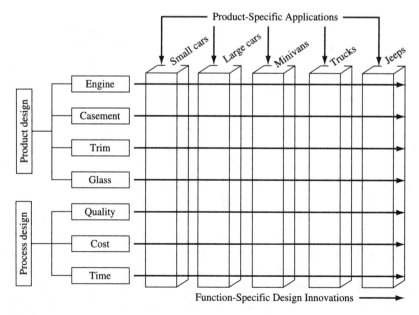

Source: Adapted from Arthur Andersen materials.

Top Management Role

A similar situation also prevails in the area of top management support. In Japanese companies, top management is actively involved and supports the target costing effort. As Exhibit 8–5 shows, Nippon Denso's unit reports directly to its top management. Similarly, at Toyota, target costing is closely tied to the strategic thrust of the corporation, and progress to targets is closely watched by top management. Arthur Andersen's survey of best practices shows that top management performs six important functions relative to target costing:

1. Deploy target costing companywide as part of hoshin (policy) deployment.
2. Support the target cost process by providing resources for training, cost tables, procurement data bases, and other items.
3. Review, approve, and clarify targets.
4. Assist with making trade-offs between quality, cost, and time.
5. Review strategic supplier plans and establish make or buy policies that recognize market conditions and core competencies.
6. Review strategic capacity and investment plans.

Despite the emerging interest in target costing in the United States, most top management is not actively involved in implementing the process. In part, this may be due to the misconception that target costing or design to cost is a finance or engineering function. It is particularly ironic to see that many companies that have adopted cost competitiveness as a key strategy have yet to integrate target costing as part of this strategic thrust.

SUMMARY

This chapter shows that target costing requires a strong cross-functional orientation in an organization. However, this does not mean remaking an existing organization or doing away with its functional specialties. Functions continue to play an important role in supporting cross-functional activity. A cross-functional culture can be built around products, customers, or processes.

Target costing is executed by four major cross-functional teams. These groups work like a relay team throughout the product development process. Teams have representation and support from functional specialists, who often continue from team to team to ensure continuity. Teams are co-ordinated by a strong program or product manager.

Effective teamwork requires that all team members understand their roles and what is expected of them. The process needs to be maintained and supported by a process owner and top management. In this last area, the practice in U.S. organizations lags far behind Japanese organizations, which typically have separate target cost offices and active top management involvement.

9

CHAPTER

Filling the Information Gap

A robust target costing system requires a great deal of information from many sources. We have previously discussed the need for pricing and competitive information (Chapter 4), cost data (Chapter 5), customer related information (Chapter 6), and supplier data (Chapter 7). This information is not routinely collected in organizations that are not using target costing. When relevant information is collected, it is often not easily accessible for target costing. An information gap exists. The challenge is to fill this gap by collecting and providing information needed for target costing.

This chapter focuses on the information gaps in target costing. The discussion is not intended to provide a comprehensive list of all information requirements for target costing. Our purpose is to highlight information not routinely collected in organizations and to suggest changes in the design of systems that will facilitate access to information available to target cost teams. We want to communicate six key messages in this chapter.

KEY MESSAGES

- The target costing process draws upon information from *five major data bases* in an organization.
- Organizations must *invest in information* that is specific to target costing and is not routinely collected.

■ Data needed for target costing must be easily *accessible* to target cost teams.

■ To support target costing, data bases should have an *open architecture* that allows multiple views of data, uses consistent definitions, and provides user defined reports.

■ Target cost participants must have *transparent connectivity* that makes access and information sharing easy.

■ Acquiring information is costly; networked and *distributed "parallel" data bases* may be a viable alternative to data warehouses.

INFORMATION REQUIREMENTS—AN OVERVIEW

Exhibit 9–1 provides an overview of the information sources typically used by target costing teams. The information is collected and maintained in functional data bases. As Exhibit 9–1 shows, target costing information draws from five major types of functional data bases: the competitive intelligence data base, the marketing data base, the cost data base, the engineering data base, and the procurement data base.

E X H I B I T   9–1

Target Cost Information Sources—An Overview

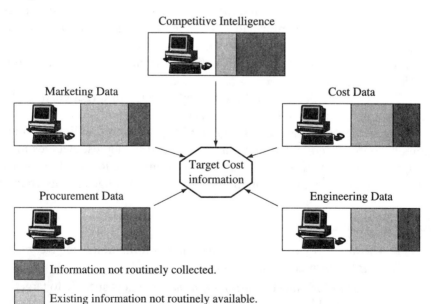

Competitive Intelligence

Marketing Data   Cost Data

Target Cost information

Procurement Data   Engineering Data

Information not routinely collected.

Existing information not routinely available.

Exhibit 9–1 shows the dependence of target costing on these five functional data bases. We use the term *data base* broadly. Not all organizations have these same five data bases. Data are not always collected by the same functional groups or stored in formal computerized data bases. In Caterpillar Corporation, competitive intelligence data are collected, and the data base is maintained by a separate competitive intelligence group. At Chrysler, competitive intelligence data are located in several functional areas, including marketing, engineering, and technical cost planning. Maintaining these data is an information processing function. The key point is that these generic information categories reside in functional organizations that often do not communicate with each other. Lack of process management makes it hard to get to this information. A method to share this information across the organization is necessary for target costing.

INVESTMENT IN NEW INFORMATION

Most organizations putting a target cost system in place for the first time will find many gaps between needed and available information. The experience of companies such as Chrysler, Boeing, Eastman-Kodak, and Texas Instruments suggests that some important types of data are not routinely available when a company first embarks on target costing. Based on their experience, we have identified a list of 13 information items that either are not collected or are not easily accessible to the target cost team. These items are shown in Exhibit 9–2.

The information items in Exhibit 9–2 are by the "type of functional data base " in which they are typically located and by "when needed" in the product development cycle. The five data bases are the same as shown in Exhibit 9–1. The timing, or when information is needed, is related to the four stages of the product development cycle. Each of these various information items is briefly described in the following pages.

Competitive Intelligence

Most organizations do not systematically collect or organize information on their competitors. The information that is collected typically is fragmented and never brought together in a useful way for target costing purposes. Firms typically track competitive product offerings, market perceptions of their own and their competitors' products, market share data, and the general financial performance of their firm relative to competition. This type of information, while useful, is not sufficient for target costing. Two major gaps in this data are competitive price and features and competitors' cost structures.

Competitive price and feature information deals with the relationship between the prices that competitors charge for their products and the features

EXHIBIT 9–2

Typical Information Gaps in Target Costing

	Product Development Cycle			
Type of Data	Product Strategy and Profit Plans	Product Concept and Feasibility	Product Design and Development	Production Logistics and Support
Competitive intelligence		Competitors' prices and features	Competitors' cost structure	
Customer and marketing	Product life cycle	Feature/price data, attribute/price data		Improvement ideas
Cost		Feature/cost data	Attribute/cost data, function/cost data	Improvement ideas
Engineering	Technology life cycle		Component/sub system interaction, VE case studies	Improvement ideas
Procurement			Supplier cost data	Improvement ideas

and functions they offer for that price. This link between prices and features is critically important to understand, particularly at the product concept stage. Information about either competitors' prices or features alone does not help a firm in its own product concept development or target costing efforts. Consider a company such as Ford. It is not enough for it to know what Chrysler charges for its minivans unless Ford also knows what features Chrysler provides for that price. If both Ford and Chrysler provide similar performance in engine, torque, drive train, and have dual air bags, the price information is useful. If, however, Chrysler provides an onboard computer, a more powerful engine, and dual climate control and charges a price $3,000 higher, the comparison becomes more difficult. The $3,000 price differential now must be decomposed into how much customers are willing to pay for the onboard computer, the engine power, and dual climate control. What makes this comparison more complicated is that Ford's minivan may have features such as aerodynamic styling, leg room, and reclining rear seats, which Chrysler may not offer. The value to a customer has to be approximated by adding the value of features offered and subtracting the value of features not offered. This type of competitive information is essential for Ford to design its own minivans to compete with Chrysler.

Competitor cost structure information is essential in the product design and development phase. In the minivan example, if Ford concludes that a Chrysler minivan provides better value to customers, it must understand how Chrysler is doing it. This is the role of good competitor cost analysis data. There are four ways in which this information can be collected for target costing purposes:

- *Financial analysis* using public data bases such as Robert Morris & Associates is one way to gather competitive cost information. Such sources provide historical and aggregated information that is useful for comparing macro categories such as return on sales ratios. For commodity products, this information can provide a good estimate of product cost. Also, many other industry specific and specialized data services provide more detailed financial data on companies.

- *Benchmarking* is another way to understand competitors' cost structures. Much has been written on this subject, and we will not go into detail here. The main point is that, as a source of competitive information, benchmarking will have limited usefulness. Competitors rarely allow such direct access to their data. If they are willing to share information about other processes, benchmarking still can be useful. However, for cost analysis, we may have to rely on publicly available benchmarking data bases.

- *Suppliers* are often useful sources for understanding competitors' cost structures. In assembly industries, such as automobiles, aircraft, or electronic equipment, the bulk of a manufacturer's cost is from suppliers. Where there are common suppliers, parts and components costs can be estimated from published prices or from the commodities market. Personal computers are a good example. Since most of the components going into a personal computer are sold as commodities, supplier prices for these components can be used to estimate a competitor's manufacturing cost. An important assumption in these cases is that suppliers are charging uniform prices to all customers. The experience of companies who acquired or merged with competitors suggests that the assumption that supplier prices are uniform in an industry is not always correct.

■ *Teardowns or reverse engineering* are often used in industries to collect competitors' cost information. These techniques consist of physically taking apart a competitor's product or reconstructing its design and then estimating the cost of materials, labor, and overhead that went into the production of each item. Teardown analysis is now common in automobile companies. At Chrysler, teardown takes the form of physically cutting open and taking apart a competitor's car. The stripped cars are then analyzed for the technology, number of assembly steps, the materials, manufacturing processes, and number of parts used. The results of the teardown allow Chrysler to determine several things: whether the competition is using better technology (such as a hydraulic vs. mechanical closing lever for the trunk door), how many steps are in the final assembly, the difference in materials for like items (such as plastic vs. metal rear mirror frames), the number of different manufacturing steps required for the car, and the number of and quality of parts used. The results of this physical process are used to determine a competitor component cost buildup by using estimates for materials, parts, processes, and assembly steps needed to manufacture these components. This process provides a rough approximation of a competitor's cost structure. Chrysler also conducts teardowns of its own cars to see how well they are holding up after specified mileage intervals. The teardown process is critical to Chrysler's technology improvement and cost reduction efforts.[1]

Customer/Marketing Data

Four types of customer or market related information typically is missing from most organizations not involved in target costing: product life cycle data, feature/price data, attribute/price data, and improvement ideas. Each is briefly explained next.

Product Life Cycle Data

Target costing manages margins and cost over a product's entire life. Without a good estimate of product life, profit margins can be adversely affected. Determining a product's life cuts across the marketing and competitive intelligence data bases. It requires projecting how long a product will be sold and whether and when the competition intends to introduce new products. Such

---

[1] For a detailed description of the teardown process used by Isuzu Motors, see Robin Cooper, *Cost Management in a Confrontation Strategy: Lessons from Japan* (Cambridge, Mass.: Harvard Business School, 1994).

data are difficult to get but very necessary. Often this issue does not get the attention it deserves from management.

Feature/Price Data

How customers trade off price and features is essential information at the product concept stage. It is also critical for value engineering efforts at the product design and development stage. Features, sometimes also called *soft functions,* are the dimensions customers use to evaluate products. An automobile is not an engine or drive train to a customer. It is "fun to drive," "safe," "corners easily," and "gets good mileage." Understanding how much more or less a customer is willing to pay for increased "fun" or "safety" is critical for making intelligent design decisions. Consumer behavior research typically collects and analyzes this type of information. It is not easy to obtain this type of information because it deals with intended purchases and not actual purchases. The information, however, is essential.

Attribute/Price Data

Attribute/price data are similar to feature/price data. They are used for simple products that do not have too many features and whose features are closely tied to physical attributes. For example, most toasters can handle either two or four pieces of bread at once. The price difference for this product can be captured by the difference in capacity, a physical attribute. For products in which product performance and physical attributes are highly related, an attribute/price relationship can serve as a good surrogate for price/feature data. The data are very useful for product concept and product design decisions but are not routinely collected.

Improvement Ideas

Organizations generate a number of improvement ideas. These ideas can come from customers, manufacturing, engineering, suppliers, and other sources. This is why we show it in multiple data bases in Exhibit 9–2. The only reason for including it here is to emphasize that the voice of the customer is the final arbiter for improvement ideas that need to be added to the data base. However, each area needs to systematically collect any ideas that will improve the product or process.

Cost Data

The type of cost data that target costing needs is significantly different from what most organizations collect routinely. Many organizations continue to have cost systems geared to inventory valuation and financial reporting needs. Even those that have management accounting systems have cost information that is typically geared to production needs. Modern cost management methods such as ABC,[2] provide useful data for parts cost, process costs, overhead costs, and other support costs related to a product. A target costing system needs a different type of cost data. Target costing requires understanding design related cost drivers. Three types of cost data that need to be collected are feature/cost data, attribute/cost data, and function/cost data.

Feature/Cost Data

Customers think of products as features. To them, a car is "fun to drive " Design engineers think of these same features as physical attributes, "torque ratio," or as functions, "engine." Cost systems have to serve both needs. Feature/cost data is a customer focused view of costs. It is particularly relevant at the product concept stage. When customers express a desire for a new feature, "plain paper color copies," Eastman-Kodak or Xerox must be able to estimate the cost of providing this additional feature in its color copiers. The cost system can estimate such data only if it can translate the feature into physical changes; that is, need for different components and processes. Plain paper copies may mean a different drum design, a new inking process, and a different type of drying element. The cost of a new drum and the two new processes have to be estimated to determine the cost of the desired feature. The cost system can do this only if it organizes data by components, processes, and features. Exhibit 9–3 shows the design of a customer focused cost data base, using the plain paper copier example. Note that the cost data are compiled by key features desired by customers as opposed to the product or activities.

Attribute/Cost Data

Attribute/cost data provide an engineering view, which relates cost to major physical attributes of a product. Attributes may be physically measurable properties or performance characteristics of a product. For the Boeing Company, two important physical attributes of an aircraft are weight and wing lift. The first is a physical attribute of an aircraft; the second is a performance related attribute. These attributes are extremely useful in parametric cost estimation (see Chapter 5). Cost systems must collect data on how costs are driven by key physical or performance parameters. Information about how costs respond to the weight, volume, area, size, density, speed, or fluctuations is commonly used in target costing systems in the aircraft, automobile, heavy machinery, and construction industries. Performance attributes are more commonly used in electronic products and home entertainment industries. In

---

[2] To learn more about ABC, see CAM-I, *Activity Based Costing: A Manager's Primer,* 1994.

Customer (Feature) Focused Cost Data

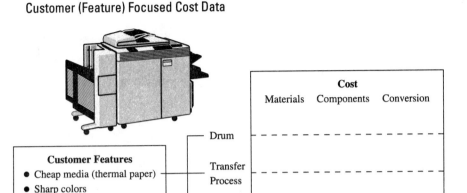

the computer industry, it is common to speak of CPU clock speeds. In the TV monitor business, an important attribute is screen refresh rates. In the stereo business, a key performance attribute is signal to noise ratio. The attribute view of costs for the heavy construction equipment industry is depicted in Exhibit 9–4. Attribute costing is more aggregate and typically is used at the concept stage, when detailed specifications for a product have not been developed.

Function/Cost Data

The functional view of costs is also an engineering view. A functional breakdown typically consists of decomposing a product into its major subsystems or "work breakdown structure." In the automobile industry, function refers to engines, chassis, drive train, and electronics. Analyzing costs by functions helps designers to provide these functions at a lower cost. A cost system must collect and report data by major product functions so each function can be assigned a target for cost reduction. The function level cost breakdown is the critical stepping stone between feature level and component level cost breakdowns. Desired customer features, such as "fun to drive," typically affect the design of more than one function. The design of the engine, drive train, and

E X H I B I T 9–4

Attribute Focused Cost Data

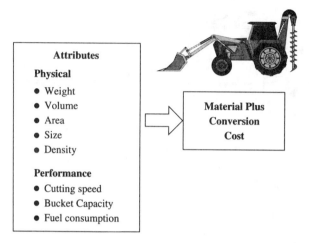

chassis may have to be modified to make a car "fun to drive." Functional costs allow a target cost to be decomposed into functions and then into components and parts. Exhibit 9–5 depicts this information flow graphically. Chapters 10 and 11 discuss how features are translated into allowable target costs for functions, components, and parts. Functional information is also used for internal benchmarking to compare the cost of a common function across multiple products of a firm. Information on functional costs is vital but typically not available from conventional cost systems.

Engineering Data

Success of target costing depends greatly on the quality of engineering related information an organization collects. Since design is central to target costing and engineers control design, it is imperative that there be good cost information to support their activities. Three key types of engineering related data that organizations do not collect routinely are technology life cycle data, component/subsystem interaction data, and value engineering case studies.

Technology Life Cycle Data

An important determinant of product strategy is the life cycle of the technology used in products. This is particularly true for technology dependent industries. Technology in place is a major determinant of the cost structure. The telephone industry uses wires for connectivity. Its cost structure is affected by

Role of Functional Cost Data

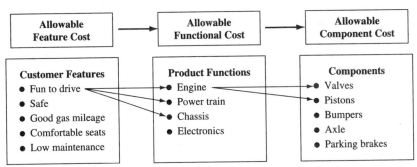

the cost of wiring. Wireless communication requires a satellite. Its cost structure is not sensitive to distance but does require a major fixed investment to get it up and running. New technology offers a chance to move to a different and lower cost structure. Indeed, NEC Japan has used this relationship to guide its target costing efforts. At NEC, when no further technological or cost improvements can be made to a product, it is time to move to the next generation of product or technology. Data on technology and its relationship to cost is important to manage and achieve target costs.

Component/Subsystems Interaction Data

As Exhibit 9–5 shows, component and part costs are the result of two levels of target decomposition. A danger exists in this decomposition because efforts to reduce component level costs may increase costs elsewhere in the product. This is due to the interaction between product components and subsystems. In the construction industry, use of PVC "bricks" instead of lumber decreases the framing cost but increases installation cost of plumbing, electricity, and drywall. Interaction between components can reduce the performance level of other components as well. In the computer industry, the use of less costly memory chips can limit the maximum efficiency obtainable from the CPU. These interaction effects are important to catalog in the engineering design data base. Studying interactions is difficult and perhaps one of the major information gaps in the practice of target costing.

VE Case Studies

Value engineering is at the core of target costing. Organizations need to systematically catalog and document their prior efforts at value engineering. A VE case study data base documents all prior process or assembly changes and their cost impacts. Consider the case of a copier. The circuit boards in a copier can be attached by screws, bolts, glued to holders, held in place by snap pins, or snapped in place in compartments. Each of these methods may have multiple variations. The VE data base catalogs the problems or difficulties in attaching the boards under each alternative. Future product generations can benefit from the successful attachment method used in the past. This VE history reduces future development time and cost because past successes and failures are documented. Design engineers can capitalize on approaches that have worked and avoid taking paths that are known dead ends.

Artificial Intelligence Driven Design Rules

A major source of data for improving designs is the accumulated knowledge base of an organization from its prior design experience. This information is vital for designers to learn from and improve product designs. A good data base that maintains knowledge driven design rules can make products easier to manufacture and assemble and can be extremely helpful in speeding the product design process and making it more cost effective. The use of artificial intelligence can turn the data base into a powerful design tool. For example, Sandia National Laboratories, a government high-technology organization, has learned that "diodes" function best when electricity flows through them in only one direction. Artificial intelligence rules can be incorporated so the designers are informed that all diodes should be placed for a linear, unidirectional electrical flow. In addition, if the diodes ordered by a designer are from a supplier that has had a history of quality or delivery problems, the artificial intelligence engine should be able to flag this for the designer.

Procurement Data

Suppliers' cost structure, margins, and performance data are important and should be collected and used as part of the target costing system. Such data tell a firm about the prior cost, quality, and time performance of suppliers. These data can be used to construct supplier cost, quality, and time indexes. Eastman-Kodak is a good example. The company maintains a cost index that compares costs across suppliers. This allows for a quick and easy evaluation of suppliers. It also routinely collects information about supplier capability and performance. These data are shared throughout the organization and incorporated in its design process. Having supplier cost and performance data allows firms to develop win-win cost reduction solutions and avoid procurement problems before they occur.

MAKING DATA AVAILABLE

Collecting data is only one part of meeting the information needs for target costing. Making that data available to target cost teams when they need it and in a form they can use are other major challenges. Meeting these challenges requires designing information systems that have an open architecture and provide a transparent connectivity to users.

Open Architecture

Three major attributes typify an information system that has an open architecture. First, it provides users with a "kaleidoscopic" view of data. Second, it uses consistent definitions of cost objects and uniform cost categories. Finally, it provides user defined reports. Caterpillar is a good example of open architecture. When Caterpillar introduced target costing, it introduced these three attributes in its information systems. Each attribute is briefly discussed next.

Kaleidoscopic View

As we discussed in Chapter 5, an information system is kaleidoscopic if it allows a user to arrange variables in different patterns. Each pattern provides a different perspective and understanding of the phenomena. Marketing data bases should allow target cost teams to understand a product as a set of customer needs, wants, and delight factors. They should also allow the team to view data from a competitive lens to evaluate the strengths and weaknesses in the product. Cost data bases should allow users to organize costs by features or functions. They should also allow life cycle and value chain based views of cost. Engineering data bases should allow users to view products as functions and interacting subsystems and components. This can be accomplished by having information elements systematized as "flexible building blocks" and collected so that no one view dominates or obscures other views of the data.

Consistent Definitions and Categories

Information systems with an open architecture use consistent definitions and categories across products and over time. This simple rule is often ignored in practice. It is difficult to collect and compare data such as customer needs or product costs if various data collection points use different definitions. In Caterpillar's case, one key feature is the use of consistent cost objects across the company. The cost object concept is taken for granted and assumed to be universally understood. However, as the Caterpillar example shows, it is often ignored in practice and must be attended to in designing information systems.

User Defined Reports

Perhaps the most universal and common complaint that users have of information systems is that they do not provide user friendly reports. This is true of most information systems in organizations. Marketing is unable to get the reports it needs because the system designers do not understand marketing needs. The accounting staff has a similar complaint when it comes to accounting reports. The situation gets worse when the accounting staff has to use engineering databases and vice versa. The ability to provide user driven reports is essential if data bases are to serve both functional and cross-functional information needs.

Transparent Connectivity

An information system is transparent and connected if it allows users access to information no matter what hardware or software was used to store the information or where it is physically located. Xerox's virtual office is an example of transparent access and connectivity to data.[3] According to Xerox vice-president Bill Pittman, its sales force was spending as much as "30 percent of their time chasing information stored on the legacy system." The entire Xerox data base has been redesigned to connect these various legacy systems. The data exist in a mainframe "warehouse," which contains customer, marketing, ordering, engineering, manufacturing, solution libraries, and other information. While the data are from different data bases, they appear unified to anyone accessing the warehouse. Salespeople can be in the field making customer calls instead of accessing information at the office.

The ease of connectivity has another advantage. It also offers a way to update information easily. This is the case with data bases designed using applications such as Lotus Notes. In these environments, design and process engineers can concurrently design products and processes. Each version of the design can be updated and stored in the central repository, allowing access by other design engineers for modification, comment, or updating.[4]

COSTS AND BENEFITS OF INFORMATION

In the previous pages we have identified information gaps in target costing. Filling these gaps by collecting new information or redesigning existing information systems is costly. Each organization must assess the costs of investing in this information and how best to get it.

---

[3] See M. Nadeau, "Not Lost in Space," *Byte,* June 1995, p. 50.

[4] An interesting example of concurrent design using engineers from across the nation was ARPA's recent MADE project. This project was an experiment in which engineers designed a "seeker" laser pointer device by exchanging versions, comments, and redesigns on the Internet. See MADE on the World Wide Web for details.

At one extreme are Xerox style *data warehouses*. They offer a practical solution to the problem but can be very costly. The design of such systems typically requires connecting existing legacy systems written in different languages and optimized for different hardware. The more legacy systems that exist, the more costly is a data warehouse solution. The cost may be justified for large organizations, but it is not cost effective for smaller organizations.

The other alternative is to use *distributed data bases* with some form of networking. These systems require a more modest level of investment. However, the challenge is to provide a common set of network standards for these data bases, so they can communicate with each other. As Internet tools become popular, the cost of distributed networking is likely to decrease, making them a more viable economic alternative.

How do we gauge the benefits of investing in new information and related technology? We propose two criteria: decision relevance and understanding of cost drivers.

Decision relevance is the property of information to change decisions and make them yield better payoffs. In the current context this means the ability to improve product designs by making them more cost effective or capable of yielding higher profit margins.

Understanding cost drivers refers to the ability of new information to enhance the understanding of the factors that causes costs to be incurred. Target costing is primarily about cost reduction and profit improvements through product design. New information, therefore, should enhance the ability to understand what drives the costs or profit margins. This is true, not just for cost data, but for all data. Customer information is useful if it helps us understand how customer requirements drive product costs. Similarly, new engineering information is useful if it helps us to understand how design changes affect cost. The same is true for process related and supplier information. Helping understand the relationship of design drivers to cost is a critical requirement of any new information.

SUMMARY

This chapter highlights the need for relevant data that help target costing teams to understand the relationship between customer requirements, competitive product offerings, product design, and product costs. A major impediment is that data for target costing often are not collected or reside in functional organizations that do not make it available to everyone. We identified key items of information that are not routinely collected. This information gap can be filled by adding the information to five different data bases within a company and connecting them together to create a seamless target cost information system. The integration also helps remove the other major impediment to target costing, lack of access to data collected.

Access to information is easier when information systems have an open architecture and provide users transparent connectivity. Open architecture is characterized by the presence of three properties: a "kaleidoscope" view that allows multiple ways of viewing a phenomenon, use of consistent definitions for objects in the data base, and ability to generate user defined reports. Transparent connectivity can be achieved by building a data warehouse, an expensive solution, or using distributed networking, a less expensive solution. The cost of doing this must be weighed against the benefits of information. New information is beneficial if it results in less costly and higher profit margin product designs and provides insights about the relationship between costs, margins, and product design.

10
CHAPTER

Supporting Tools and Techniques

This chapter discusses *core* target costing tools and techniques. We limit the discussion to core tools because it is beyond the scope of this book to discuss all tools and techniques that support target costing. Appendix C provides an overview of when and how these other tools assist the target costing process. Here, we describe the core tools and discuss the possible size of investment needed to acquire them. We also show when in the target costing process various tools come into play and where in the organization to find the functional expertise for these tools. We want to leave you with three key messages from this chapter.

KEY MESSAGES

- Target costing requires several core tools that work in conjunction with other process tools already available in many organizations. These tools are interrelated and often used together for maximum effectiveness.
- New organizations may have to invest in new tools to varying degrees. Not all tools are essential for all organizations. There is a trade-off between the cost and the benefit of investing in tools.
- Using the right support tools and techniques at the right stage of the target cost process greatly increases the effectiveness of the process.

TARGET COSTING TOOLS AND TECHNIQUES

The target costing process is supported by two types of tools and techniques:

- *Core* tools are those support tools that are central. Absence of these tools can seriously hinder target costing. Some of these tools, such as design for manufacturability, may already exist and can be employed easily for target costing. Others, such as value engineering, may require investment on the part of an organization.
- *Other process* tools refer to tools and techniques that support other business processes as well as target costing. Included in this category are tools such as capacity measurement, supplier ratings, process testing, waste and yield analysis, CAD/CAM, ABM, Pareto analysis, failure mode and effect analysis, make or buy models, regression analysis, net present value analysis, and discriminant analysis. Most businesses are fairly familiar with these tools.

E X H I B I T   10-1

Target Costing Core Tools and Product Development

Functional Expertise for Tools	Product Strategy	Concept and Feasibility	Design and Development	Production and Logistics
	← Product Development Cycle (when tools are used) →			
Planning	Multiyear Product Plan			Multiyear Product Plan
Marketing	Benchmarking QFD			
Costing	Cost Tables	Function Cost Feature Costing QFD	Component Cost Process Costing	
Engineering		Value Engineering DTC QFD	Value Engineering DFMA, DTC QFD	Value Analysis
Procurement		Supplier Based Value Engineering	Supplier Based Value Engineering	

As the process model in Appendix B shows, all tools come into play during the new product development cycle. They require different functional expertise. Exhibit 10–1 shows the core tools by when they are used and where the functional expertise for the tool typically is located.

There are nine core target costing tools: value engineering and value analysis, quality function deployment, design for manufacturing and assembly and design to cost, cost tables, feature to function costing, component cost analysis, process (operations) costing, multiyear product and profit planning, and benchmarking. These nine tools are described in this section.

Value engineering (VE) and value analysis (VA) differ only in their timing. Value engineering occurs at the design phase for a new product, while value analysis typically occurs after production has started. Both are organized efforts directed at analyzing the functions of products, processes, and services to achieve these functions at the lowest overall cost with no reduction in required performance, reliability, maintainability, quality, safety, recyclability, and usability.

Value engineering typically is conducted in four stages: feature to function analysis, creative thinking and problem solving, analysis, and idea development. Each stage is discussed next.

Feature to function analysis is the first step in VE. Features desired by customers are mapped to product functions, as described in Chapter 5. The functions are described, classified as to their worth, and arrayed by the cost of providing them. The purpose of functional analysis is to determine what function an item performs, what it costs, and what it is worth to a customer. Value is typically expressed as degree of importance to a customer, which is determined by the contribution of a function to a product's features. Cost is expressed as percentage of total cost devoted to each function. The ratio of degree of importance to percent of cost is called the *value index*. Functions or components with a value index of less than 1 are typically prime candidates for value engineering.

To illustrate how a value index is constructed, we will use an electric pencil sharpener as an example. Assume that a customer desires three features in an electric pencil sharpener: speed of sharpening, ease of cleaning scrapings, and appearance. Four components provide these features: motor, blade assembly, drawer, and outer casing. Motor and blade assembly contribute 75 and 25 percent each to the speed of sharpening.

Exhibit 10–2 summarizes the relevant data. It shows the customers' rankings for these three features on a scale of 1 to 5 in column 4. The contribution of each function to the product features is mapped in columns 1 and 2 of the exhibit. Column 3 shows the relative cost of each component. Column 5 is the transformation of the customer rankings into relative importance rankings for the four functions. The last column shows the value index.

Components that have small value indexes are prime candidates for

E X H I B I T   10–2

Feature to Function Analysis for a Pencil Sharpener

(1) Feature or Function	(2) Component Contribution	(3) Component Cost	(4) Customer Ranking	(5) Relative Importance (col. 2 × 4)	(6) Value Index (col. 5 ÷ 3)
Speed	Motor (75%)	$1.60 (40%)	4(40%)	30%	0.75
	Blades (25%)	0.80 (20%)	4 (40%)	10%	0.50
Cleaning	Drawer (100%)	0.60 (15%)	4 (40%)	40%	2.67
Appearance	Casing (100%)	1.00 (25%)	2 (20%)	20%	0.80
		$ 4.00 (100%)	10 (100%)	100%	

value engineering. Components with high value are candidates for enhancement, since we are spending far too little for a feature that is important to a customer. These components present an opportunity to enhance the product. We can plot the two variables in the value index, cost and relative importance, on a graph (Exhibit 10–3). The optimal zone indicates the control band in which deviations are accepted. The upper left part of the graph indicates the components that are candidates for cost reduction

E X H I B I T   10–3

Value Index Chart

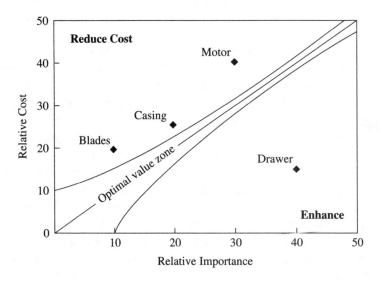

and the items on the right are items that are candidates for enhancement.

Creative thinking is the second step in VE. The purpose is to brainstorm about cost reduction ideas for functions or components that have a low value index. These functions are critically evaluated to determine if they can be eliminated, simplified, or reduced so the needed functionality can be provided at less cost. Exhibit 10–4 shows a sample list of brainstorming questions that are typically used for identifying functions that are best candidates for redesign and for generating product or process cost reduction ideas.

Analysis of the most promising cost reduction ideas is the third stage in VE. Ideas that are most likely to reduce cost are identified for further study. Selected ideas must be technically feasible and acceptable to a customer.

Development of selected ideas into concrete cost reduction proposals is the last stage of VE. The purpose is take these ideas and convert them into concrete proposals for changes in product or process design or specifications.

Quality function deployment (QFD) is a systematic way of arraying information about important objectives in any business decision. The term *QFD* is used broadly in the quality literature as the process of ensuring that product design and quality meet customer requirements. We use it narrowly as a matrix data array tool. The use of QFD in product concept stages of target costing is a way to bring together the relationships between competitive offerings, customer requirements, and design parameters. A matrix is used to array the information on these three variables. The QFD matrix is used iteratively throughout the process. After the design requirements have been determined at the concept stage, the QFD matrix can be used to relate part and component characteristics and process needs to the design. These, in turn, can be used to plan the actual production system. A sample QFD matrix for a hypothetical fax machine is shown in Exhibit 10–5.

Design for manufacture and assembly (DFMA) refers to engineering processes designed to optimize the relationship between materials, parts, and manufacturing processes. Its purpose is to reduce cost, increase quality, and reduce time to market by making it easier to manufacture or assemble parts or to eliminate them. A good example of DFMA is the productivity evaluation system used by Fujitsu.[1]

The Fujitsu system consists of the following four step sequence:

1. Designers select parts and specify their assembly sequence.

---

[1] The example is adapted from A. Miyazawa, "Productivity Evaluation System," *Fujitsu Scientific and Technical Journal,* 29 (December 1993), pp. 425–431.

E X H I B I T   10–4

Brainstorming about Cost Reduction Ideas in Value Engineering

I, *Identifying Potential Functions as Redesign Candidates*

The following list provides some sample questions that can be used to identify functions that are strong candidates for product or process redesign. Except for the last two questions, if the answer to a question is yes, then that particular function is a candidate for redesign.

	Yes	**No**

Can we do without this function?

If this were not done, would anything of consequence happen?

Is it doing more than the customer requires?

Do others produce it at less cost or in less time?

Is there a simpler way of meeting this need?

Can another firm's standard part or process be used?

Does it cost more or take more time than is reasonable?

Are we trying for too much reliability?

If you were a customer, would you omit this?

Is this the only way to do this?

Is this the best way to do this?

What critical function does it perform for a customer? List below.

II, Generating Ideas for Product or Process Redesign

The following list is a way to generate options for product or process simplification and redesign.

Adapt	What else is like this?
	What could we copy?
	What is out there that we can adapt?
Combine	Can we combine steps?
	Can we combine purposes?
	Can we combine functions?
Magnify	What can we add?
	Can we do it more frequently?
	Should we enlarge the scope?
Minimize	What can we reduce?
	What can we omit?
	What can we streamline?
Rearrange	Can we interchange steps?
	Can we do these in a different sequence?
	Can we change the timing?
	Can we rearrange steps in a different pattern?
	Can we schedule steps differently?

Exhibit 10–4 Concluded

Reverse	What is the opposite?
	Can we turn it around?
	Can we do it upside down or backward?
	Can we reverse roles or functions or steps?
Modify	What new twist can we add?
Substitute	What can we use instead?
	What else can do this?
	Can we take another approach?

---

2. Pre-existing guidelines are used to evaluate ease of (time for) assembly.
3. Parts are reduced or their ease of assembly is improved.
4. Designs are reviewed against prior design experiences stored in a design data base.

Steps 2 and 3 are concurrent and not sequential. The process is depicted in Exhibit 10–6.

DFMA is a tool used in conjunction with value engineering and "design to cost" (DTC) efforts. Unlike value engineering, which maximizes customer value, a DTC approach attempts to minimize cost by using it as a constraint. A designer must design to a realistic but difficult cost objective. Market information or customer value and worth are not part of either DFMA or DTC analysis. Nor are these tools typically cross-functional in their application. In this respect, both DFMA and DTC are useful tools but not the same as value engineering because they lack customer focus. They can be used within the target costing process, however.

Cost tables are data bases of detailed cost information. They enable timely cost estimates for new products. Cost tables include data on cost elements, such as raw materials, purchased parts, processing costs, overhead, and depreciation on new investments as well as cost models. Most Japanese companies have detailed cost tables that are updated on a regular basis. Regular updating is important if the cost tables are to be useful. Well-designed cost tables usually contain very specific information on both internal and supplier manufacturing processes. Information includes machine hour rates, labor rates, scrap rates, cycle times, and cost of operations. Major cost drivers are identified and documented. Some typical cost drivers that are used in the construction of cost tables are:

E X H I B I T   10–5

A Sample QFD Matrix in Product Development: Example of a Fax Machine

Design Parameters Customer Requirements	Display Panel	Print Engine	Modem Speed	Paper Tray	Memory Board	Interface Card	Competitor Ranking Low High 1 2 3 4 5	Customer Ranking
Ease of setup	◆					●	□ ■	5
Memory			◆		●	◆	■ □	3
Receive/send speed			◆		◆		□ ■	4
Printing speed		◆				○	■ □	4
Copy settings	●				◆		■ □	3
Handset	◆					○	■□	2
Paper supply		●		◆			□ ■	3
PC Interface			○		●	◆	□ ■	2

Correlation of design   Comparative competitive rankings
parameters and rankings.

Customer requirements

◆ = Strong correlation   ■ = Competitor ranking
● = Moderate correlation   □ = Our ranking
○ = Weak correlation

Physical attributes (e.g., size),

Material or component substitution,

Manufacturing method,

Function, and

Parts used.

Feature to function costing is a way to cost the various features and functions of a product. The purpose of feature to function costing is to pro-

EXHIBIT 10–6

Fujitsu's DFMA System

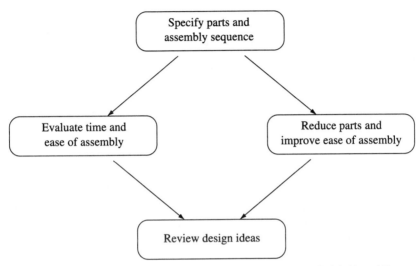

Source: Adapted from A. Miyazawa, "Productivity Evaluation System," *Fujitsu Scientific and Technical Journal*, 29 (December 1993).

vide information about the costs of providing a function that in turn satisfies a feature desired by customers. When more than one function is needed to provide a feature, the cost must sum across all these functions. Also, this addition must allocate the cost of a function among features. In the pencil sharpener example in Exhibit 10–2, if the motor supported two features, speed and cleaning, then we would have to allocate the motor cost of $1.60 to both these features. Note that this would change the value index for these components.

Component cost analysis is particularly important for assembly industries that purchase thousands of components, parts, and subassemblies. The purpose of component analysis is threefold. First, it identifies the costly components in a product. Second, it focuses on the cost relationships between components. The purpose is to determine if decreasing the cost of one component increases the cost of another. For example, in construction, the use of steel studs instead of lumber can increase materials cost but decrease electrical wiring and window installation costs because of the predrilled holes. Finally, it ensures that no outdated or soon out of production components are used. The use of such components can increase product costs significantly.

E X H I B I T   10–7

Component Cost Analysis

Components	C_1	C_2	C_3	C_4	C_n	Cost	Available Until
C_1		+	-	+		$aaa	1997
C_2	+			-		bbb	1999
C_3	-					ccc	1996
C_4		-				ddd	2005
C_n	+					nnn	2004

Exhibit 10–7 shows a sample component cost matrix. The Cost column shows the cost of a component. The Availability column shows the last available date for the component before it is no longer available. The plus or minus entries indicate whether there is a positive or negative relationship between the costs of components. A plus sign indicates that, as the cost of the component in row 1 goes down, the cost of the component in the column goes up. For example, when we decrease the cost of component C_1, the cost component C_2 goes up but the cost of component C_3 goes down.

Process (operational) costing is the analysis of costs by manufacturing processes. The term *process costing* should not be confused with its usage in cost accounting. Product costing in mass production process industries (chemicals, oil) is also called *process costing*. We use the term to mean "operations costing." The purpose of process or operations costing is to understand the cost drivers for each step in the manufacturing process. This provides information that allows management to eliminate or modify costly or non-value added operations. Consider the semiconductor industry. The "burn-in" testing of semiconductors is an expensive process. The longer the burn-in, the higher is the cost. Without operations costing, it would be easy to overspecify burn-in since there is no cost information to guide this decision.

Multiyear product and profit planning integrates many important business planning dimensions. This tool is used to integrate information on revenues, spending, and investment for a firm's product portfolio over a three to seven year period. The exact time frame varies by the nature of the planning cycle in a given industry. The plan shows the products (or services) to be developed and introduced over this time horizon. A multiyear profit plan

E X H I B I T   10–8

Multiyear Product and Profit Plans

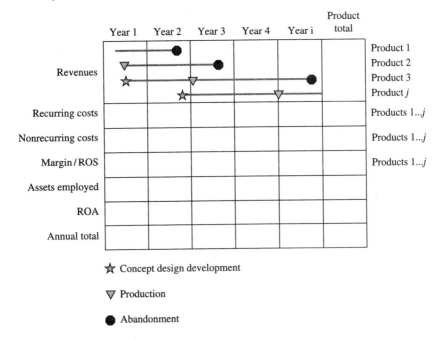

★ Concept design development

▽ Production

● Abandonment

integrates long-range forecasts of product markets, technology, and investment plans into a product strategy. Product strategies are defined for multiple business groups. These strategies describe product goals and opportunities and competitive threats for product lines and particular products. The product strategy is then turned into projections of revenues and costs to produce a multiyear profit plan.

A key consideration in the plan is the length of product life cycles for both existing and new products. The other element of the plan is to couple product introductions and deletions with projected sales and profit margins from these products over their life. The final output, shown in Exhibit 10–8, is an annual product mix that shows aggregate profits by year for each product. The sum of all products in a given year is the annual profit plan, while the total of the annual profits by products is the product life cycle profit. The product level profit includes all directly traceable recurring costs such as materials and conversion and nonrecurring traceable fixed costs such as special tooling, dedicated machinery, and other costs.

Benchmarking is a well-established business tool that can be used for target costing. Pioneered by Xerox, benchmarking requires comparing processes or operations in a business against the "best in class." The best in class may be another business in the same industry or any other organization with a comparable process. For example, Xerox used L. L. Bean's order filling process as a benchmark against which to compare its own order filling process. The importance of benchmarking for target costing is its ability to provide estimates of competitive product offerings, prices, margins, and costs. In addition, information about competitor support processes and product features can be used to enhance all stages of target costing.

INVESTMENT IN CORE TOOLS

The level of investment required to acquire core tools will vary for each firm. In general, process and component costing tools are the easiest to acquire. These tools are different ways of accumulating and arraying cost data. The only investment required may be for software and accounting system redesign so that the cost data is readily available. Other core tools such as feature to function costing, benchmarking, DFMA, and multiyear product and profit plans require a higher level of investment. These tools require new data, systems redesign, and new software and training. Investment in software can be high or low depending on whether off the shelf software can be used.[2] The highest level of investment is in cost tables, QFD, and value engineering. These tools require significant amounts of data, system redesign, custom designed simulation software, data networking capabilities, CAD/CAM, and sophisticated market research tools. All these items typically are expensive. The list in Exhibit 10–9 can be used as a guide for the level of investment required in target cost core tools.

SUMMARY

Having the right tools is critical to the success of target costing. In this chapter, we presented the core tools that support the target costing process. Nine such tools were described. The most critical tool is value engineering. It is at the heart of cost planning and cost reduction. The nine core tools require dif-

---

[2] A good example of using off-the-shelf software is Siemens Solar Industry. The company was able to use Promodel, a Windows based software package, to simulate its new clean room fabrication facility. The model was used by engineering students from California State University, San Luis Obispo, as part of a class project. Siemens provided them with a live site for the test. As a result, the company had to invest little in developing an in-house simulation capability. See J. Vacca, "Faking It, Then Making It," *Byte Magazine* (November, 1995), pp. 66–72.

Core Tools by Level of Investment Required

Investment Level Required	Core Tools
Low	Process costing,
	Component costing
Medium	Feature to function costing,
	Design for Manufacturability and Assembly, (DFMA)
	Benchmarking,
	Multiyear product/profit plan matrix
High	Cost tables,
	Value engineering,
	Quality Function Deployment (QFD)

ferent levels of investment, depending on the extent to which an organization has them in place. Typically, costing tools are the least expensive while design and simulation tools are the most expensive to acquire.

11

C H A P T E R

Target Costing—An Illustration

The previous chapters of this book have discussed the need for target costing and presented the structures, tools, and processes that must exist for its use. This chapter illustrates the key activities at each stage of the target costing process with the help of a hypothetical company, Kitchenhelp Inc.[1] Our purpose is to provide an integrating framework for the discussion in the prior chapters.

KITCHENHELP INC.

Kitchenhelp is a manufacturer of small kitchen appliances, such as toasters, coffeemakers, grinders, blenders, juicers, electric carving knives, and can openers. Competition is tough, with major brand names on the market, including Mr.Coffee, Moulinex, Braun, Krups, Sharp, and Toshiba. The company is looking for market opportunities to exploit in their various products. One such product is their coffeemaker line. Currently, Kitchenhelp makes a conventional drip coffee maker and an espresso/cappuccino maker. How can the company apply the target costing process to its coffeemaker line?

---

[1] This example was developed for and is contained in a teaching module, "Target Costing," in S. Ansari, J. Bell, T. Klammer, and C. Lawrence Management Accounting A Modular Series, (Burr Ridge, Ill.: Richard D. Irwin, 1996).

ESTABLISHING TARGET COSTS

In Chapter 3, we provided an overview of the target costing process. Exhibit 11–1, which reproduces Exhibit 3–3, will remind readers that the first phase of target costing is establishing target costs. This requires conducting market research, performing a competitive analysis, and defining a market niche.

Assume that Kitchenhelp's market research and analysis discovers an upwardly mobile college educated consumer who is interested in more "gourmet" types of food at home. The company decides to go after this "home gourmet" market niche. Further market research by the company results in the discovery that one area in which the "home gourmet" market niche can be exploited is through its coffeemaker line.

Kitchenhelp has determined that there is a market for a coffeemaker that provides "espresso" quality coffee but is not as complex and time consuming to operate as an espresso/cappuccino maker. Also there is little competition in this market segment.

Kitchenhelp must form a cross-functional team to come up with an initial product concept and test its feasibility. Assume that Kitchenhelp's product team proposes an initial product concept that combines a coffee grinder and a drip system into a single coffeemaker. The new design will grind fresh coffee beans and push extremely hot water through the grinder basket to make a coffee that smells and tastes more like espresso.

If this type of coffeemaker is technically and financially feasible, then the next steps for the product team are to understand customer requirements and define product features, as shown in Exhibit 11–2.

E X H I B I T   11–1

Beginning Steps in Establishing Target Costs

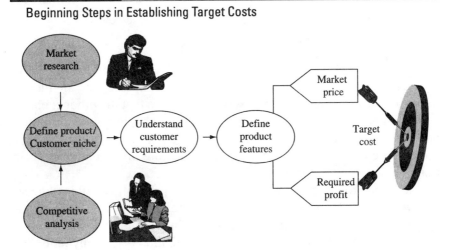

E X H I B I T   11–2

Next Steps in Establishing Target Costs

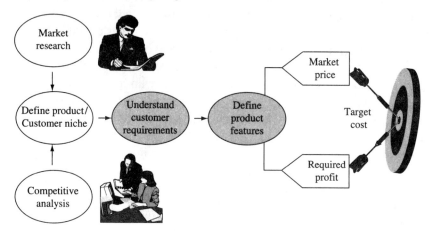

Market research aimed at coffee drinking consumers is needed to better understand customer requirements. This topic was covered extensively in Chapter 6. Assume that, based on surveys and focus groups, Kitchenhelp has identified eight features important to customers:

- Coffee tastes and smells like espresso.
- The unit is easy to take apart and clean.
- It has a six+ cup capacity.
- Coffeemaker looks nice.
- It has a clock timer to start automatically at a designated time.
- It performs well with different grinds of coffee beans.
- It keeps the coffee warm after making it.
- It automatically shuts off the unit after a designated time period.

These customer requirements become the basis for the engineering design of the coffeemaker. Engineers must ensure that the product encompasses all the features important to customers. This initial set of features becomes the first product definition for design purposes. The product team now must convert this customer input into a more precise product definition.

For the proposed coffeemaker, the product definition will include specific items such as an eight cup coffee carafe, grinder size, blade rotation speeds, size and shape of the coffeemaker, the heating unit size, the water heater specifications, and so on. A product definition is typically in the form

EXHIBIT   11–3

Final Steps in Establishing Target Costs

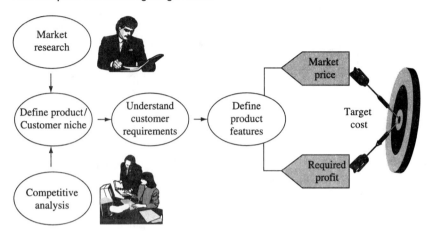

of a blueprint, a computer designed drawing or model, or an actual scale model.

The last two steps in establishing the target cost for the proposed coffee maker are to set price and profit margin, as shown in Exhibit 11–3. Methods for doing this were presented in Chapter 4.

Kitchenhelp's market research shows that the market price for an eight cup drip coffeemaker with a clock timer is currently $69. A stand-alone coffee grinder sells for $15. Since the two features are being combined, and the coffee taste is being enhanced, Kitchenhelp can charge a price slightly higher than $84. Given its desire to capture a 20 percent market share, assume that Kitchenhelp can set the target price at $100.[2]

The final step is to establish a target profit by determining the desired rate of return for the coffeemaker. The common return on sales in the small appliance industry is 7–10 percent. Kitchenhelp decides to set a target profit margin of 10 percent on the product. The target cost for this new coffeemaker, therefore, is $90 (100 − 10). This is also referred to as the *allowable* cost for the product.

---

[2] To keep the example simple, we have not introduced multiyear planning. Clearly, the price projection will have to be over the life of this product and it will be a declining price, since competitors are likely to introduce their own products. Cost reduction therefore will be more important over time for this product than at its introduction.

E X H I B I T 11–4

Steps in Attaining Target Costs

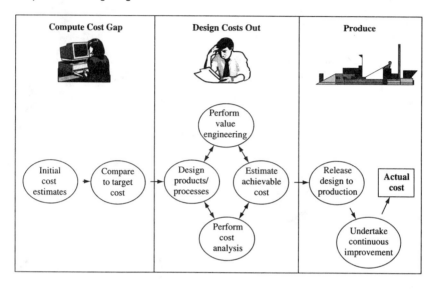

ATTAINING TARGET COSTS

The second phase of target costing addresses how to attain the $90 target cost. That is, how do we turn this *allowable* cost into an *achievable* cost? This recaps the discussion in Chapter 5.

There are three steps in attaining target costs: Compute cost gap, design costs out of a product, and release the design for manufacturing and perform continuous improvement. These three steps are shown in Exhibit 11–4.

Computing the Cost Gap

Determining the difference between the *allowable cost* and the *current cost* is the first step in attaining target costs. For Kitchenhelp's coffee maker, the allowable (target) cost is $90. *Note that this is total product cost and not just manufacturing cost.* The current cost is the initial "as-is" estimate of the cost of producing the coffeemaker based on current cost factors or models. The overall gap between allowable and current costs must be decomposed by life cycle and value chain. A life cycle decomposition assigns total product cost into birth to death categories of research, manufacturing, distribution, service, general support, and disposal. A value chain decomposition breaks down the cost by whether it is incurred by Kitchenhelp or by one of its value chain members such as suppliers, dealers, or disposers.

Exhibit 11–5 provides an assumed breakdown of the allowable and current costs by life cycle and value chain for Kitchenhelp's coffeemaker. How did the company arrive at these cost breakdowns? The breakdown of allowable costs by life cycle typically requires estimating the costs to be incurred on research and development, manufacturing, marketing, distribution, repairs and other support, and disposition costs at the end of the product's life. The value chain requires estimating the costs incurred within a firm and those incurred by its suppliers, dealers, and recyclers. A company can use its past historical average as an initial estimate for these costs.

For example, Kitchenhelp's past experience shows that manufacturing costs typically are 41 percent of the total product cost for small appliances. Further, of the 41 percent, inside costs are 17 percent and the remaining 24 percent are for components purchased from suppliers. These percentages can be used as a starting point to set the allowable cost for the coffee maker for each category in the life cycle and value chain of costs.

Exhibit 11–5 shows these estimates for Kitchenhelp's proposed coffeemaker. It shows that the life cycle breakdown as a percent of the allowable cost of $90 is as follows: R&D (4%), manufacturing (41%), selling and distribution (20%), service and support (10%), general business overhead (20%), and recycling (5%). It also shows 62 percent of the allowable cost of $90, or $55.80, is within Kitchenhelp and 38 percent, or $34.20, is in the value chain.

Kitchenhelp's initial estimate also shows that the total product cost of the new coffeemaker will be $114 or a gap of $24 (114 − 90). The total $114 consists of $67 inside (gap = $11.20) and $47 outside (gap = $ 12.80).

The information in Exhibit 11–5 shows us that the three largest cost gaps exist in external manufacturing costs ($8.40), internal manufacturing costs ($4.70), and external selling and distribution ($4.40). It is clear that Kitchenhelp's cost reduction efforts must be focused both externally and internally. It needs to work closely with its suppliers and dealers and involve them actively in cost planning and reduction efforts. This means partnership and mutual trust and sharing of information with these various entities, as discussed in Chapter 7. Some ideas for reducing costs in the value chain include the following:

- Reduce supplier's cycle time.
- Reduce the distance parts and products have to travel.
- Give incentives for cost reduction ideas; make all solutions win-win.
- Involve value chain members in lean production exercises.
- Reduce the uncertainty value chain members face; share production estimates and scheduling with them.
- Involve value chain members in total quality management programs.

EXHIBIT 11-5

Comparing Allowable and Current Costs: Life Cycle and Value Chain Breakdowns

Value Chain

Life Cycle	Inside			Outside			Total		
	Allowable	Current	Gap	Allowable	Current	Gap	Allowable	Current	Gap
Research and development	$3.60 (4%)	$5	$1.40				$3.60	$5.00	$1.40
Manufacturing	15.30 (17%)	20	4.70	$21.60 (24%)	$30	$8.40	36.90	50.00	13.10
Selling and distribution	5.40 (6%)	6	0.60	12.60 (14%)	17	4.40	18.00	23.00	5.00
Service and support	9.00 (10%)	10	1.00				9.00	10.00	1.00
General business overhead	18.00 (20%)	19	1.00				18.00	19.0	1.00
Recycling costs	4.50 (5%)	7	2.50				4.50	7.00	2.50
Total	$55.80 (62%)	$67	$11.20	$34.20 (38%)	$47	$12.80	$90.00	$114	$24

Designing Out Costs

Reduction of cost through product design is the most critical step in attaining target costs. The key to cost reduction is to ask one simple question: How does the design of this product affect all costs associated with the product from its inception to its final disposal? To include all costs, and not just manufacturing costs, may appear farfetched at first. However, many "downstream" costs such as distribution, selling, warehousing, service, support, and recycling can be greatly affected by product design.

Cost reduction relies on four major activities: product design, cost analysis, value engineering, and cost estimation. These four activities will be explained in greater detail later in the next section. Cost reduction is recursive, since the activities cycle back several times as the product goes from an initial concept to a final design. The recursion is a characteristic of target costing. The purpose of the recursion is to generate a cost effective design and not to correct design errors.

HOW COST REDUCTION OCCURS

This section illustrates the process of cost planning and reduction. Cost reduction would be a trivial task if no constraints were placed on the features and functions offered in a product and the time to develop it. For example, Kitchenhelp can simply delete the coffee grinder from its coffeemaker and probably reach its target cost of $90. However, this defeats the basic product concept of providing a fresh espresso taste in the coffee. The challenge, therefore, is to reduce costs without sacrificing any of the features important to a customer.

We demonstrate how to reduce costs using the four step recursive activity cycle shown in Exhibit 11–6. This cycle, which is design → cost analysis → value engineering → cost estimation is combined with the data from Exhibit 11–5 to show how to attain the target manufacturing cost of $36.90 from the currently estimated level of $50. Note that the target includes both inside and outside manufacturing costs, because suppliers are part of the product team during this cost reduction phase.

Design Product and Processes

In the case of Kitchenhelp, the coffeemaker and the manufacturing process that will be used to produce it are designed and considered at the same time. This avoids costly changes later because machines may not be available or capable of executing a product as designed.

E X H I B I T 11–6

Steps in Attaining Target Costs

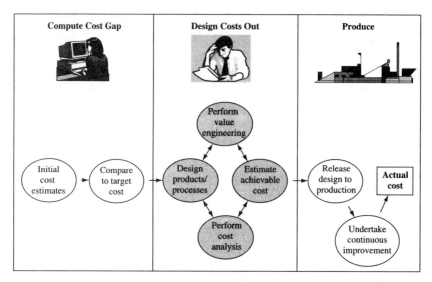

Common tools used at this stage are computer-aided design (CAD) and computer-aided manufacturing (CAM). Cost parameters sometimes are built into these computer models so the cost impact of design changes can be simulated concurrently. Product design goes through several iterations before it is released for manufacturing.

Perform Cost Analysis

Cost analysis consists of determining what components to target for cost reduction and assigning individual cost targets to the major subcomponents and parts of a product. For Kitchenhelp, it means deciding what components of the coffeemaker (heating element, control panel, grinder, etc.) to target for cost reduction and then assigning a cost target to each of these components.

Cost analysis also focuses on the interaction between components and parts. Often a reduction in the cost of one component more than offsets the cost increase elsewhere. For example, decreasing the cost of the outer shell of the coffeemaker by making it small may increase the costs of the control panel, electronic circuitry, and heating element. If these cost increases are large, no net cost saving accrues from decreasing the outer shell.

Cost analysis requires five major subactivities. These are discussed next.

1. *Develop a List of Product Components and Functions.* Cost reduction efforts start by listing the various product components, identifying the functions that they perform and their current estimated cost. The initial product design and cost estimates provide this information. The list shows what components and functions are needed to satisfy customer requirements and what the cost to provide these functions might be. Exhibit 11–7 shows a diagram of the various components of the proposed coffeemaker.

2. *Do a functional cost breakdown.* Each of the various parts and components of the coffeemaker performs a specific function. The next step is to identify that function and estimate its cost. This is shown in Exhibit 11–8. For example, the function of the brew basket assembly is to grind and filter coffee. Its current estimated cost is $9, which represents 18 percent of the total manufacturing cost for this product.

To keep the example simple, we have combined several functions and components for the coffeemaker. At a detailed level, the brew basket or the electronic control panel will be broken into several subcomponents. The total for all components is $50, which is the same as the manufacturing cost estimate shown in Exhibit 11–5.

3. *Determine Relative Ranking of Customer Requirements.* The functions of the coffeemaker form the engineers' view of the product. This

EXHIBIT 11–7

Major Components of Kitchenhelp's Proposed Coffeemaker

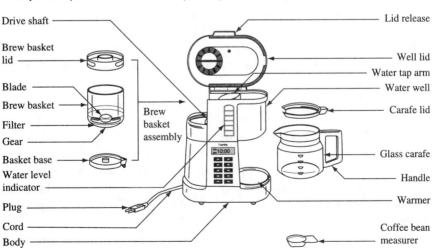

Source: This example is based on a coffee machine first introduced by Toshiba Corporation. The company still produces these coffee makers though it does not sell them in North America.

EXHIBIT 11–8

Functional Cost Breakdown for Kitchenhelp's Coffee Maker

		Cost	
Component	Function	Amount	Percent
Brew basket	Grinds and filters coffee	$9	18%
Carafe	Holds and keeps coffee warm	2	4
Coffee warmer	Keeps coffee warm	3	6
Body shape and water well	Holds water and encasement	9	18
Heating element	Warms water and pushes it	4	8
Electronic display panel	Controls brew and clock settings	23	46
Total		$50	100%

is not the customers' view. You will recall that Kitchenhelp had identified eight features important to its customers. The engineers' view of a product as functions must be reconciled with the customers' view of a product as a set of features. We must relate product functions to the features customers want. To do this we must first assess the relative importance that customers place on the various features. A formal survey of prospective customers asking them to rank the importance of these eight features can be used to rank customer requirements. An assumed ranking for each feature, based on survey results, is shown in Exhibit 11–9. The importance ranking is based on a five point scale. A score of 5 means the feature is very important, a score of 1 indicates that it is not important. For instance, the taste and smell of coffee is the most important feature and multiple grinder settings is the least.

The last column of Exhibit 11–9 converts the raw scores for the importance of features into a *relative ranking of features*. This is done by first adding together the raw scores for the eight functions (5 + 4 + 2 + 3 + 4 + 1 + 3 + 3) = 25. Each function's score is then expressed as a percentage of this total score of 25. For example, coffee taste has a score of 5 out of 25. The relative ranking, therefore, is 5/25 = 20 percent. It says that, of the total value a customer derives from this coffee maker, 20 percent comes from the way the coffee tastes.

4. *Relate Features to Functions.* The relative ranks of features must be converted into an importance rank for each function. Since components carry out the functions of a product and are the key design parameters, this step re-

EXHIBIT   11–9

Customer Feature Ranking for Kitchenhelp's Coffeemaker

Customer Requirements	Customer Ranking		Relative Ranking (%)
	1 (not important)	5 (very important)	
Coffee tastes and smells like espresso		5	20%
Easy to clean		4	16
Looks nice	2		8
Has 6+ cup capacity		3	12
Starts automatically at designated time		4	16
Works well with different coffee beans	1		4
Keeps the coffee warm		3	12
Automatically shuts off		3	12
Total			100%

lates customer ranks to the components that best meet that particular requirement. Quality function deployment (QFD) is typically used for systematically arraying information about these three variables, features, functions (components), and competitive evaluation, in a matrix format.

The QFD matrix is a useful tool for target costing because it highlights the relationships among competitive offerings, customer requirements, and design parameters. The QFD matrix summarizes the information about product functions from Exhibit 11–8 with customer ranks from Exhibit 11–9. It adds two other pieces of information collected in the market research phase. First, it adds the correlation between a component or design parameter and customer requirements. Second, it adds information about how customers evaluate competitors' offerings of these same features.

A QFD matrix for Kitchenhelp's coffeemaker is shown in Ehibit11–10. It shows, for instance, that the requirement that coffee taste like espresso has a high correlation with the design of the brew basket and the heating element. Similarly, how many cups the coffeemaker can hold is correlated to the water well and the carafe size. Taste is also the most important feature to a customer, and it is currently rated at 3 for Kitchenhelp and 2 for its competitor. This tells Kitchenhelp that, although it is ahead of the competition, it is still far from what the customer would like to see as far as taste goes. On

EXHIBIT 11–10

A QFD Matrix for Kitchenhelp's Coffeemaker

Components or Functions / Customer Requirements	Brew Basket	Carafe	Coffee Warmer	Body/ Water Well	Heating Element	Display panel	Competitor Ranking Low High 1 2 3 4 5	Customer Ranking
Tastes/smells like expresso	◆				◆		■ □	5
Easy to clean	●	●		◆			□ ■	4
Looks nice				◆		◆	□ ■	2
Has 6+ cup capacity		◆		◆			■□	3
Starts automatically on time						◆	□ ■	4
Works with different beans	○					◆	■□	1
Keeps the coffee warm		●	◆				■ □	3
Automatic shutoff						◆	□■	3

Correlation of design   Comparative competitor
parameters and   rankings
customer requirements

◆ = Strong correlation   ■ = Competitor ranking
● = Moderate correlation   □ = Our ranking
○ = Weak correlation

appearance, the competition obviously has a better looking product with a rating of 5. However, the customer ranking for this feature is 2, which suggests that it is not worth spending too much in improving the appearance of the coffeemaker.

5. *Develop Relative Functional Ranking.* The QFD matrix allows converting feature ranks into functional or component ranks. This is critical, because customers think in terms of features but products are designed in terms of functions and components. For the conversion, we need one other piece of information, the percentage contribution of each component to a customer feature. This information is shown as a general correlation in Exhibit 11–10.

Engineers have to convert this correlation data into specific contribution percentages. Such a breakdown for the coffeemaker is shown in Exhibit 11–11, and the information is interpreted as follows. The feature "tastes like espresso" is a function of the brew basket and heating element design. (You can verify this from Exhibit 11–10.) Engineers feel that both these components contribute equally to this "taste" feature. We, therefore, assign equal (50%) weight to each function's contribution to taste. The relative value ranking of the "taste" feature is 20 percent. Therefore, since both components contribute equally, we assign each component a value rank of 10 percent.

The last row of Exhibit 11–11 adds the value contributions of a component to all features to arrive at that component's approximate value to a customer. The brew basket is assigned a value, based on a customer importance

EXHIBIT 11–11

Kitchenhelp Inc.'s Coffeemaker: Functional Cost Analysis of Components

	Component						
Customer Requirements	**Brew Basket**	**Carafe**	**Coffee Warmer**	**Body/ Water Well**	**Heating Element**	**Display Panel**	**Relative Feature Ranking**
Tastes/smells like espresso	.5 × 20% = 10%				.5 × 20% = 10%		20%
Easy to clean	.3 × 16% = 4.8%	.1 × 16% = 1.6%		.6 × 16% = 9.6%			16%
Looks nice				.6 × 8% = 4.8%		.4 × 8% = 3.2%	8%
Has 6+ cup capacity		.5 × 12% = 6.%		.5 × 12% = 6%			12%
Starts automatically on time						1 × 16% = 16%	16%
Has multiple grinder settings	.05 × 4% = 0.2%					.95 × 4% = 3.8%	4%
Keeps the coffee warm		.2 × 12% = 2.4%	.8 × 12% = 9.6%				12%
Automatic shutoff						1 × 12% = 12%	12%
Converted component	15.0%	10.0%	9.6%	20.4%	10.0%	35.0%	100%

rank, of 15 percent; the carafe has a value of 10 percent; and so on. Note that the last row and last column both add up to 100 percent. They are simply different views of customer values. The column represents value of features, and the row represents the value of components.

Perform Value Engineering

To achieve the cost targets, Kitchenhelp must analyze the various components to determine how to provide their functions at the lowest overall cost with no reduction in required performance, reliability, maintainability, quality, safety, recyclability, and usability of the coffeemaker. For example, the function of the heating element is to bring water temperature to a specified level. Value engineering asks how the water temperature can be raised to 110° in three minutes at a lower cost. It generates ideas for simplifying both the design of the coffeemaker and the processes used to manufacture it. Value engineering consists of three steps.

The first step is to *identify components for cost reduction*. Choosing which components to select requires computing a value index. This is a ratio of the value (degree of importance) to customer and percentage of total cost devoted to each component. For the coffeemaker, the value information is in the last row of Exhibit 11–11 and the relative cost information is in the last column of Exhibit 11–8. Both quantities are expressed as percentages. Exhibit 11–12 computes the value index and shows its implications for cost reduction.

E X H I B I T   11–12

Value Index for Kitchenhelp's Coffeemaker

(1) Component or Function	(2) Component Cost (EX. 11–8) (% of total)	(3) Relative Importance (EX. 11–11) (%)	(4) Value Index (Col. 3 ÷ 2)	(5) Action Implied
Brew basket	18	15.0	0.83	Reduce cost
Carafe	4	10.0	2.50	Enhance
Coffee warmer	6	9.6	1.60	Enhance
Body shape and water well	18	20.4	1.13	O.K.
Heating element	8	10.0	1.25	Enhance
Electronic display panel	46	35.0	0.76	Reduce cost
	100%	100%		

As Exhibit 11–12 shows, components with a value index of less than 1 typically are prime candidates for value engineering. Components with high values are candidates for enhancement, since far too little is being spent for a feature important to customers. These components present an opportunity to enhance the product. The two variables in the value index, cost and relative importance, are plotted on the graph shown in Exhibit 11–13.

An optimal value zone in Exhibit 11–13 indicates the value band in which no action is necessary. The optimal value zone is based on the experience and opinion of the target costing team members. The zone is usually wider at the bottom of the value index chart, where low importance and low cost occur, and narrower at the top, where features are important and cost variations larger. The area of the graph above the optimal value zone indicates components that are candidates for cost reduction. Items below the zone are candidates for enhancement.

The second VE activity is *generating cost reduction ideas,* which requires creative thinking and brainstorming. The purpose is to ask what can be reduced, eliminated, combined, substituted, rearranged, or enhanced to provide the same level of functionality from a component at less cost. Exhibit 11–14 lists some sample cost reduction ideas that Kitchenhelp might consider to reduce the cost of the electronic display panel, the prime target for cost reduction identified by the value index.

E X H I B I T   11–13

Value Index Chart for Kitchenhelp's Coffeemaker

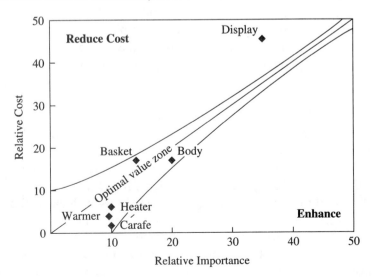

E X H I B I T   11–14

Kitchenhelp Coffeemaker Electronic Display Panel: Value Engineering Ideas to
Reduce Cost

Panel Subcomponent	Cost Reduction Idea
Power supply	*Reduce* wattage; more than needed in current design
Flexible circuit	*Eliminate* flexible circuit; use wiring harness
Printed wire board	*Standardize* board specifications; use mass produced unit
Clock timer	*Combine* with printed wire board
Central processor chip	*Substitute* standard 8088 chip instead of custom design
Heater connector	*Rearrange* layout of board to heater connection

Note that the cost reduction ideas in Exhibit 11–14 contain some general principles that can be applied to many different situations. These ideas
focus on reducing the number of parts, simplifying the assembly, using common or standard parts, keeping the design simple, not using soon to be obsolete parts, and not overengineering the product beyond what will meet
customers' needs. A cross-functional team is essential because these types of
engineering design choices must be guided by customer and financial input.

Engineers need to know quickly and reliably if the cost reduction
ideas they are considering are worthwhile from a financial standpoint. For
example, considering whether to eliminate the flexible circuit requires a
good idea of its purchase cost as well as good cost tables that can estimate
what a flexible circuit adds to the other manufacturing costs of the coffeemaker.

The last VE activity is *testing and implementing promising ideas,*
which requires determining if cost reduction ideas are technically feasible
and acceptable to customers. Those ideas that meet this test are further developed and incorporated into the product or process design and cataloged
in a VE ideas data base so they are available for future design efforts.

One tool often used for testing the feasibility of ideas is the component interaction matrix. This matrix, which helps to identify the impact of
changing one component on other components, requires cost data. It
ensures that no current or soon out of production components are used.
The use of such components can increase product costs significantly. Ex-

E X H I B I T   11–15

Component Interaction Matrix

			Components					
Components	**Basket**	**Coffee Carafe**	**Warmer**	**Body**	**Heater**	**Display**	**Cost**	**Available Until**
Brew basket					√		$9	2004
Carafe	√			√			2	2010
Coffee warmer	√			√			3	2010
Body		√	√			√	9	2008
Heater						√	4	2010
Display panel				√			23	2005

hibit 11–15 shows a sample component interaction matrix for Kitchenhelp's coffeemaker.

The Cost column of Exhibit 11–15 shows the cost of a component. The Availability column shows the date on which the component is expected to be obsolete. A √ entry indicates a relationship between the components. Kitchenhelp must determine whether the relationship between the components is positive or negative. For example, decreasing the size of the brew basket may decrease the cost of the heater, which does not have to use as much water heating power. Similarly, we may find that the display panel cost goes up as the body cost goes down. In this case, the savings in body may be wiped out by the increase in panel cost. In determining these costs, we must keep the life cycle for all components consistent. For example, we may have engineered a body to last for 15 years when the display panel will last only 7 years.[3]

Release Design for Production

Ideally, Kitchenhelp will release the design of the new coffeemaker for manufacturing when it is satisfied that the estimated achievable cost is equal to the allowable cost. If this is not the case, it has three options: remove some of

---

[3] Many appliance companies have made this mistake in recent years. For instance, one maker of dishwashers uses a 25 year steel wash tub with a 7 year electronic control panel. The replacement cost of the panel is 75 percent of the cost of a new dishwasher. Clearly, the company could have reduced the cost of the tub by using materials other than steel that do not last as long or increase the life of the panel to match that of the tub.

the features, increase the market price, or get cost savings from continuous improvement. The first two actions are feasible only if they will not adversely affect the sales of the coffeemaker. The last action requires serious evaluation of the manufacturing processes, defect rates produced, yield experienced, cycle time for manufacturing, storage, transportation, and other areas to determine whether any waste can be eliminated. These continuous improvements may be used to fill any shortfall between allowable and achievable target cost.

SUMMARY

This chapter provided an illustration of the target costing process by using a hypothetical company, Kitchenhelp. We used this illustration to recap the discussion in the prior chapters of this book in concrete terms. A coffeemaker was used to illustrate the steps in target costing: formulating a product strategy, defining a product, setting its target cost, taking steps to achieve that cost, and its final release for manufacturing.

12

CHAPTER

Deploying Target Costing

The central message of this book is that, to compete effectively, organizations need to adopt target costing as a strategic initiative. Believing in the need for target costing is only a first step in institutionalizing this initiative. Integrating target costing in the daily actions of an organization requires more than a belief; it requires organization–wide deployment. How to deploy target costing is the subject of this last chapter, which contains four key messages.

KEY MESSAGES

- Target costing deployment will not happen because management thinks it is a good idea. It requires organizational readiness, a conceptual plan, and an action plan.
- Before proceeding with deployment, one must create acceptance for target costing, provide a common understanding of it, and use it to link daily action with organizational strategies.
- Target cost deployment requires determining the technical and structural changes needed; the behaviors desired; the cultural values, symbols, and mind-sets to be reinforced; and the political issues that need to be addressed.

- A deployment plan is needed that specifies how to meet the technical, behavioral, cultural, and political requirements for acceptance and success of target costing.

A CONCEPTUAL MODEL FOR DEPLOYMENT OF TARGET COSTING[1]

Deploying strategic initiatives is not a simple, tidy process. Managers tend to underestimate its difficulty. They use a "field of dreams" approach: If an initiative is rational and logical to them, deployment will follow from the obvious force of logic.

Not everyone in an organization will embrace the need for a new initiative or recognize its importance, however. Many organizations found out the hard way that worthwhile initiatives such as total quality management or activity based management have failed to be successfully deployed because management underestimated the difficulty of the deployment task. In some cases, the organization was not ready for the initiative. In others, deployment failed because of poor communication, lack of resources, rejection by significant interest groups, or lack of management support.

Deployment requires careful planning that is guided by a sound conceptual approach. We propose the CAM-I conceptual model as a framework for thinking about deployment,[2] which is reproduced in Exhibit 12–1.

The CAM-I conceptual model uses the game of baseball as an analogy for deployment. Before play can proceed, the players must be ready to play, the climate and ground conditions must be right, and everyone must understand the rules of the game. Scoring a run requires taking four bases.

So, too, in deployment. The organization must be ready to accept target costing as an important strategic need, all key participants must be ready to proceed and must be clear about what needs to happen. They must be willing to take all four bases. The four bases in our analogy are these:

- *The technical or structural base* covers the task-oriented requirements for target costing, including collecting and providing information, developing process metrics, investing in needed tools, and organizing for cross-functional teams.
- *The behavioral base* deals with the behaviors needed to succeed at target costing, including issues of employee motivation, morale, and performance measurement and evaluation.

---

[1] Much of the discussion here draws from the CAM-I field research project on strategy deployment. See S. Ansari, J. Bell, and J. Blumenthal, *Strategy Deployment In Organizations,* Research Monograph, (Arlington, Texas: CAM-I, 1993).

[2] For a full description and discussion of the CAM-I conceptual deployment model, see ibid.

E X H I B I T   12–1

The CAM-I Conceptual Deployment Model

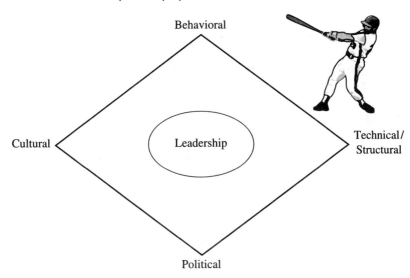

- *The cultural base* covers the values, meanings, symbols, stories, and mind-sets that reinforce the need for target costing and facilitate its acceptance and adoption.
- *The political base* encompasses dealing with the groups in an organization whose interest may be served or set back by the use of target costing.

As Exhibit 12–1 shows, leadership is at the center of this conceptual strategy "diamond," our analog for the coach and umpire rolled into one. The remainder of this chapter elaborates on how to use this conceptual deployment framework to think through and plan for target costing deployment.

ARE WE READY FOR TARGET COSTING?

Before trying to get to any base, the "conditions" for play must be right and the team must be motivated, with each player clear on "what the game" is about. Games are lost if the coach is not attentive to these two preconditions. In our model, the leaders are the coaches. No leader can or should attempt to deploy target costing if the time or place is not right or if the expectations are unclear to the players. Participants should have a common conception about the nature, purpose, and the need for target costing.

The first step in deployment, therefore, is to do a "readiness assessment." The following seven questions can be used for such an assessment.

1. *Have we made the reason for target costing clear? Is its connection to business strategy clear?* For successful deployment, organizational participants must have a shared conception of target costing. They must be clear about its strategic need, and they must be able to see target costing as the connection between their daily actions and the overall strategy. If not, target costing will be viewed as a quick fix or as another "flavor of the month" initiative. When Chrysler launched target costing, the company made it clear that the use of target costing was a matter of company survival. In addition, it used a 12-panel objectives chart. This chart was designed to connect target costing with overall strategic objectives of responding to customer needs (quality), selling the car at a competitive price (cost), and bringing the product to market faster (time).

2. *Does top management support target costing?* Target costing needs considerable cross-functional cooperation. This can occur only if top management is strongly behind the initiative. An important part of assessing readiness is to ensure that top management supports target costing both in word and deed. The Neon project at Chrysler was sold first to the chairman, Lee Iacocca. The championship of top management created the necessary awareness for target costing and enabled teams to get the resources for doing things, such as flying engineering teams to the Chrysler Technology Center on a chartered plane.

3. *Is this the right time to introduce target costing?* Quite often, organizations overburden employees with too many initiatives. In recent years, organizations have seen TQM, ABM, BPR, and a host of other initiatives introduced with overlapping implementations. This often leaves employees exhausted and feeling that no strategic priority is being followed.

4. *Are people ready for change?* People do not accept change easily. An imperative for change must be present. The most obvious one is survival. The need to survive was an important motivation at Caterpillar and Chrysler. Komatsu had made significant inroads into Caterpillar's markets. Chrysler was strapped for cash in 1990, and its stock prices were at an all time low. Both organizations were acutely aware of the need for change. In addition to survival, positive challenges that appeal to employee values also can help

create an imperative for change. Organizations with traditions of engineering excellence can present target costing as an engineering challenge to produce lean designs. Those that value customer service may want to present target costing as a customer-focused initiative.

5. *Is there a readiness to embrace the key principles of target costing?* In Chapter 2, we presented several important principles of target costing. These principles represent a significant shift in cost management thinking. For target costing to be successfully deployed, we must ensure that these principles are acceptable to all key functional groups and managers. Accounting or finance has to embrace the idea of cost management through design. If traditional costing, budgeting, and legal reporting systems dominate an organization, target costing systems will be competing with them and may not survive. Similarly, the engineering community must use concurrent engineering instead of the traditional linear design processes. These principles cannot be accepted casually. The "we have always done it this way" mentality is dangerous.

6. *Is the organization ready to commit the necessary resources?* Target costing deployment requires resources to be expended for training, system redesign, collection of new information, and other related changes. If an organization is unwilling to commit resources, deployment may not be feasible. Thinking through the resource implications early reduces the risk of abandoning target costing for lack of resources later.

7. *Are all management levels ready for "catch ball"?* Japanese companies use the game of rugby as an analogy for deployment. This catch-ball view of deployment is designed to signal that each party in the process must do his or her part rapidly. Playing catch-ball means that, as lower level managers ask higher level managers to make decisions, resolve differences, or commit resources, the latter will do so quickly. The analogy also recognizes that this game is played in several successive rounds. If management is not ready to respond quickly, the target costing initiative may languish and wither before taking hold.

These seven questions help to determine whether an organization is ready for deployment and also determines the scope, breadth, and speed of deployment if only some parts of the organization are ready. If the answer to most of these questions is no, then a significant amount of preparation has to be done before launching target costing. When these questions have been addressed affirmatively, a company can proceed to play and start thinking about how to take the four bases.

MEETING TECHNICAL AND STRUCTURAL REQUIREMENTS

Taking the first base requires making the technical and structural changes needed for target costing. This book has spelled out in great detail many of these elements.

We have discussed how to determine prices and required return targets (Chapter 4), the need for cost system redesign, (Chapter 5), incorporating customer inputs (Chapter 6), new ways of organizing suppliers and other external relationships (Chapter 7), internal organizational changes (Chapter 8), information system changes (Chapter 9), and new investment in target costing tools (Chapter 10). All these technical and structural changes are necessary if target costing is to perform well. The key enablers for the technical base are shown in Exhibit 12–2.

Taking the technical base means examining the four enablers shown in Exhibit 12–2 and translating them into specific changes needed. For instance, the enabler invest in tools means acquisition of tools such as VE, QFD, cost tables, and the like. The next step is to identify the "gap" between what is needed in each enabling area against what an organization currently has in place. An organization that has been using QFD does not need to invest in this tool. To document this "gap" between the technical or structural enablers needed and those already in place, we can use an assessment tool similar to the one shown in Appendix E. A complete version of this tool lists all the

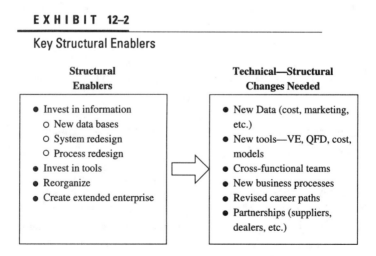

EXHIBIT 12–2

Key Structural Enablers

Structural Enablers	Technical—Structural Changes Needed

• Invest in information
  o New data bases
  o System redesign
  o Process redesign
• Invest in tools
• Reorganize
• Create extended enterprise
	• New Data (cost, marketing, etc.)
	• New tools—VE, QFD, cost, models
	• Cross-functional teams
	• New business processes
	• Revised career paths
	• Partnerships (suppliers, dealers, etc.)

technical requirements for target costing, the area that is responsible for ensuring it is in place, and whether others in the organization agree that the responsible area has that capability. An example is component cost data. As Appendix E shows, accounting is primarily responsible and *should* have the data but does not. Others who should have *access* to the data are design and manufacturing, and they do not have the data. Procurement does have the data even though it is not that area's primary responsibility.

GETTING DESIRED BEHAVIORS

The second base in our conceptual deployment diamond is the behavioral base. The focus here is on the human side of the organization. To take this base, we need to know what behaviors we "desire" for successful target costing, how to "obtain and sustain" these behaviors, and how to avoid "dysfunctional" behaviors.

Behaviors Desired

Target costing is a different way of doing things and requires many behavioral changes. To a certain extent each organization must list the behavioral changes it needs, based on the behaviors in place. Most organizations, however, may find the need for the six major behavioral changes discussed next:

- *Early involvement of functional areas is primary.* In most businesses, functional areas typically get involved sequentially in business processes. Manufacturing engineers do not want to consider equipment changes until a design is final. Service and support people do not want to provide input until the drawings are final. Accountants do not want to estimate costs until all design parameters and procurement issues have been resolved. Early involvement is considered a waste of time, since designs can change. These behaviors, once considered functional or efficient, are the antithesis of what is needed from functional groups in a target costing environment.

- *Engineering needs to take cost ownership.* Traditionally engineers have not assumed responsibility for costs. Accountants are supposed to "control" costs. Target costing emphasizes the prime role of design. Engineers, therefore, are central for managing costs. An important behavioral change is to make engineers aware of and accept responsibility for cost management. They need to incorporate new technology into products only if it is cost effective and driven by market needs. A good example is a Danish manufacturer of optical scanners that has adopted the slogan "state of the market" technology. What it means is that new technology is introduced in its products not because it is "state of the art" but because customers are willing to pay for it.

- *Marketing must evaluate trade-offs not just sell.* Marketing people are traditionally oriented to selling products. More features at a lower price make their work easier. They behave as consumer advocates. For target costing, marketing people must balance cost and features against a customer's ability and willingness to pay for the features. They must assist trade-off and affordability analysis. This means taking a consumer view *and* a producer's view of the product.

- *Targets are commitments.* Often targets are viewed as negotiable and approximately achievable. An important behavioral change is to make participants accept targets as serious commitments. Actual behaviors, not just good intentions, must be directed at achieving cost targets.

- *Cross-functional cooperation is essential.* Functional experts have traditionally protected their turf by keeping information and expertise to themselves. Accounting information is sometimes deliberately kept obscure or not shared with others. Similarly, procurement data bases are not accessible to outsiders. Target costing requires a high degree of cross-functional cooperation. Expertise and information should be provided by the functional specialists. Targets need to be smoothly passed on from team to team.

- *Accountants must be business partners.* The traditional role of the accounting staff is to act as "corporate policemen."[3] The emphasis is on providing "verifiable" rather than "relevant" information and behaving as "auditors" and not as "business partners." This bias stems from the traditional preoccupation of accounting with external financial and tax reporting. Target costing requires that accounting provide more relevant (even if less precise) information and act as "business advisors" instead of auditors.

Enablers of Desired Behaviors

Communication and motivation are instrumental in obtaining desired behaviors. Communication informs and provides feedback to participants about what behaviors are considered functional for target costing. Performance measurement and rewards motivate the behaviors target costing needs. Com-

---

[3] See Jablonsky, S. and Keating, P. , "Management Communication and Control Systems: Two Competing Models of Financial Management" *Management Accounting,* (February, 1995), pp. 21–25.

EXHIBIT 12–3

Enablers of Desired Target Costing Behaviors

**Enablers of
Behavior**

Communication
- Command media
  - o Newsletters, videos
  - o Policy manuals
- Training
  - o General
  - o Specific

Motivation
- Performance measurement
  - o Process measures
  - o Output measures
- Rewards
  - o Extrinsic
  - o Intrinsic

**Desired
Behaviors**

- Early involvement of functions
- Engineers own costs
- Marketing does feature trade-offs
- Targets are commitments
- Cross-functional cooperation
- Finance acts as "business advisor"

munication can be done using an organization's command media and through training. Employees can be motivated through performance measurement and by rewards. These key enablers for obtaining desired behaviors are shown in Exhibit 12–3 and discussed in this section.

- ■ *Command media* refers to the use of all in-house media available in an organization. These include newsletters, internal memoranda, videos, and policy manuals. Top management frequently uses these as a way to communicate the behaviors needed for new initiatives. While they are important and useful, we need to remember that deployment requires more than just sending out a message. Just because target costing appears in an organization's command media, wall posters, or banners does not mean people understand what it is about or are willing to do what is needed to carry out its intent. Effective communication is a two-way street. It provides information to intended recipients and gets feedback from them as well.

- ■ *Training* is a more effective form of two-way communication for technically complex initiatives, such as target costing. Two types of training are required. *General training* focuses on imparting the need for target costing and an understanding of its general principles. Its purpose is to create a critical mass of people in the organization who understand and facilitate interaction between the various functional groups. This type of training should mix teams from various functions in a single class, which will allow for both downward and lateral communication. *Specific training* focuses on communicating specific skills and behaviors desired. Many Japanese companies offer formal instruction in VE at three different levels: beginner, intermediate, and advanced. The Boeing Company offers a VE class that uses materials and instructors from the company as well as faculty from universities.

■ *Performance measurement* is another way to obtain desired behaviors. We know that people attend and respond to what is measured by an organization. Performance metrics can be a powerful way to motivate desired behaviors. Good metrics start with a specification of desired behaviors then build measures that are likely to generate such behaviors. Two types of measures commonly used are process measures and output measures.[4] *Process measures* provide information about how well a process is working. The target costing framework in Appendix A provides details of the process steps. Each major process step requires behaviors such as cross-functional cooperation, customer input, and feature trade-offs. Process measures should be developed to measure behaviors desired for target costing. It is beyond the scope of this chapter to specify detailed metrics. The main point is that the selection of process metrics should be guided by the desired behaviors.[5] *Output measures* provide a final test on whether desired behaviors are also producing desired results. The desired behaviors for target costing should include reduced cycle time for producing designs, improved quality, decreased product and process costs, and increased profit margins. These results can be operationalized in several different metrics. Again the guiding principle is to use metrics that will motivate the desired behaviors.

■ *Rewards* promote desired behaviors by reinforcing performance measures. This is why many organizations link rewards to

---

[4] For a detailed discussion of process and output measures, see S. Hronec, *Vital Signs: Using Quality, Cost and Time Performance Measures to Chart Your Company's Future* (Arthur Andersen & Co., Chicago, 1993).

[5] A good example of measuring behaviors is the ITT performance measurement instrument for corporate controllers. This instrument consists of 1600 questions in 30 areas that provide a detailed specification of what ITT considers desired controllership behaviors. See "International Telephone & Telegraph Company," Harvard Business School Case 478–022, (Cambridge, Mass.: Harvard Case Clearing House, 1968).

performance metrics.[6] Rewards can be *extrinsic, (*pay, promotion, job security) or *intrinsic* (job satisfaction, self-actualization, self esteem). Both must be used so that the reward system promotes the desired target costing behaviors.

Avoiding Dysfunctional Behaviors

Target costing, if not employed correctly, can lead to undesirable behavioral consequences. Kato et al.[7] report four behavioral problems experienced by Japanese companies that have installed target costing. These problems, and how to avoid them, are discussed next.

- *Longer development times.* In some companies, an overemphasis on design led to a longer product development cycle and delayed the product from reaching the market on time. This behavioral dysfunction can be avoided by setting simultaneous targets for quality, cost, and time. Behavior must be driven to all three targets and not just cost.

- *Employee burnout.* Pressure to attain targets, particularly demanding ones, can cause employee burnout and frustration. If after working many hours of overtime and doing their best, employees fail to attain targets, it is likely to reduce their aspiration levels in future periods or may lead to rejection of targets as unattainable. There are three ways to reduce the likelihood of these types of adverse behavioral consequences. *Use employee participation in setting targets.* Research on the effects of participation are mixed.[8] However, it does suggest that employees, particularly professionals such as engineers, are better motivated to attain targets when they have a voice in setting those targets. *Create and manage slack.* In their pioneering work on organizations, March and Simon[9] argued that a certain amount of slack is functional because it allows organizations to harness extra energy for crisis periods. It may be in an organization's best interest not to operate in a constant crisis mode but instead to create a certain

---

[6] Readers should be aware that many, including Edward Deming, question this assumption. It is beyond the scope of this chapter to examine the pros and cons of performance-based reward systems. The literature on performance measurement and organizational culture discusses this issue in greater detail.

[7] The discussion of these four consequences comes from Y. Kato, G. Boer, and C. Chow, "Target Costing: An Integrative Management Process," *Journal of Cost Management,* Spring 1995.

[8] For a summary of research findings on the effects of participation, see P. Brownell, "Participation in the Budgetary Process, When It Works and When It Doesn't," *Journal of Accounting Literature,* Spring 1982, pp. 124–153.

[9] See J. G. March and H. A. Simon, *Organizations* (New York: John Wiley, 1958).

amount of "acceptable" slack in targets whenever possible. *Focus on continuous improvement and not radical changes.* Learning reinforcement theory suggests that frequent positive reinforcement is a useful way to motivate and keep behaviors on a desired path. Continuous improvement is one way to use frequent positive reinforcement. Making small incremental improvements provides employees a sense of accomplishment in the near term. Individuals need not meet an entire target before they are rewarded for their efforts. This incremental move toward targets can mitigate some of the pressure for meeting targets.

- *Market confusion.* Uncritically attending to customer requirements can cause "feature creep." That is, additional features are added on without regard to cost and product models proliferate causing market confusion. Management accountants can help avoid this by making certain that engineers are aware of the costs of new features and that marketing does not just produce a customer "wish list." Both disciplines should be guided to consider cost trade-offs so that features are added only when customers are willing to pay for them.

- *Organizational conflict.* The traditional focus of target costing is product design. Other costs, such as marketing or general business support (overhead), are either exempt from cost targets or are treated as "fixed" by prior decisions and part of the "legacy" of the existing cost system. Design engineers feel that other parts of the organization are getting a free ride while they try to squeeze every penny out of a product. This leads to internal conflict, which can be avoided by taking the following two steps. First, we should set targets for all costs and not just manufacturing costs. This makes sense both from a cost management perspective and a behavioral perspective. Just as we cannot exceed a certain amount to manufacture a product, we cannot exceed a target for advertising and promoting that product as well. These costs need to be managed as part of achieving overall profit targets. Second, we can apply the target costing philosophy to manage "fixed" or "legacy" costs as well. Target costing represents a philosophy that says costs are driven by the way products and processes are designed. This philosophy can be used to manage all costs by looking at the design of these support functions and processes. Indeed activity-based management and business process re-engineering are two techniques that employ the same design orientation to manage the cost of processes.

BUILDING A SUPPORTIVE CULTURE

Performance evaluation and rewards can ensure short-term compliance. Sustaining desired behaviors in the long run is possible only if an organization or society's culture supports these behaviors. To take the cultural base, target costing must create or appeal to symbols, mind-sets, values, and worldviews that create the kind of culture that is needed. Exhibit 12–4 shows the relationship between cultural enablers and desired cultural attributes for target costing.

Desired Cultural Attributes

As Exhibit 12–4 shows, four cultural attributes are required for target costing:

- *Customer focus* is an important value needed for target costing. An organization must clearly adopt listening to and meeting customer needs as an important value within its culture so it becomes ingrained and internalized over time.
- *Cross-functional cooperation* is not just a behavioral issue but also an important value to be internalized. The organization must strive to create a culture in which parochial concerns are forgotten and cross-functional cooperation is achieved. Leadership must make certain that teamwork is the norm and that parochial behavior is not rewarded, tolerated, or encouraged.
- *Openness* requires creating a culture in which people share information. This is extremely important, not just as a behavior but also as a value. Employees must feel that the culture rewards sharing information and knowledge. Only then is it possible to have

E X H I B I T   12–4

Cultural Enablers of Target Costing

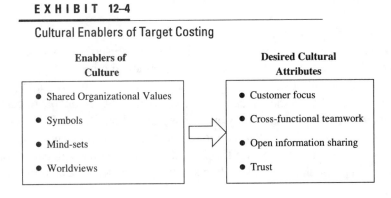

the open sharing of information critical to the success of target costing.

■ *Trust* is an important component for building the effective extended enterprise essential for target costing. Without trust, it is hard to envision suppliers opening their processes or books to manufacturers. Without trust, it is inconceivable that dealers will report customer issues fairly and be responsive to their needs. Trust must be a centerpiece of any value system around which an organization builds its culture.

Creating the Right Culture

Creating these four attributes is perhaps the least understood and most problematic base in deployment. Changing cultures is difficult because people have deep-seated values and convictions that they bring to the workplace. Organizational culture can appeal to these values; changing them is fairly difficult. It is easier to change values if they are consistent with the values of the larger culture and society. It is leadership's role to ensure that this happens as much as possible.

Appealing to the Right Values

A very effective way to get cultural acceptance for a new idea is to emphasize its link to pre-existing values within a culture. This is a more effective way to deploy target costing because it is introduced as appealing to a higher set of values. The presentation by Robert Marcell, Chrysler's general manager, to the Neon project team members is a good example of this approach. In his presentation, given against the backdrop of a cash-strapped Chrysler Corporation, Marcell showed slides and talked about life in his hometown of Iron River, Michigan. These slides show life in Iron River while he was growing up: a town with 50 working iron mines, lots of railroad activity, a prosperous community amid beautiful lakes and woods. Later in the talk he showed pictures of Iron River as it is today: a ghost town of largely abandoned mine shafts and a population less than half of what it was in the early 1960s, with more than 75 percent of the residents below the poverty line. Iron River had been unable to compete against imports from Brazil and Canada. As Marcell put it, Iron River's inability to compete made it into "an economic Chernobyl." The talk ended with Marcell asking the team members if the present-day auto industry in America, and Chrysler in particular, were likely to become like Iron River. Could they rise to the challenge and disprove critics who think the U.S. auto industry is "soft, lazy, dumb . . . and can't compete." He ended by exhorting Chrysler to become competitive and not just save themselves and the auto industry but, maybe in a small way, make a significant contribution to the United States as well.

The Chrysler story shows a masterful use of symbols and values to drive home the necessity for building small cars cost effectively. It has all the elements of an appealing story. The slides of small-town USA invoke the symbols of a nostalgic past. These are the images that Norman Rockwell has burned into the American consciousness forever. Add to this an element of a challenge from Japanese and European automakers. The image of a sleeping giant awakening (World War II) provides a rich subtext. There is a villain to be proven wrong. The infamous "they" (the media, foreign critics, U.S. citizens, and top management) are those who have lost faith in the company's ability to do things right. Finally, it ends with a Kennedy-style appeal to do something for the country. Taken together, the Chrysler speech has all the images, symbols, values, and emotions that appeal to a midwestern work force.

MEETING POLITICAL CHALLENGES

Getting to home plate involves addressing political issues. Politics may be the killer that strikes down more good ideas than any other single factor in organizational life. People are understandably negative about politics and therefore prefer to avoid addressing the political side of deployment. This is naive. It is a mistake to assume that rational or sound solutions will be enough to win the day. We must clearly identify the political objectives of deployment and the means and ways of achieving these objectives. Exhibit 12–5 depicts the desired political outcomes for deployment and their enablers.

EXHIBIT   12–5

Political Objectives and Enablers

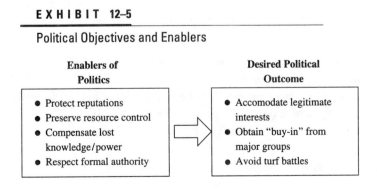

Enablers of Politics	Desired Political Outcome
• Protect reputations • Preserve resource control • Compensate lost knowledge/power • Respect formal authority	• Accomodate legitimate interests • Obtain "buy-in" from major groups • Avoid turf battles

Desired Political Outcomes

As a new initiative, target costing will affect the interests of organizational participants in material and psychological ways. It also will disturb existing patterns of power and influence. This may evoke a negative reaction strong enough for interest groups to form and block implementation. A successful deployment has three political objectives:

- *Accommodate genuine interests.* Where genuine interests are hurt, they must be recognized and provided for. A new initiative, such as target costing, can create a threat of job losses or feelings of inadequacy because of the new skills being demanded. These are genuine fears, and they must be met to avoid opposition to target costing.

- *Get "buy-in" from major groups.* Key power groups in an organization, such as engineering, manufacturing, procurement, accounting, and marketing, must "buy" into target costing if it is to succeed. Getting this buy-in may involve a process of mutual negotiation and give and take, so resource losses or power sharing arrangements can be re-established.

- *Avoid turf battles.* Target costing requires new forms of organizing and information sharing. If authority or information are the sources of power, then those who rely on them are likely to be political losers. We need to recognize these sources of power and make plans to offset them through other means.

Achieving Political Objectives

These political outcomes can be achieved by being sensitive to the power and influence game in organizations. We must understand how target costing will affect the sources of power and influence in an organization and then work to counter these threats. The key enablers that allow us to address these political objectives stem from the four major sources of power and influence in organizations:[10]

- *Protect reputations.* Power in organizations is often the result of reputations built on past successes. A new initiative, by definition, is an implicit admission that the old ways are not working. Target costing is no exception. It is implicitly critical of past cost control, product design, and procurement efforts. Existing managers may

---

[10] For a discussion of these and other sources of power, see J. Pfeffer, *Managing With Power* (Boston, Mass., Harvard Business School Press, 1992).

have their egos hurt by this repudiation. Things can be made worse by criticizing past systems or actions or by demanding public success stories of how the new initiative has pinpointed past failures or mistakes.

- *Offset resource losses.* Those who control resources have power. One source of power for procurement comes from awarding contracts to suppliers. This power source is considerably weakened and reduced when strategic suppliers are brought in as partners. Target cost deployment must be aware of these power shifts from the loss of control of resources. These losses have to be considered and somehow mitigated.

- *Replace knowledge power.* Control over information and knowledge is another source of power. When marketing opens up customer interface to others and when accounting makes the cost data transparent, they lose some of the power they enjoy from controlling information that others need and they have. Political solutions have to be found to make these losses more palatable to these groups.

- *Respect formal authority.* Formal authority is another major source of power in organizations. Target costing requires a cross-functional organization managed by powerful project managers. This shifts power from functional managers to project managers. Be prepared to mitigate any resentment from functional managers at this power shift, find ways to reassure them, and give them an important role in the target costing process.

BACK TO THE PAST—THINKING HOLISTICALLY

As enablers are put into place and used to take the technical, behavioral, cultural, and political bases, their interrelationships also must be managed. We return to the theme of systems or holistic thinking presented in Chapter 2. The four bases in deployment are subsystems within the larger organizational system. To deploy target costing, these subsystems must work together in harmony. One subsystem cannot be an impediment to the others. We must not allow them to become disconnected from the overall objective of deployment or with each other.

This internal disconnection is a major reason why most organizations have difficulty with deployment. We want to accomplish goal A but we organize to do B, measure C, and reward D. Other times, we optimize one subsystem at the expense of or by ignoring others. To avoid this type of disconnection, it is a good idea to critically evaluate the deployment plan by asking the following questions: Do my planned structural, behavioral, cultural, and political changes support target costing? Are these structural, behavioral, cultural, and political changes going to work together or at cross purposes? In what ways will they support each other? In what ways will they impede each other?

DEPLOYMENT—FROM PLANNING TO ACTION

Conceptual planning identifies the gaps deployment has to address. We now need an action plan to make the changes happen. The action plan must summarize and set priorities among the gaps, determine the scope and depth of deployment, develop an action item list, and execute and follow-up on actions. These steps are described next.

Gap Analysis

The four bases in our conceptual deployment diamond identify what needs to be done for successful deployment. Many of these items may already exist in the organization. Items not present constitute the "gaps" that must be filled. Information on gaps should be formalized in a diagnostic summary. This summary should indicate the nature of the gap, where in the organization it exists, and who in the organization should be responsible for addressing it. Appendix E addresses this issue and provides a sample form for this purpose. The items listed on this sample form are *not a comprehensive list* of all deployment items. They are intended only to illustrate how to organize gap information obtained during the conceptual deployment planning phase.

Scope of Deployment

The gap analysis information allows determining the scope and breadth of deployment. We know what requirements have to be met. We also know which ones are more important and need to be addressed first. The next step is to decide where in the organization to begin deployment. We also need to determine the scope of deployment. There are four choices regarding scope:

- *Selected business unit deployment* can be used when there are differences in the "readiness" and "gaps" across business units. This allows a firm to introduce target costing in its centers of excellence first and work out the deployment issues in a relatively benign environment. Business unit deployment is a fairly common practice. Caterpillar, for instance, has differences between its Peoria and Aurora, Illinois, plants in the degree to which target costing has been successfully implemented in these two units.

- *Program-based deployment* can be used to test deployment when there are multiple programs and not all of them are ready for deployment. Typically, a new program, such as Chrysler's Neon or Boeing's 777, lends itself well to first site deployment. The advantage of program-based deployment is that it forces cross-functional integration faster because programs by their nature are cross-functional.

- *Companywide deployment* is usually too ambitious for a new initiative such as target costing. It is costly and bears a high risk. However, it does have the merit of forcing change throughout the organization without having to deal with the problem of "old ways of doing business" existing alongside the new ways. It provides a clear direction for the organization and moves the initiative from "let's try and see" to "what will make this work."

- *Value-chain deployment* extends target costing deployment to value-chain participants. Like organizationwide deployment, it is costly and risky. However, without it, the organization cannot reap full benefits. When dependence on suppliers is high, it may be a good idea to bring them into target costing deployment early.

If the scope of deployment is partial—that is, business unit or program based—it is important not to pressure the unit or program for early success stories. Quite often, those pushing a new idea have a need to demonstrate that they were right by pointing to quick successes. Target costing is not a quick fix. It takes time to produce results. Even Japanese companies who have used target costing for years are finding out that it is difficult to export these ideas quickly to their overseas subsidiaries.[11] They have had to deploy target costing slowly and sometimes partially in their global ventures. For instance, many Japanese automakers still rely on their Japanese suppliers for their North American operations.

Action Item List

The last planning step in deployment is to convert the "gap analysis" into a detailed action item checklist. The action item checklist specifies the many tasks or activities needed to address each gap area. These tasks are then assigned to individuals or subteams. This is done using a "who" and "when"

---

[11] For a discussion of the problems that Japanese companies face in globalizing target costing, see Y. Iwabuchi, "Target Costing as Japanese-Style Cost Control," *Konan Management Study,* 33 (March 1993), pp. 169–188 [in Japanese].

matrix tool of the type shown in Appendix E. The first column of this sample matrix breaks down each gap into specific action items. The next two columns list "who" is responsible for primary and secondary performance of these tasks. The choices are (1) individual members of the cross-functional deployment team, (2) another subteam, (3) top management, or (4) the entire deployment team. The next column shows the liaison or "inform" category, of people who need to know of the changes. This is followed by a projected deadline or completion date column. Finally, the last column is a periodic (weekly or biweekly) status update column for monitoring progress toward completion.

Execution

The action item checklist culminates the planning phase of deployment and moves it into execution. The execution phase must monitor actions and make certain that deadlines are being met. The catch-ball model must proceed smoothly, and continuity of team membership must be maintained. A common deployment problem is the attrition of team members to other assignments before deployment is complete. An important part of deployment is to make certain that this does not happen.

The entire deployment process is summarized in Exhibit 12–6.

Exhibit 12–6 provides an overview of the many detailed issues that organizations must tackle in deploying target. These issues have not been addressed in this book. They are the subjects of future research projects expected to be undertaken by CAM-I.

While deployment is difficult and requires planning, we should not be overwhelmed by it. Most situations do not need everything to be planned beforehand or to be executed flawlessly. Nor is it essential that all items be in place immediately. Errors and omissions are likely to occur. However, the key is to avoid fatal errors. As a general rule, political and symbolic errors are fatal. Once an initiative is mired in politics or associated with bad symbols, it is difficult to recover. These two bases, therefore, need more attention and planning initially. Technical and behavioral items typically emerge as deployment unfolds and can be taken care of concurrently. Errors in these areas are recoverable and can be rectified during deployment.

SUMMARY

This last chapter deals with how to deploy target costing in an organization. Using the CAM-I conceptual "deployment diamond" as a framework, we have presented a conceptual approach to deployment. The first step in de-

The Target Costing Deployment Process

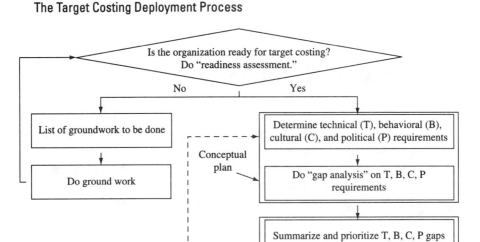

ployment is to determine an organization's *readiness* to deploy target costing. If the organization is not ready, further groundwork needs to be done. If it is ready, then we need to plan on taking four bases: technical, behavioral, cultural, and political. We need to identify the technical, behavioral, cultural, and political requirements for deploying target costing. A *gap analysis* should be done to determine what requirements the organization cannot currently meet. The gaps should be addressed by an action item plan. This plan determines the depth and breadth of deployment and breaks down each gap to be filled into a detailed task list.

The Target Cost Process Map

This appendix contains a detailed description of the target costing process. It captures the many processes and subprocesses in target costing as they occur within the four stage product development cycle. The main processes are numbered 1–4. The subprocesses share the first digit in their number with the main process. A subprocess with the letter C indicates a concurrent process. Each process step has a purpose statement followed by five field descriptors, which are

- Input: Data, action, or output of prior process.
- Description: Activities and tasks undertaken at a process step.
- Output: Results of actions taken at this process step.
- Who participates: Teams, functions, or indivduals who participate.
- Supporting tools: Tools needed to obtain desired outputs.

The entire process is summarized in a integrated flow diagram at the end of the appendix. Abbreviations used in the process charts are explained next and an overview of the process is presented in Exhibit A–1.

EXHIBIT A–1

The Target Costing Process—An Overview

Voice of the Customer

←——— Establish Target Costs ———→

←——— Attain Target Costs ———→

1.0	2.0	3.0	4.0
Product strategy and profit plans	Product concept and feasibility	Product design and development	Production and logistics

Extended Enterprise Participation

EXPLANATION OF ABBREVIATIONS USED

- ABC/M: Activity based costing/management.
- CAD: Computer aided design.
- CAM: Computer aided manufacturing.
- CPM: Critical path method.
- DFMA: Design for manufacturability and assembly.
- EVA: Economic value added.
- FMEA: Failure mode and effect analysis.
- ISO: International Organization for Standardization.
- IRR: Internal rate of return.
- JIT: Just in time inventory system.
- MRP: Materials requisition planning systems.
- NPV: Net present value.
- PERT: Program evaluation and review technique.
- QFD: Quality function deployment.
- ROS: Return on sales.
- SPC: Statistical process control.
- VA: Value analysis.
- VE: Value engineering.

THE TARGET COSTING PROCESS—A DETAILED VIEW

Process 1.0. Determination of Product Strategy and Profit Plans (Exhibit A–2)

   1.1   Establish and deploy enterprise and business level strategy.

   1.C.1 Establish technology plan.

   1.2   Select customers and identify their quality, cost, and time needs.

   1.3   Define product line market size and share objectives.

   1.4   Develop multiyear product portfolio profit plans.

E X H I B I T   A–2

Process 1.0

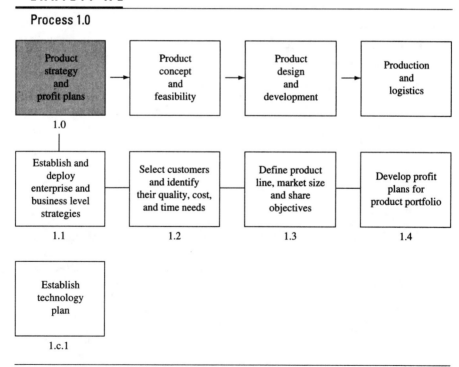

Process Model: Subprocess 1.1

Process: 1.0. Product strategy and profit planning.

Subprocess: 1.1. Establish and deploy enterprise and business level strategies.

Purpose is to determine the overall strategy of the firm. It provides a single vision, defines the strategic intent, and translates into goals and objectives. It determines the technology to be used, investment needs, and research and development required to support products. The process also communicates the strategy, gets buy-in from key groups, identifies structural and measurement issues, specifies behaviors required, and encourages values important in the organizational culture so that the strategy is effectively deployed.

	Input	Process Description	Output	Who Participates	Supporting Tools	Remarks
a	External data on market trends and threats; other social, cultural, and political expectations	Define vision, values, goals, and objectives	Vision, mission, goals, and objectives statement	Business planning team	Market analysis, economic analysis, political analysis	Provides the overall framework and context for target costing
b	Data on industry, competition, internal strengths and weaknesses, external opportunities and threats	Determine business level strategy	Business strategy statement	Business planning team	Competitive analysis strategic assessment	Establishes customers, markets, and, constraints; provides "competitive intelligence"
c	Review of existing structures, policies, values, interests, and behavioral patterns	Deploy strategy	Deployment plan	All employees	Performance measures, hoshin planning, or policy deployment	Communication, feedback, performance managment, motivation, etc., to deploy strategy

EXHIBIT A-4

Process Model: Subprocess 1.1.C.1

Process: 1.0. Product strategy and profit planning.

Subprocess: 1.1.C.1. Establish technology plan.

Purpose is to translate the overall business strategy and core competencies into a technology strategy. Future R&D spending is determined. A plan to turn technologies into commercially viable products is also part of the technology plan. Also included is a consideration of future processes.

	Input	Process Description	Output	Who Participates	Supporting Tools	Remarks
a	Business strategy	Review technology alternatives	Core competence statement	Engineering, R&D, manufacuting, business planning team	Technology assessments, relational matrices	
b	Supplier presentations, technology options	Review outside technology alternatives	Technology options	Engineering, R&D, manufacturing, business planning team	Technology assessments	
c	Technology options	Select a technology direction	Technology plan	Engineering, R&D, manufacturing, business planning team	Decision tools, hoshin planning tools	
d	Technology plan	Develop R & D and new processx new	R&D spending plan, process spending plan	Engineering, R&D, manufacturing, business planning team	Decision tools	

EXHIBIT A–5

Process Model: Subprocess 1.2

Process: 1.0. Product strategy and profit planning.

Subprocess: 1.2. Select target customers and identify their quality, cost, and time requirements.

Purpose is to translate overall firm strategy to a product or service and niche market level. It defines the particular product, service, and market share goals. It defines product life cycles, new product introduction timetables, and new business opportunities.

	Input	Description	Process Output	Who Participates	Supporting Tools	Remarks
a	Business strategy, objectives statement, industry data, and competitive analysis	Define product, service,and market niche goals	Statement of goals and opportunities for product groups	Business planning team	Market analysis, competitive intelligence financial analysis	Defines the markets and related constraints for target cost system
b	Evaluation of internal strengths and weaknesses, opportunities and threats; customer preference data.	Define customer requirements, competitive strategy by product lines	Competitive plan; general description of price, quality, functions, and competitive terms such as cost,quality, time	Business planning team	Market analysis Competitive intelligence, financial analysis, survey research methods	Uses data from "market intelligence" to define key parameters in target costing
c	Data on product market and competition and customers, competitive plan, general description of price, quality, functions, time	Define competitive strategy at product level and customer needs	Product level plans; initial product space definition.	Business planning team	Investment analysis, QFD, new product plans; feature to function analysis	Price, quality, and function data by product is a key input for target costing

EXHIBIT A-6

Process Model: Subprocess 1.3

Process: 1.0. Product strategy and profit planning.

Subprocess: 1.3. Define product line market size and share objectives.

Purpose is to settle on a market size and share for a firm's selected portfolio of products and services. It determines the capacity plan based upon the existing and anticipated portfolio of products or services. Market and sales forecasts are developed as is information on competitive prices and possible countermoves by competition.

	Input	Process Description	Output	Who Participates	Supporting Tools	Remarks
a	Product level plans, development and replacement cycle	Define market share goals	Market share targets by product lines	Product team	Market analysis, competitive intelligence, customer analysis	Establishes market segmentation; defines "volume" for target cost
b	Market share targets by product lines; competitive plan; general description of price, quality, function, and competitive terms such as cost, quality, and time	Analyze pricing trends	Price/margin forecast	Product team	Market analysis, competitive, intelligenge regression analysis	Provides "pricing/volume data" for target costs
c	Data on industry, competition, and market	Developing a sales/marketing forecast	Sales Forecast business planning team	Product team, competitive intelligence, econometric forecasting	Market analysis, by products	Provides "market share"
d	Technology plans, investment plans, capacity use data, product level plans	Determine available capacity	Capacity investment and use plan; make or buy strategic sourcing plan	Product team, manufacturing team	CAM-I capacity model	Focuses target costing efforts by identifying "make vs. buy" items

EXHIBIT A-7

Process Model: Subprocess 1.4

Process: 1.0. Product strategy and profit planning.

Subprocess: 1.4. Develop profit plans for product portfolio.

Purpose is to create an integrated business plan, generally in a three to seven year horizon, that brings together the sales and profit plans for the various products and services offered by a firm under a single umbrella. The plan sets the target contributions from the various products in a firm's portfolio by defining their margins and prices.

	Input	Process Description	Output	Who Participates	Supporting Tools	Remarks
a	Sales forecast	Develop portfolio level product mix plan	Product mix and volume commitments	Business planning team	Market analysis, competitive intelligence, financial analysis	Defines product mix for target costs
b	Sales forecast, data on competition, price margin forecast	Forecast individual product prices for mix	Product price forecast	Business planning team financial analysis	Market analysis, competitive, intelligence, for target costs	Provides "pricing data"
c	Product mix, product price forecast, cost history	Develop an integrated profit plan for company	Profit plan	Business planning team, product team	Financial analysis, market analysis, scenario and sensitivity	Provides "profit is target" that the goal of the target cost system
d	Product market share data	Define preliminary market share	Market share goal for for product	Product team market analysis product	Profit simulations,	Provides market share desired for target costing
e	Product mix, product price forecast, sales forecast, profit plan	Define preliminary profit margin required of product	Profit margin goal for product	Product team, finance, marketing	Financial analysis, scenario and sensitivity cost has to achieve	Provides the specific profit margin that target
f	Product mix, profit plan, product price forecast, market share goal	Define integrated businessplan	Multiyear product, profit, and cost plan	Product team, business planning team	NPV, IRR, EVA	Provides the mid-term product portfolio plan.

187

Process 2.0   Product Concept Development and Feasibility (Exhibit A–8)

2.1   Prepare product concept plan.

2.1.a.   Define product concept.

2.1.b.   Confirm price/margin goals for preliminary design.

2.1.c.   Set product investment plan.

2.2.   Estimate product and process costs.

2.3.   Identify improvement opportunities.

2.4   Initiate value engineering.

2.5   Confirm concept feasibility.

EXHIBIT A–8

Process 2.0

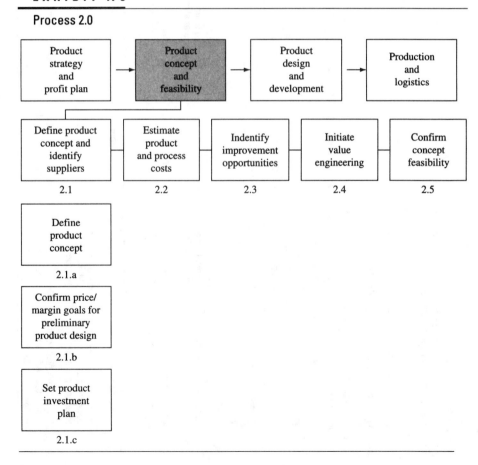

EXHIBIT A-9

Process Model: Subprocess 2.1

Process: 2.0. Concept development and feasibility.

Subprocess: 2.1. Prepare product concept plan.

Purpose is to develop a plan for the organization, project management, changes in infrastructures, information and tooling needed, and potential suppliers to effectively complete the Product Development Process for new or modified products.

	Input	Process Description	Output	Who Participates	Supporting Tools	Remarks
a	Multiyear product, profit, and cost plan; market data; technology data	Define product concept	Product concept	Product team, manufacturing team	Matrix analysis	
b	Product concept	Form subsystem teams	Project critical path and responsibilities	Product team	Priority matrix, PERT/CPM	
c	Volume estimates, life cycle issues, market share goal for product	Determine available production capacity	Capacity requirements manufacturing team	Product team, CAM-I capacity model	Cost-volume models,	
d	Supplier rating data, capacity requirements, market share goal for product	Identify key suppliers; do initial make or buy decision for product	Supplier sourcing list	Product team, suppliers	Supplier assessment	

E X H I B I T   A–10

Process Model: Subprocess 2.1.a

Process: 2.0. Concept development and feasibility.
Subprocess: 2.1.a. Define product concept.

Purpose is to provide the basic conceptual design direction for the product based on satisfying customer requirements and meeting corporate objectives.

	Input	Process Description	Output	Who Participates	Supporting Tools	Remarks
a	Multiyear product plans	Develop an overall concept	Product/profit plan, approved product direction	Product team, business planning team	QFD, CAD/CAM	Develops preliminary product cost goal
b	Product planning research	Define initial price, net of quality and functionality discounts	Preliminary assessment of price, quality and functionality	Product team, design team	QFD, functional analysis	Relating voice of the customer to product specifications
c	Competitive reference data	Develop preliminary product specifications	Feasible design	Product team, design team	Product models, CAD/CAM, simulation	Allowable targets, price, cost, margins
d	Approved product direction	Preliminary product design	Product concept	Design team, product team	Style tools, models, drawings	Initial cost estimates

Process Model: Subprocess 2.1.b

Process: 2.0. Concept development and feasibility.
Subprocess: 2.1.b. Confirm price/margin goals for preliminary product design.

Purpose is to confirm the proposed sales volumes, prices, and margins for products identified in the profit plan. The process is recursive; it sifts through the proposed concepts and selects those few that meet required standards.

	Input	Process Description	Output	Who Participates	Supporting Tools	Remarks
a	Preliminary design	Confirm product profit targets	Approved product hurdle rate or margin	Product team, business planning team	Product planning	Objective parameters
b	Competitive product information	Set target price estimates	Approved pricing structure	Product team, business planning team	Scenario and sensitivity analysis, QFD	Pricing input
c	Market segment data, approved price	Determine market share goals	Required volume	Product team, business planning team	Factor analysis	Provides price/ volume for "desired market share"
d	Industry information	Establish profitability data	Economic forecast, pro forma financials, product profit plan	Business planning team	Financial simulations	Margin input

EXHIBIT A-12

Process Model: Subprocess 2.1.c

Process: 2.0. Concept development and feasibility.
Subprocess: 2.1.c. Set product investment plan.

Purpose is to establish long lead spending approvals of all consolidated product activities required for developing the product per customer specifications. It also determines whether all or only part of the proposed capital spending will be charged to the lead products.

	Input	Process Description	Output	Who Participates	Supporting Tools	Remarks
a	Product profit plan, capacity requirements, capacity investment and use plan	Develop capital and training investment budget	Preliminary product spending plan	Product team, business planning team	IRR, NPV, ROS, EVA	"Cost trade-offs" are affected by approved capital reqests
b	Preliminary request for funding	Identify early product spending	Long lead funding requirements, investment plans	Product team, design team, manufacturing team	Budgeting	
c	Investment plans, product profit plan, appropriation request	Get funding approvals	Funding decision, development budget	Manufacturing team, business planning team	Budgeting	

Process Model: Subprocess 2.2

Process: 2.0. Concept development and feasibility.

Subprocess: 2.2. Estimate product/process costs.

Purpose is to provide preliminary cost estimates based on early product specifications. This enables senior management to decide whether to continue with a particular product development or to abandon it.

	Input	Process Description	Output	Who Participates	Supporting Tools	Remarks
a	Preliminary design and product description	Develop preliminary cost estimates	Initial cost estimate	Product team, business planning team	Cost tables, parametric estimation, regression analysis, ABM/ABC	This provides a revised "design to cost" target
b	Market share and margin target	Develop "initial" price and target costs	Initial price and drifting cost estimate	Product team, business planning team	Cost tables, matrices, regression analysis	
c	Preliminary profit plan	Integrate estimates in profit plan	Updated product and profit plan	Design team, product team, business planning team		
d	Updated profit and product plan	Confirm financial feasibility	Go or no go decision	Product team, senior unit managers		This check is key to target costing

Process Model: Subprocess 2.3

Process: 2.0. Concept development and feasibility
Subprocess: 2.3. Identify improvement opportunities.

Purpose is to analyze customer preferences and distributor and supplier feedback about competitive product offerings to compare to our own product offering. The customer and competition information helps designers and engineers identify areas to focus on and improvement opportunities in product and process design. It also provides data for evaluating the life cycle cost performance and unanticipated uses of the product by a customer

	Input	Process Description	Output	Who Participates	Supporting Tools	Remarks
a	Data on competition	Analyze competition's technology and cost structure	Comparative statement of strenghts and weaknesses, opportunities and threats; competitor cost assessment	Business planning team, product team, design team	Competitive intelligence, competitor cost analysis, teardown analysis, reverse engineering, QFD	Provides competitive ntelligence and market feedback essential for target costing
b	Customer and distributor feedback	Improve current product definition	Product design changes	Planning team, design team	Discriminant analysis, functional anaylsis	Voice of the customer check
c	Supplier feedback	Identify areas for VE on new ideas and VA on existing products	Cost reduction and process improvement ideas	Product team, design team	Functional analysis, value engineering, CAM-I capacity model	Provides ideas for continuous product and process improvements

E X H I B I T A–15

Process Model: Subprocess 2.4

Process: 2.0. Concept development and feasibility.
Subprocess: 2.4. Initiate value engineering.

Purpose is to initiate value engineering. It takes ideas for improvements generated earlier and cuts costs and maintains value by focusing on features, functions, components, weight, volume, processability, manufacturability, and the like of a new product. Integrated product and process design is a key element of value engineering.

	Input	Process Description	Output	Who Participates	Supporting Tools	Remarks
a	Feasible product design	Evaluate functions, features, and components	Cost/value index,	Design team, product team	Functional analysis QFD, Component Costing	This is key to achieving customer satisfaction and cost targets
b	Cost/value index, improvement ideas	Brainstorm about redesign options	Target costs by components, functions, and features	Design team, product team	QFD, matrix tools, VE idea data base	Implements "ideas for improvement" and performs design to cost
c	Cost targets	Refine product price, quality, and function specifications	Revised product design	Design team, product team	QFD, VE, CAD/CAM, functional costing, process costing	

E X H I B I T A–16

Process Model: Subprocess 2.5

Process: 2.0. Concept development and feasibility.

Subprocess: 2.5. Confirm concept feasibility.

Purpose is to confirm and finalize the basic design direction for the product. A well-defined product design that has been subjected to initial value analysis emerges from this phase. Any remaining technical and financial issues are resolved, and the concept is evaluated to ensure that it meets customer requirements, target costs, and profit targets.

	Input	Process Description	Output	Who Participates	Supporting Tools	Remarks
a	Revised product design	Develop cost reduction alternatives	Cost reduction targets	Product team, suppliers idea data base	QFD, value engineering, VE	
b	Cost reduction targets	Analyze cross effects of cost reduction options	Cost impact report	Product team, suppliers	QFD, value engineering, matrix analysis	
c	Cost impact report	Revise product specifications and description	Revised product specifications	Product team, suppliers	Value engineering	
d	Product planning research	Reassess quality and functionality	Revised product design	Product team, suppliers	QFD, CAD/CAM, simulation	
e	Revised product design	Obtain customer feedback	Confirmed product concept and target costs	Product Team, Suppliers customer surveys	Prototypes, models, focus groups,	This check is critical for customer satisfaction

Process 3.0.   Product Design and Development (Exhibit A–17)

3.1.   Prepare development plan and confirm suppliers.

3.2.   Finalize design.

3.3.1.   Validate design.

3.3.2.   Validate process.

3.3.3.   Plan production system.

3.C.1.   Continue value engineering

3.C.2.   Monitor performance and review and update status.

EXHIBIT   A–17

Process 3.0

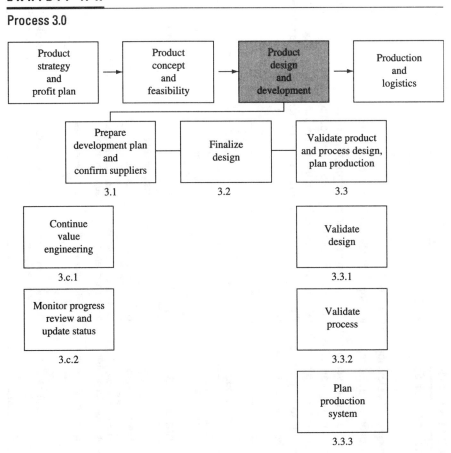

E X H I B I T   A-18

Process Model: Subprocess 3.1

Process: 3.0. Development phase.

Subprocess: 3.1. Prepare development plan and confirm suppliers.

Purpose is to develop a plan for organizing and managing the project and identify needed changes in infrastructure, information systems, and other areas to effectively complete the product development steps for new or modified products. An implementation team takes over from the product team. The team leader should be chosen from the product team. Other members of the product team will continue to play key roles. This process brings suppliers in as partners early in the process, starts negotiations with suppliers, and sets up the structure to manage them.

	Input	Process Description	Output	Who Participates	Supporting Tools	Remarks
a	Final product concept	Identify a product development approach	QCT targets, product development approach	Product team, manufacturing team	GANTT charts, risk analysis	
b	QCT targets	Form subsystem team	Project critical path and responsibilities	Design team, product team	Prioritization matrix, PERT/CPM	"Ownership of targets" is assigned to an implementation team
c	Initial supplier list, initial make or buy decision, parts list, supplier reliability	Confirm suppliers and finalize make or buy decision; negotiate pricing and terms	Parts list (internal and external), long-term supplier agreements	Procurement, design team product team	Histograms, matrices, cost tables	Communicates "design parameters" and performance intent
d	Supplier agreements	Provide support to suppliers	Supplier process analysis	Design team, manufacturing team	Value engineering	Full "supply chain" participation in product improvements
f	Outputs (a–d)	Complete product development plan	Product development plan	Product team, manufacturing team	Project management tools	Plan is critical to success

Process Model: Subprocess 3.2

Process: 3.0. Development phase.

Subprocess: 3.2. Finalize design.

Purpose is to use design for manufacturability concepts to finalize the design of the product. The final design must meet customers' needs for time, quality, functionality, and cost.

	Input	Process Description	Output	Who Participates	Supporting Tools	Remarks
a	Revised product design	Manage final design to meet targets	Detailed design	Design team, product team	Design for manufacture, CAD/CAE/CAM	Provides "QCT trade-offs"; empowers designers and avoids problems
b	Process capabilities, detailed design	Check design against requirements; review with senior management	Approved final design	Design team, product team, suppliers	FMEA, CAD/CAE/CAM, simulation	Reviews "status of design" against cost

E X H I B I T   A–20

Process Model: Subprocess 3.3.1

Process: 3.0. Development phase
Subprocess: 3.3.1. Validate Design

Purpose is to test the design to be used to make the product to ensure that all product attributes and QCT goals are being met simultaneously. Suppliers perform a similar validation for their part of the product.

	Input	Process Description	Output	Who Participates	Supporting Tools	Remarks
a	Customer requirements	Get customer feedback	Design changes or verified design	Design team, product team	Statistical tools, market analysis	This tests if "customer satisfaction" goals are being met
b	Cost estimates	Profitability check	Verified profit plan	Business planning team, product team	Cost estimation models	"Profitability" check is the goal here
c	Product designs	Design, build and evaluate prototypes	Design changes or verified design	Manufacturing team, product team	Alpha, beta tests	"Status check" to see performance v. targets
d	Production parts and tools	Evaluate production parts and tools	Design changes or verified design	Manufacturing team, product team	Relationship matrices	
e	Product attribute test results	Check product QCT dimensions	Design changes or verified design	Manufacturing team, product team	Functional testing tools	Minimizes unnecessary design changes
f	Product attribute test results	Check reliability, durability, and other attributes	Design changes or verified design	Manufacturing team, product team	Reliability tests, maintainability and durability tests	

Process Model: Subprocess 3.3.2

Process: 3.0. Development phase.

Subprocess: 3.3.2. Validate process.

Purpose is to test the processes that will be used to make the product to ensure that QCT goals will be met simultaneously and that opportunities for value analysis in production will ensure continuous improvement. This takes places with suppliers as well.

	Input	Process Description	Output	Who Participates	Supporting Tools	Remarks
a	Process plan	Complete process specifications	Process control plan	Manufacturing team, product team	ISO 9000, ABM, cost tables, process costing	Simultaneous "process and product design"
b	Production alternatives	Evaluate production alternatives	Process path priorities	Manufacturing team, design team	Functional analysis, theory of constraints	Use of process "cost tables" to support production
c	Process layout, volume, and mix; capacity information; process capabilities; historical learning	Simulate processes or prototype processes	Verified layout, throughput rate, learning rate	Manufacturing team, design team	Dynamic simulation, process analysis, DFMA	Establishment of metrics before production begins
d	Bill of material; process routing	Develop cost element and process standards	Unit production costs	Manufacturing team, design team	Process costing, cost tables	
e	Departmental budgets, cost driver information,	Confirm plant processing budgets	Fixed cost and variable cost	All departments	ABC/ABM	Cost tables and ABC may provide

Process Model: Subprocess 3.3.3

Process: 3.0. Development phase.
Subprocess: 3.3.3. Plan production system.

Purpose is to identify the production facilities that will be used to make the product and prepare tooling, production plans, alternate plant layout, supplier schedules, labor requirements, distribution requirements, and performance measures to begin production.

	Input	Process Description	Output	Who Participates	Supporting Tools	Remarks
a	Tooling test results	Finalize tooling and equipment plan	Acquisition and installation schedule for tooling and equipment	Manufacturing team	Priority matrices	Tooling and equipment to be included in target product costs
b	Capacity analysis	Finalize equipment capacity plan	Capacity assignments	Manufacturing team	CAM-I capacity model	Capacity costs are included in target cost
c	Production requirements	Finalize production plan	Unit production forecasts	Manufacturing team	Shop floor exercises	
d	Approved suppliers	Finalize supplier and logistics plans	Part delivery schedules	Manufacturing team	MRP, JIT, supplier ratings	Sets up JIT deliveries schedule
e	Labor requirements	Finalize staff and training plan	Hiring and training schedules	Manufacturing team	Process analysis	Empowered and trained work force
f	Shipping requirements	Finalize distribution plan	Warehousing, transport orders, and metrics	Manufacturing team	ABC, dynamic simulation	Logistics costs are included in target costs
g	Estimated metrics	Verify QCT achievement	Confirmed metrics	Top management		No launch until QCT goals are met
h	Outputs b–f	Complete integrated production plan	Integrated production plan	Product team, manufacturing team	Project management, CAM	Integrates in-plant and out-plant processes

EXHIBIT A-23

Process Model: Subprocesses 3.c.1

Process: 3.0. Development phase.

Subprocess: 3.C.1. Continue value engineering.

Purpose is to utilize value engineering and value analysis tools to reduce costs out of the preproduction design and continuously improve costs in production while meeting or exceeding customer expectations.

	Input	Process Description	Output	Who Participates	Supporting Tools	Remarks
a	Design issues alternate materials	Identify VE opportunities	Revised design	Procurement, manufacturing team, design team	Cost tables, QFD, DFM, root cause analysis	VE performed during design to achieve QCT targets
b	Process issues alternate equipment	Identify VA opportunities	Revised process	Manufacturing team, product team	Cost variances, process control charts, parts analysis, planning matrices	VA performed during production to achieve continuous improvement targets
c	Numbers of anticipated projects	Identify and assign VE and VA resources	Revised quality and time targets	Human resources, top management		
d	Supplier actual cost to target cost gaps	Set up VE and VA support for suppliers	Reduced supplier cost	Procurement, product team	Function analysis	Support suppliers in achieving QCT targets
e	Kaizen improvement	Establish VA communication	Kaizen projects	Product team, manufacturing team,	Hoshin planning tools	Improvement programs are planned

203

EXHIBIT A-24

Process Model: Subprocess 3.C.2

Process: 3.0. Development phase.

Subprocess: 3.C.2 Monitor performance and review and update status.

Purpose is to establish a project management system with a program manager who measures the achievement of QCT goals, volumes, other economic assumptions, and manages design trade-offs.

	Input	Process Description	Output	Who Participates	Supporting Tools	Remarks
a	Design results, QCT	Development progress	Target measurements and action plans	Program manager, product team	Design reviews	Proactive problem avoidance
b	Actual and estimated design costs	Cost confirmation process	Cost gaps	Product team	Cost tracking, cost tables	Cost sensitive design
c	Volume, pricing, and time estimates	Market and economic assumptions	Revisions to targets	Product team, program manager	Dynamic financial models	Links designs, market, economic assumptions, and go or no-go decisions
d	Final product target cost	Target cost decomposition	Subassembly targets, component targets, purchased parts targets	Product team, procurement	QFD, conjoint analysis, competitive information, cost tables	Cost targets developed at lowest level and sensitive to customer value perceptions
e	Product and process design	Cost estimating	Cost/function, input to design, teams	Product team, program manager	Cost tables, ABC	Focus on forward looking relevant costs
f	Design alternatives	Manage trade-offs alternatives	Set priorities on QCT cross-funtional team,	Chief engineer, customer values, finance	Priority matrix, "feature creep" estimated costs	Avoids and makes visible

Process 4.0.   Launch Production (Exhibit A–25)

4.1.1. Launch production.

4.1.2. Implement sales, distribution, and service plans.

4.2.1. Manage supplier relationships.

4.2.2. Manage continuous improvement.

4 C.1. Monitor competitive environment.

4.C.2. Monitor performance against targets.

E X H I B I T   A–25

Process 4.0

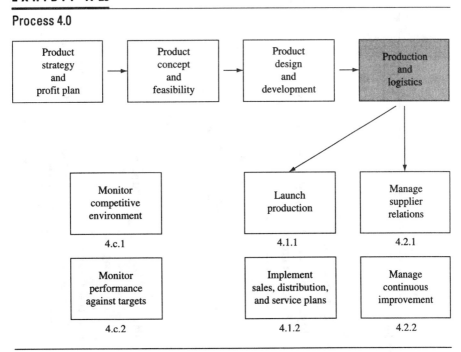

EXHIBIT A-26

Target Cost Process Model

Process: 4.0. Production.
Subprocess 4.1.1. Launch production.

Purpose is to train employees and get them and other things ready for production in mass volume. These activities occur in the plant designated to build the product.

	Input	Process Description	Output	Who Participates	Supporting Tools	Remarks
a	Part specifications, machine capacity, required output, raw materials	Quality testing	Quality verification, equipment verification, production process verification, conformance to target	Manufacturing team, suppliers,	Root cause analysis design team	
b	Product cost target	Train employees	Trained people	Manufacturing team, product team	Process training	
c	Product and process failures	Make engineering changes to product and processes	Revised product and processes	Manufacturing team, suppliers, design team	Root cause analysis	Improve productivity, minimize learning curve
d	Revised product and processes	Produce product in volume	Product financial data, corporate profit input	Plant personnel	Component costing, process costing	Continuous "process improvement" to meet targets

E X H I B I T A-27

Process Model: Subprocess 4.1.2

Process: 4.0. Production.

Subprocess: 4.1.2. Implement sales, distribution, and service plans.

Purpose is to implement sales, service, and distribution plans that focuses on customer satisfaction by providing product and services when the customers want them.

	Input	Process Description	Output	Who Participates	Supporting Tools	Remarks
a	Customer requirements	Service profit plan	Final service profit plan	Customer service, product team, design team	Life cycle costing, VA/VE, ABC/ABM	
b	Integrated business plan	Determine final spares requirements	Updated production plan, inventory plan, component costs data	Service and support suppliers, dealers; manufacturing team	Supply chain analysis, yield analysis	
c	Final service profit plan and product plan	Put in place delivery network	Service plan profit, customer and dealer interface requirements	Dealer service, materials, finance	Value index margin analysis (actual vs. targets)	

E X H I B I T A-28

Process Model: Subprocess 4.2.1

Process: 4.0. Production.
Subprocess: 4.2.1. Manage supplier relationships.

Purpose is to assure that an effective and efficient process is in place to manage the supply chain so it can support production.

	Input	Process Description	Output	Who Participates	Supporting Tools	Remarks
a	Production requirements	Evaluate supplier performance	Actual performance data on QCT	Product team, manufacturing team, business planning team	Supplier evaluation tools, learning curve analysis	Provides cost awareness thoughout the "value chain" to reduce costs
b	Performance to targets data	Encourage supplier continuous improvement	Improvement progress on QCT	Product team, manufacturing team, business planning team	Process analysis, FMEA, Cost analysis, DOE, VA/VE, CPK, cycle time analysis, tolerance analysis	Link to kaizen

E X H I B I T A-29

Process Model: Subprocess 4.2.2

Process: 4.0. Production.

Subprocess: 4.2.2. Manage continuous improvement.

Purpose is to set up continual monitoring of processes, cost reviews, and change management in an overall cost reduction effort. It ensures that cost, quality, and time targets are being achieved on a continuous basis.

	Input	Process Description	Output	Who Participates	Supporting Tools	Remarks
a	QCT improvement ideas	Set improvement targets	Improvement targets	Product team	Market research tools	This is an ongoing program for cost reduction and quality
b	Improvement targets	Define improvement plans	Improvement plans design team, suppliers	Product team, VA/VE	Shop floor exercises,	improvement; its focus is on large or small improvement areas such as waste reduction,
c	Improvement plans	Execute improvement plans	Improvement results	Product team, design team, suppliers	ABM, SPC, VA/VE, hoshin tools, process analysis	yield increases, and feature improvements using customer feedback
d	Improvement results	Compare results to targets	Improvement evaluation	Product team, suppliers		
e	Improvement evaluation	Define and execute action plans	Improvement results	Product team		
f	Production plan	Evaluate supplier performance	Updated supplier rating	Product team, manufacturing team	Supplier evaluation tools	

Process Model: Subprocess 4.C.1

Process: 4.0. Production.

Subprocess: 4 C.1. Monitor competitive environment.

Purpose is to monitor competition and the legal or regulatory environment to ensure early reaction to changes in the competitive environment. This information is used to take corrective action for existing products or to alter future products.

	Input	Process Description	Output	Who Participates	Supporting Tools	Remarks
a	Changes in competitive environment	Review product design and production methods	Product enhancement	Product team benchmarking, industry benchtrending, teardown or reverse engineering	Market analysis,	Quick reaction to change provides a competitive edge
b	Legal issues	Protect proprietary information and intellectual property	Legal actions, revised product plans	Product team, legal, design team	Legal Analysis	Feedforward to "next generation" product design
c	Change in government requirements and technology	Review product design and production methods	New developments report	Design team	Regulatory analysis, technology analysis	
d	Customer feedback and dealer feedback	Monitor customer requirements	Long-range production plans	Business planning team	Pareto analysis, benchmarking, survey research	Feedforward to "next generation" product design

Process Model: Subprocess

Process: 4.0. Production.
Subprocess: 4.C.2. Monitor performance against targets.

Purpose is to identify and measure key attributes of a product program and monitor its performance relative to customer requirements. The output of this process is used to measure and reward team efforts, an essential requirement for target costing. Portions of this activity are also referred to as *kaizen costing*.

	Input	Process Description	Output	Who Participates	Supporting Tools	Remarks
a	Product targets and objectives	Assess target attainment	Target achievement report	Product team	Financial and non-financial analysis	Different metrics are used at different stages of this process
b	Process targets and objectives	Assess target attainment	Target achievement report	Manufacturing team	Financial and non-financial analysis	
c	Final data	Provide feedforward to next generation product	Final product feedback report.	Product team		Next product's "initial" cost
d	Target achievement report, production plan	Set new targets	New product and process targets	Product team		

EXHIBIT A-32

Target Cost Process—Interactive Flow Diagram

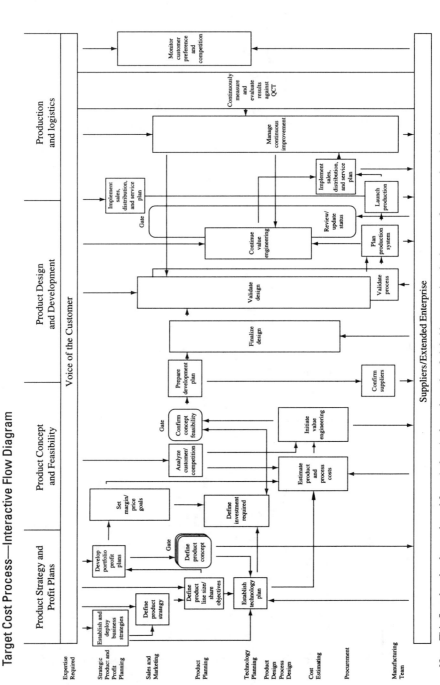

Note: This flowchart has been adapted from Arthur Andersen's study of global best practices in the area of new product development processes.

Relations with Other Business Processes

This appendix describes the relationship of target costing to other business processes in an organization. We focus on nine key processes that provide critical support to a firm's target costing efforts. These processes come into play at various stages of the product development cycle and, hence, become salient for target costing at different times. Exhibit B–1 shows the relationship of these processes to the product development cycle and to the two phases of target costing.

STRATEGIC PLANNING

Strategic planning defines the markets and customers to be served. It positions the product within a competitive product space and provides information about what price customers are willing to pay, the quality (features and

EXHIBIT B–1

Target Cost Phases and Support Processes

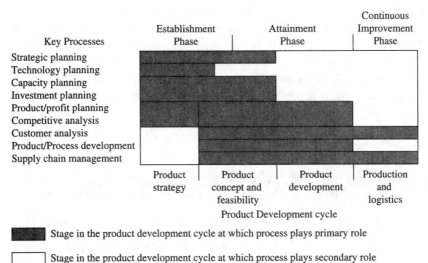

Key Processes	Establishment Phase	Attainment Phase	Continuous Improvement Phase
Strategic planning			
Technology planning			
Capacity planning			
Investment planning			
Product/profit planning			
Competitive analysis			
Customer analysis			
Product/Process development			
Supply chain management			

| Product strategy | Product concept and feasibility | Product development | Production and logistics |

Product Development cycle

■ Stage in the product development cycle at which process plays primary role

☐ Stage in the product development cycle at which process plays secondary role

performance) they expect, and when customers need it, (i.e., the time to market). Strategic planning provides the critical external focus for target costing. A strategic plan also defines the target market share and profit margins a firm seeks. These are the critical internal parameters for target costing.

TECHNOLOGY PLANNING

The purpose of technology planning is to assess technology directions and core technology competence of a firm. It assesses future directions of technology and application of technology to new or existing products. Technology review includes evaluating product obsolescence and spinning-off products from existing technologies.[1] Technology planning is related to target costing in two ways. First, technology creates rigid or flexible cost structures for firms. A cost structure is more flexible when it allows increases in volumes without the need for large one-time nonrecurring costs. One way of achieving flexibility is to invest in equipment that can be introduced sequentially or invest in multiple-use equipment. Flexibility allows a firm to meet target costs despite fluctuations in volume, since excess capacity can be put to other use. Second, technology planning is used to project the end of a product's life cycle. This information is necessary for multiyear profit planning, which determines target costs.

CAPACITY PLANNING

Capacity planning is another major consideration in target costing. In establishing target costs, a firm must proceed with the assurance that capacity is available, within both the firm and its value chain, now and in the future. Robust capacity planning highlights the manufacturing, marketing, and logistics capacity available. If capacity bottlenecks exist, then target costs will have to be adjusted or must provide for the cost of remedial measures to remove this excess capacity. If capacity has to be acquired, it can have a major impact on product costs, since capacity costs are frequently step functions. Measuring unused capacity and understanding its causes also helps kaizen costing efforts aimed at continuous cost reduction.[2] It can also help value engineering efforts

---

[1] For an excellent discussion of the use of technology for spinning off new prodcuts, see J. Alic, L. Branscomb, H. Brooks, A. Carter, and G. Epstein, *Beyond Spinoff* (Boston, Harvard Business School Press, 1992).

[2] For more information on measuring and reporting capacity, see Klammer, Thomas and CAM-I, *Capacity Measurement and Improvement* (Burr Ridge, Ill.: Richard D. Irwin, 1996). The CAM-I model measures and reports idle, nonproductive, and productive capacity. Nonproductive capacity can be eliminated by redesigning processes and thus reducing costs. Idle capacity signals capacity available for adding new products.

aimed at reducing process costs. A product strategy that considers bottlenecks in the entire chain is likely to be more cost effective in the long run. Available unused capacity is useful in planning new product offerings. If future products can use existing unused capacity then there is little need to build or invest in new capacity. Good capacity information is essential for sound product planning and target costing.

INVESTMENT PLANNING

Investment plans are crucial for target costing in several ways. First, they spell out spending on R&D, new technologies, new types of manufacturing plant and equipment, and training and support for a firms' product portfolio. These inputs determine the long-lead-time spending necessary for product planning and cost planning efforts. Second, investment plans provide the only chance for reducing equipment and other costs that lock a firm into a long-term cost structure and inhibit its flexibility. Investment planning can assist target costing greatly by making investments in assets that are flexible, multipurpose, and capitalize on a firm's core competencies. Finally, investment analysis helps to establish a product's target costs. The size and rate of return used in investment plans provides a key parameter for setting target costs. The rate of return used for investment justifications ideally should be the same rate that is used to determine the desired profit margin in the target cost equation, price minus margin equals cost.

PROFIT AND PRODUCT PLANNING

This process translates strategic market niche choices into specific *multiyear product and profit plans*. It includes determining product portfolios, product life cycles, and profit margin requirements and assigning profit margins to individual products within a product family. Initial pricing strategy for products is also part of this planning. New products are conceptualized and existing products are enhanced. All of this is brought together in a product level profit plan, which results in the allowable cost for each major product.

COMPETITIVE ANALYSIS

An evaluation of competition is part of strategic planning. For target costing purposes, competitive evaluation focuses on understanding market perceptions of competitors' product offerings. Also, it attempts to learn from competitors by performing product teardowns or reverse engineering. Finally, competitive analysis also aims at predicting competitors' reactions to the company's product and pricing decisions through activities such as scenario development and sensitivity analysis.

CUSTOMER ANALYSIS

Incorporating the voice of the customer is one of the most important aspects of target costing. It involves understanding customer needs and translating these needs into a specific product profile. The customer analysis process helps to evaluate the value and relative importance that customers place on product features and functions. It helps a company determine the price and value trade-offs necessary for deciding which features and functions to include in a product.

PRODUCT DEVELOPMENT AND MANAGEMENT

This process includes the management of design and manufacturing processes needed for a product. It includes development of product design, validation of processes, evaluation of productive capacity, planning of production, training and development of plant personnel, development of bill of materials, and all other activities that are needed to launch production.

SUPPLY CHAIN MANAGEMENT

The success of target costing in most industries requires early and active supplier involvement in attaining target costs. Long-term supplier partnerships play a critical role. Partnerships bring suppliers into the design process early. The partnering process also creates trust and "open-book" relationships that allow first-tier partners to share cost and margin data.

Tools and Process Milestones

Target costing core tools are used in conjunction with many other tools that also provide critical support to the target costing process. This appendix shows when in the target costing process both these sets of tools are used. Our purpose is not to provide an exhaustive list of all tools, but only to highlight the major tools used. In the Exhibits that follow, all core target costing tools are shown in bold face and all support tools are normal type.

The target costing process occurs within the product development cycle. In Appendix A, we described the process in detail. Here, we will simplify the product development process into *eight* discrete milestones. We will use these eight milestones to show how and when the various target costing tools are used.

The eight milestones are

- Business strategy developed
- Product concept approved
- Product feasibility confirmed
- Product design finalized
- Production process validated
- Production plan developed
- Production launched
- Post-launch environment changes monitored

MILESTONE 1. BUSINESS STRATEGY DEVELOPED

The first milestone is the development of a business strategy. The business strategy provides the product strategy that starts the target costing process. The planning process used for strategy development requires six broad types of analyses: market conditions, economic outlook, technology forecasts, competitive intelligence, investment analysis, and financial analysis. Several tool groups are available for performing these types of analysis. They vary from econometric methods to matrix analysis of market data. The core tools

E X H I B I T   C–1

Business and Product Strategy Tools

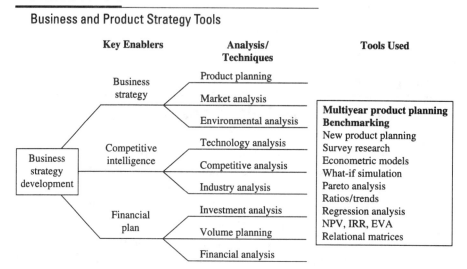

Key Enablers	Analysis/Techniques	Tools Used

of multiyear product planning and benchmarking come into play at this stage. The major tools are summarized in Exhibit C–1.

MILESTONE 2. PRODUCT CONCEPT APPROVED

Defining a product concept requires analyzing the product mix. This involves analyzing margins, prices, and volume of the various products. It means costing possible functions and features to be provided. Quality function deployment (QFD) is a prime tool here. It translates customer preferences into design attributes of a product. Cost estimates for this initial design are developed. Technology is reviewed, capacity is measured, regulatory constraints are studied, suppliers are identified, legal research is reviewed, and conceptual models of the product are developed. As Exhibit C–2 shows, a wide variety of tools and techniques come into play at this stage.

MILESTONE 3. PRODUCT FEASIBILITY CONFIRMED

Milestone 3 is reached when a feasible product design that meets cost and profit margin targets is achieved. Product features and functions have been analyzed and a preliminary bill of materials at the product level is in place. The design incorporates supplier input and customer requirements. Value en-

E X H I B I T   C–2

Product Concept Tools

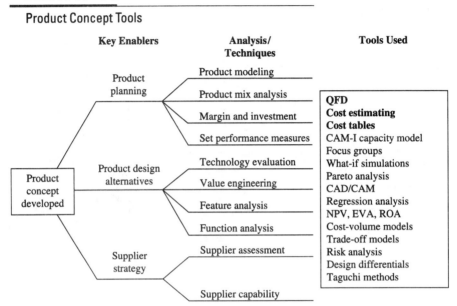

Key Enablers	Analysis/Techniques	Tools Used

gineering is used to ensure that the product can meet both customer requirements and financial hurdles. Exhibit C–3 shows the techniques and tools used at this stage.

MILESTONE 4. PRODUCT DESIGN FINALIZED

The release of the final design requires completion of detailed cost estimates, feature and function trade-offs, and investment analysis for new product development. The decision to go with a design requires complete cost estimates, a detailed bill of materials, make or buy decisions, and models and prototypes of products. Also, parts costs must be reduced and suppliers must start their own part analyses. Exhibit C–4 shows the major techniques and tools needed at this phase of the target cost process.

MILESTONE 5. PRODUCTION PROCESS VALIDATED

This milestone is achieved when the production process required for the new product is validated. The validation ensures that the process is capable of producing the product at the targeted cost and margins. Process validation

E X H I B I T C–3

Product Feasibility Tools

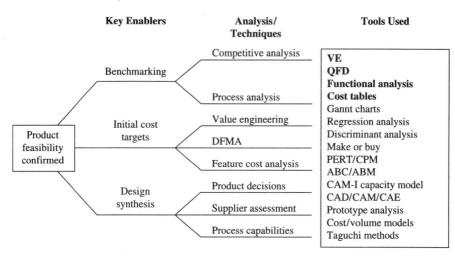

E X H I B I T C–4

Product Design Tools

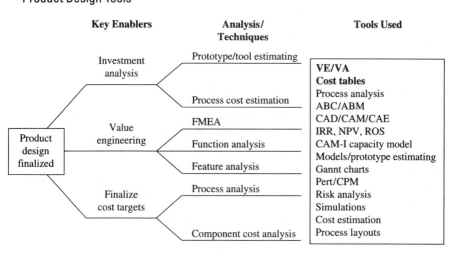

EXHIBIT C–5

Process Validation Tools

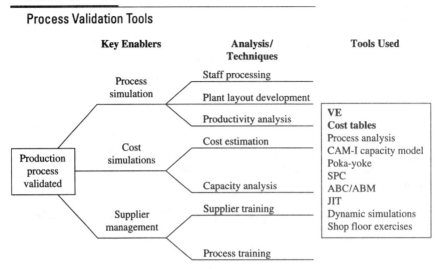

Key Enablers	Analysis/Techniques	Tools Used

- Production process validated
  - Process simulation
    - Staff processing
    - Plant layout development
  - Cost simulations
    - Productivity analysis
    - Cost estimation
    - Capacity analysis
  - Supplier management
    - Supplier training
    - Process training

Tools Used:
VE
Cost tables
Process analysis
CAM-I capacity model
Poka-yoke
SPC
ABC/ABM
JIT
Dynamic simulations
Shop floor exercises

requires testing for cycle time variations, interference, capacity bottlenecks, quality, and performance. These tests can be done through test runs or by computer simulations. Outside suppliers begin the hard tooling they need to support production. Exhibit C–5 shows the techniques and tools that help validate the process.

MILESTONE 6. PRODUCTION PLAN FINALIZED

This milestone is reached when the production plan is released and documentation is issued for procuring parts. It allows manufacturing to process and build test or pilot products. The key analyses needed at this stage are change analysis, supplier analysis, and value analysis. Internal and external capacity issues are resolved and process decisions are finalized. The techniques and tools used are shown in Exhibit C–6.

MILESTONE 7. PRODUCTION LAUNCHED

Milestone 7 is marked by the start of normal volume production. The tools and techniques used at this stage are primarily kaizen costing and continuous improvement. They are shown in Exhibit C–7.

E X H I B I T   C–6

Product Planning Tools

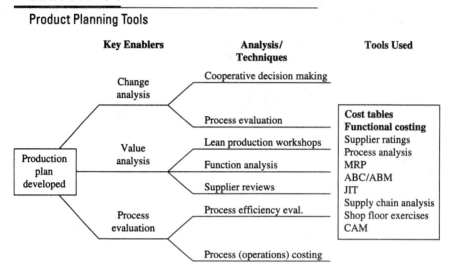

Key Enablers	Analysis/ Techniques	Tools Used

Change analysis — Cooperative decision making / Process evaluation

Value analysis — Lean production workshops / Function analysis / Supplier reviews

Production plan developed

Process evaluation — Process efficiency eval. / Process (operations) costing

Tools Used:
Cost tables
Functional costing
Supplier ratings
Process analysis
MRP
ABC/ABM
JIT
Supply chain analysis
Shop floor exercises
CAM

E X H I B I T   C–7

Production Launch Tools

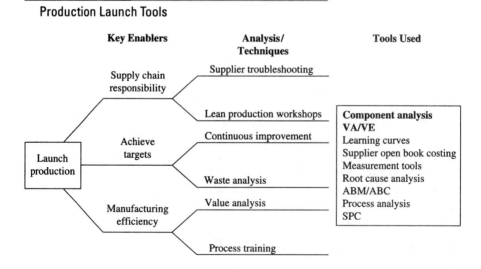

Key Enablers	Analysis/ Techniques	Tools Used

Supply chain responsibility — Supplier troubleshooting / Lean production workshops

Achieve targets — Continuous improvement / Waste analysis

Launch production

Manufacturing efficiency — Value analysis / Process training

Tools Used:
Component analysis
VA/VE
Learning curves
Supplier open book costing
Measurement tools
Root cause analysis
ABM/ABC
Process analysis
SPC

MILESTONE 8. MONITORING THE POST-LAUNCH ENVIRONMENT

The last milestone is also the first step in the next product development cycle. It requires monitoring the reaction of customers to the product, service history, sales reached, profit projections achieved, and reaction by competitors, regulatory agencies and others. The techniques and tools used at this stage are shown in Exhibit C–8.

EXHIBIT   C–8

Post-Launch Tools

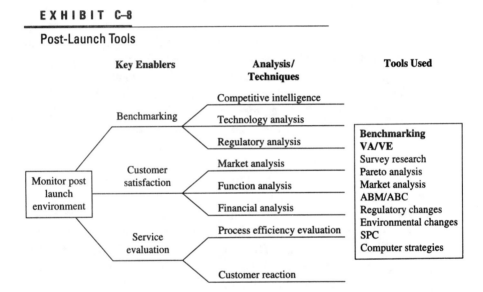

Target Costing and Legacy Costs
An Illustration

Target costing is often perceived to be relevant only for planning new and recurring product costs. This is because these costs are most intimately related to product design. Legacy costs, those that exist from an organization's prior decisions, are often treated as fixed or sunk and not amenable to critical cost planning. For many products, these costs can be very significant. In the case of telecommunications or broadcasting, a new product that uses an existing satellite has to pay for this legacy cost of several hundred million dollars that is already in place. The cost of renting transponder space on this satellite may be significant compared to the other costs for a firm in the data communication or broadcast business.

Ignoring legacy costs can create an undue burden on product designers. It can also severely cut into a firm's profit and return potential. How can a firm address these legacy costs? This subject is addressed in this appendix. Using the telecommunications industry as an example, we will show that legacy costs are not always inflexible and that a good product design can sometimes better utilize or reduce a product's share of legacy costs.

Like other costs, legacy costs can be planned and managed through product design or through activity based management. We will use a company called Datacom[1] Inc. to illustrate these methods and to show their impact on profits.

Datacom Inc. is a telecommunications company that offers satellite-based data communication services. The data network uses very small aperture terminals (VSAT) to link remote sites (such as bank branches) with corporate headquarters. Datacom assembles these terminals at its own plant and leases them to customers. The network is used for data transfers and video broadcasting. The company currently leases two 18 MHz. transponders on a communications satellite. Each transponder rents for $3 million per

---

[1] Datacom is a fictitious name for a real company. The name has been disguised to preserve confidential information provided by the company.

year. A typical video application uses 9 MHz for transmitting an analog signal. A digital signal takes less space, particularly if it is compressed video. Datacom wants to offer video teleconferencing as a new product.

The company's projected product line income statement for the video conferencing line is shown in Exhibit D–1. Datacom expects to make $253,000 profit on a sales of $10.1 million for a 2.5 percent return on sales (ROS). It has $5.26 million in assets, so asset turnover is 1.9, and the return on assets (ROA) is 4.8 percent. The profit from the product line is below the global industry average of around 8–15 percent. This profit needs to be higher if the video conferencing product line is to look attractive.

An important variable affecting the profitability of video conferencing is the $1.5 million charge for transponder rental. This represents one half of the annual $3 million rental. Video conferencing has been allocated half because it expects to use 9 out of 18 MHz of the transponder space. In addition,

EXHIBIT D–1

Datacom Projected Income Statement (in 000)

Revenues		$10,100
Manufacturing/network costs		6,000
Gross margin		4,100
Sales and support expenses		2,200
G & A expense		1,500
Operating expenses		3,700
Operating income		400
Interest expense	8%	147
Net profit		$253
Assets:		
Receivable turnover in days	45	$1,263
Inventory turnover in turns	4	1,500
Fixed assets		2,500
Total assets		$5,263
Key Rates of Returns		
Return on sales		2.50%
Asset turnover		1.9
Return on assets		4.8%
Assumptions Used		
Debt/equity ratio		35.00%

it also is paying its allocated share of existing marketing and business support costs.

To improve the profit picture, Datacom must address all costs, including legacy costs, associated with the video conferencing product. These latter are 36 percent of total costs. What can it do about these costs?

Target costing can be used to address some of these legacy costs. Transponder rental is a good example. The use of transponder space depends on the design of the VSAT terminals. If they were designed to handle compressed video, then the space requirements could shrink considerably. Assume that digital compression can reduce the space needed to 6 MHz or two thirds of its former size. This will reduce the transponder rental to $1 million or a reduction of $500,000. This represents a significant reduction in the network operating costs. The redesign of VSATs to handle compressed video will mean an increase in R&D costs of nearly 20 percent.

Other cost management tools such as ABM, BPR, or JIT can be used to address legacy costs not influenced by product design. These costs can be used to examine the level of support the product needs and whether it can use alternative methods of distribution.

Exhibit D–2 shows hypothetical results of using these two approaches for Datacom.

By redesigning its VSAT terminals, the company gets a net cost savings of 13 percent (increase of 20% for R&D on digital technology and 33% decrease in transponder rental). The use of BPR and ABM on distribution and business support costs yields another 3 percent savings in costs. Together there is a reduction in legacy costs of 16 percent and in new costs of 5 percent. Note that the company has been able to obtain a cost reduction in legacy costs that is more than three times higher than its cost savings on new costs. The combined effect of addressing both new and legacy costs results in a dramatic improvement in the profit picture. The ROS increases from 2.5 to 8.5 percent. The ROA increases from 4.8 to 18.6 percent.

We not do not mean to imply that, in all cases, legacy costs can be decreased more than new costs. However, our point is that they should not be ignored in the profit planning process and sometimes they do offer significant opportunities. Datacom is a good case in point. The communications industry has significantly boosted existing satellite capacity through the use of digital compression technology. Other side benefits have accrued as well. The recent introduction of direct broadcast television by Hughes is a good example of the new product opportunities created by compressed video technologies that were originally designed to solve the legacy cost problem of broadcasters.

When used for both new and legacy costs, target costing allows a company to think of costs in a broader "economic value chain," "life cycle," and "time" context. It forces us to ask questions such as these:

EXHIBIT D-2

Impact On New and Legacy Costs

Kaleidoscopic View of Costs		Amount (000s)	(%) of cost		Effect (%)	Revised Results
Total revenues		$10,100				$10,100
R&D costs: inside, Legacy		100	1	R&D for compression	20.0	120
Component cost: inside, New		400	4	VE	−2.0	392
Transponder rental: inside, Legacy		1,500	15	VE	−33.3	1,000
Material costs: suppliers, New		3,700	38	Supplier Based VE	−2.0	3,626
Distribution costs: inside, Legacy		300	3	ABM	−1.5	296
Distribution costs: dealers, New		1,200	12	Dealer Based BPR	−0.1	1,199
Business process costs: Legacy		1,900	19	ABM	−1.5	1,872
Warranty costs: inside, New		300	3	VE	−0.1	300
Warranty costs: dealers, New		100	1	Dealer Based VE	−0.1	100
Recycling costs: New		200	2	"Green" Design	−0.5	199
Interest expense: New	8%	147	1	Process + BPR		144
Total costs		9,847	100		−21.1	9,246
Profit		$253				$854

Assets

Receivable turnover (days)	45	$1,263		BPR	45	1,263
Inventory turnover (turns)	4	1,500		JIT	6	836
Fixed assets		2,500				2,500
Total assets		$5,263				$4,599
Return on sales		2.53%				8.5%
Asset turnover		1.9				2.2
Return on assets		4.8%				18.6%
Debt/equity ratio		35.0%				35.0%

- How do we maximize flexibility *and* utilization of plant capacity?
- How well will the product perform in use? How high will warranty costs be?
- How safe is the product? Will it create product liability?
- How will we dispose of the product? Will it create a later cost exposure?
- What by-products or processes are created? Is there a market or liability related to these products or processes?

A second major benefit of focusing on all costs is that the costs of running a business is brought into central focus. This not only relieves some of the burden for cost reduction from manufacturing and suppliers, it allows us to think about business process "design" issues such as these:

- How much time and effort is spent "administering the business"?
- What information technology do we need to run as an integrated enterprise?
- What is the best way to deliver products to customers?
- How do we package and store the product?
- How do we manage our assets?

The answers to these questions can result in a more efficient, integrated, and lean organization that can provide a cost and competitive advantage for a company.

Sample Deployment Tools

This appendix presents two useful tools for deploying target costing. The first is a gap analysis form that can be used for assessing deployment gaps. The other is an action item plan to track progress toward deployment.

A sample gap analysis instrument is shown in Exhibit E–1. It represents a summary of forms filled out by several respondents. We can illustrate the interpretation of the sample entries in the summary form shown in that exhibit. The first two lines of the sample summary form indicates the identity of the respondent. Column 1 lists the technical, behavioral, cultural, and political requirements or enablers for target costing deployment. The remaining columns identify the various functional areas involved in target costing deployment. For each functional area, we have two columns. The first column, titled *should,* indicates whether this functional area is affected by a requirement and should be involved with it. The symbol λ is used to capture this. The symbol Φ in a column means that the functional area not only should be involved but has the primarily responsibility for fulfilling that requirement. The second column, titled *does,* has a yes or no entry. This indicates the extent to which the affected functional area has that enabler in place.

The form is filled out by personnel from all functional areas. This allows us to evaluate self and peer assessments of requirement gaps. The combined data can be used to compare responses across functional areas. This comparison allows us not only to know what gaps must be filled, but also where we have communication and perceptual differences between functional groups.

Consider some sample entries from the Exhibit E–1. Line 9, under behavioral requirements, shows that marketing has the primary responsibility for providing data about feature/cost trade-offs. The yes entry means that marketing thinks it is accomplishing this. However, the design and accounting departments need information on these trade-offs to do their jobs. Their responses indicate that they do not think marketing is collecting this information or providing it to them. Similarly, line 2, under technical requirements, indicates that ranking customer needs is marketing's responsibility and it is currently

E X H I B I T E–1

A Sample Gap Analysis Tool for Target Costing Deployment

Respondent's Rank:

Respondent's Department:

Deployment Requirements (Enablers)	Marketing		Design	
	Should	Does	Should	Does
Technical Requirements:				
1. Do we have clearly delineated product line objectives?				
2. Do we have a ranking of customer needs?	Φ	Yes	λ	No
3. Do we have VE training?			λ	Yes
4. Do we have a cost breakdown of components used?			λ	No
5. Have we set up cross-functional teams?				
6. Have we identified a list of critical suppiers?			λ	No
Behavioral Requirements:				
7. Are all functions ready to participate in design activity?	λ	No	λ	No
8. Do our engineers use cost data?			λ	No
9. Is marketing willing and able to do feature trade-offs?	Φ	Yes	λ	No
10. Are we willing to share information across functions?	λ	No	λ	No
11. Is accounting ready to act as business advisor?				
Culture/Symbolic Requirements:				
12. Does target costing have a positive meaning for us?	λ	Yes	λ	Yes
13. Does our culture support open sharing of information?	λ	No	λ	No
14. Is target costing consistent with our organizational culture?	λ	Yes	λ	Yes
15. Do we value customer input in our culture?	λ	Yes	λ	No
16. Do we value cross-functional teamwork?	λ	No	λ	No
Political Requirements:				
17. Does it preserve our vital interests:	λ	Yes	λ	
18. Will the target cost initiative reduce our power?	λ	No	λ	No
19. Will those who have formal power support target costing?	λ	No	λ	
20. Will target costing adversely affect our resource base?	λ	No	λ	

Key: Φ = Functional area primarily responsible for or affected by a deployment requirement.

	Functional Area Involved								
Manufacturing		Service		Accounting		Procurement		Top Management	
Should	Does	Should	Does	Should	Does	Should	Does	Should	Does
								Φ	No
λ	No								
λ	No			λ	No	λ	Yes		
								Φ	Yes
λ	No					Φ	No		
λ	Yes	λ	No	λ	No	λ	No		
					No				
				λ	No				
λ	Yes	λ	Yes	λ	No	λ	No		No
				Φ	No				
λ	No	λ	No	λ	Yes	λ	Yes	Φ	Yes
λ	Yes	λ	Yes	λ	No	λ	Yes	Φ	No
λ	Yes	λ	No	λ	No	λ	Yes	Φ	Yes
λ	Yes	λ	Yes	λ	Yes	λ	Yes	Φ	No
λ	Yes	λ	No	λ	Yes	λ	Yes	Φ	Yes
λ		λ		λ				λ	Yes
λ		λ		λ				λ	Yes
λ		λ		λ				λ	No
λ		λ		λ				λ	No

λ = Area affected by deployment requirement.

doing the job. However, design engineering disagrees. It does not think that marketing is ranking customer needs.

The sample form in Exhibit E–2 shows the decomposition of two of the deployment gaps in Exhibit E–1 into a task breakdown. The first item is VE training (item 3) and the second is open information sharing (item 10). Both these items are broken into detailed tasks, which are shown in the first column of Exhibit E–2. The second and third columns show the primary and secondary persons responsible for carrying out the task. The fourth column shows who needs to be consulted or kept informed. The next column is the completion deadline for the task. The last column is the current status of the task. By updating this form frequently, the deployment team can keep up with progress made and can add actions that arise during the deployment process.

EXHIBIT E-2

A Sample Action Item Plan

Last Update: June 21, 1997

Task	Primary Responsibility	Secondary Responsibility	Consult/ Inform	Deadline	Status
Set up VE Training:					
Get trainee names	Alice, Ben	Deployment team	Area heads	Feb. 15, 1997	Done
Prepare course syllabus	Charlene	Deployment team	VP training	Feb. 15, 1997	Done
Contact Professor Lynn	Charlene	Alice		Feb. 20, 1997	In progress
Select training site	Alice	Ben		Feb. 20, 1997	Need new site
Prepare training materials	Charlene, David	Greg	VP training	April 15, 1997	In progress
Reproduce training materials	Greg	Maria		April 21, 1997	
Mail materials to trainees	Greg	Maria		April 25, 1997	
Get CEO to launch training	Maria	Greg		Feg. 15, 1997	done
Line up guest speakers	Maria	Greg	VP training	Feb. 15, 1997	2 yes; 3 more needed
Obtain training films	Ben	Maria		April 1, 1997	In mail
Create Open Information:					
Form systems design team	Nancy	IT subteam	VP IT	Feb. 15, 1996	Done
Set up user team	Nancy, Tanaka	Chang	VP IT	Feb. 15, 1996	In progress
Identify "change" consultants	Siva, Jose	Kate	VP IT	May. 31, 1996	2 interviewed
Set up facilitation sessions	Ingrid	La Pierre	VP HR	May. 31, 1996	In progress
Purchase software	Ingrid	La Pierre	VP HR	May. 31, 1996	
Install software	Ephrahim	Banovsky		June 1, 1996	
Start software training	Jamal	Teresa		June 8, 1996	
	Jamal	Teresa			Tested

233

G L O S S A R Y

Activity   An activity is the work (series of tasks) performed in an organization. It represents what we do, such as unload a truck, open a letter, or write a check. (See the process diagram.)

Activity based costing (ABC)   A method of costing in which activities are the primary cost objects. ABC measures cost and performance of activities and assigns the costs of those activities to other cost objects, such as products or customers, based on their use of the activities.

Activity based management (ABM)   The use of activity cost data to manage activities. The purpose of ABM is to analyze whether activities are of (add) value to customers and how they can be performed to maximize customer value.

Actual cost of work performed   The costs actually incurred and recorded in accomplishing the work performed within a given time period.

Affordable   The selling price of a product that provides the value or worth customers want and is within their ability to pay.

Agile manufacturing   The ability of a company to thrive and prosper in a competitive environment of continuous change and to respond quickly to rapidly changing markets. The term also refers to the ability of a company to customize products and produce them in relatively small lot sizes.

Allocation   An allocation is an apportionment or distribution of a common cost between two or more cost objects. In accounting, allocation is usually a way of assigning a cost between cost objects (products, departments, or processes) that share that common cost. An allocation involves dividing the cost we want to allocate by some physical quantity (ideally a cost driver).

Allowable cost   An early estimate of a target cost. It is determined by subtracting a required profit from a competitive market price. The allowable cost is the maximum that can be *committed* to a product in the product planning process.

Benchmarking   The process of investigating and identifying "best practices" and using them as a standard to improve one's own processes and activities.

Best practices   The establishment of criteria to evaluate whether an activity or process is best of its kind. Best practices are used as benchmarks by which similar activities are judged.

Budget   A quantitative plan of action that helps an organization coordinate resource inflows and outflows for a specific time period. Budgets are usually financial but may also include nonfinancial operating information.

Capacity   Capacity refers to having the physical facilities, personnel, supplier contacts, and processes necessary to meet the product or service needs of customers.

Committed cost   A cost the organization will incur because of a prior decision. A particular design decision or equipment purchase commits a firm to certain types of costs.

Competitive analysis   A tool that enables companies to quantify how their performance and costs compare to those of competitors, understand why their performance and costs are different, and apply that insight to strengthen competitive responses and implement proactive plans.

Continuous improvement program   A program to continuously and incrementally improve yields, eliminate waste, reduce response time, simplify design of both products and processes, and improve quality on a continuous incremental basis.

Cost   A measure of the amount paid, charged, or incurred. Strategically, we use the term to mean the total cost to the customer, including the initial cost, the cost of maintaining, and the cost of disposing of a product.

Cost control   (See Cost management.)

Cost estimation   A tool and process used to estimate product costs by understanding their underlying causes or drivers.

Cost management   The systematic analysis of cost drivers to understand how to reduce or control costs.

Cost object   Any item (activity, customer, project, work unit, product, channel, or service) for which a measurement of cost is desired.

Cost tables   Data bases of detailed cost information based on various manufacturing variables. Cost tables represent an easily accessible source of information about the effect on product costs of using different productive resources, manufacturing methods, functions, product designs, and materials.

Culture   The collective beliefs, values, ethics, and mind-sets of the members of an organization, clan, or society that is subconsciously used to interpret events and take action. Some authors define *culture* as the collective programming of the subconscious mind.

Current cost   The cost of producing a *new* or *redesigned* product with existing technology, specifications, and processes.

Customer value   The difference between customer realization and sacrifice. *Realization* is what the customer receives, which includes product features, reliability, usability, safety, dependability, and service. *Sacrifice* is what the customer gives up, which includes the amount the customer pays for the product plus time and effort spent acquiring the product and learning how to use it, maintain it, and dispose of it.

Design for manufacture and assembly (DFMA)   A simultaneous engineering process that optimizes the relationship between materials, manufacturing technology, assembly process, functionality, and economics. It seeks to ease manufacture and assembly of parts or eliminate parts.

Design to cost (DTC)   A method to ensure that product designs meet a stated cost objective. Cost is addressed on a continuing basis as part of product or process design. The technique embodies early establishment of realistic but difficult cost objectives, goals, and thresholds and then manages the design until it converges on these objectives.

Development cost   The nonrecurring cost to design and develop a product.

Discounted cash flow   A technique used to evaluate the present value of future cash flows generated by a capital investment. Discounted cash flow is computed by applying a rate representing cost of capital to future cash flows.

Drifting cost   (See Current cost.)

Driver   Any event, circumstance, or condition that causes activities within a process to commence or a factor that causes a change because it has a direct cause/effect relationship on a cost object. For example, a cost driver is the factor(s) that changes the cost of an activity.

Extended enterprise   The organization and its customers, suppliers, dealers, and recyclers. There are interdependencies across these separate organizations.

Failure mode and effect analysis (FMEA)   An analysis of each part to determine what could go wrong and how serious the consequences would be.

Features   The attributes, physical or aesthetic, of a product as viewed by customers.

Fixed cost   A cost element that does not vary with changes in cost drivers such as volume in the short run. The property taxes on factory building is an example of a fixed production cost.

Flexible manufacturing systems (FMS)   An integrated system of machine tools and material-handling equipment designed to manufacture a variety of parts at low or medium volumes.

Function   The physical actions associated with a component or subassembly of a product. It is also used to refer to discrete components or subassemblies that are the focus of engineering design. For example, the engine and chassis are functions of a car. *Function* is also used to refer to specialist departments or units in an organization such as sales, marketing, and engineering.

Functional worth   Lowest cost for providing a basic function in a product.

Historical cost   The original or past cost of a product or service.

Incentives/reward systems   The use of incentives and rewards, such as salary increases, incentive compensation, promotions, key assignments, recognition, or praise.

Incremental cost   1. The cost associated with increasing the output of an activity or project above some base level. 2. The additional cost associated with selecting one economic or business alternative over another, such as difference between working overtime or subcontracting the work.

Incurred cost   An expenditure the firm has made.

Indirect costs   1. Costs common to a multiple set of cost objects and not directly traceable to such objects in a specific time period. Such costs are usually allocated by systematic and consistent techniques to products, processes, or time periods. 2. Costs that are not directly assignable or traceable to the product or process.

Internal rate of return   The rate of return at which the present value of future cash flows equal the present value of costs.

Investment management   Planning and development of a product's process, including the selection and acquisition of the technology used to make the product.

Just-in-time (JIT) inventory management   A logistics approach designed to result in minimum inventory and waste during the manufacturing process.

Kaizen costing   A method for managing continuous cost improvement through cross-functional, team oriented problem solving with a customer focus.

Lean production   A manufacturing process that allows firms to quickly turn out small batches of customized products. (*Agile* or *flexible manufacturing* are other terms sometimes used for lean production.).

Life cycle costing   Accumulation of costs for activities that occur over the entire life cycle of a product from its inception to abandonment.

Market price   The price at which a customer is willing to buy a product over that of a competitor. It is determined by taking into account the market factors and by measuring customer trade-offs between price and features required.

Mass production   The process of making a large number of identical products, typically using linear or sequential assembly lines.

Non-value added activity   An activity that does not contribute to customer value or the organization's needs. The designation reflects a belief that the activity can be redesigned, reduced, or eliminated without reducing the quantity, responsiveness, or quality of the output required by the customer or the organization.

Pareto analysis   The identification and interpretation of significant factors using Pareto's rule that 20 percent of a set of independent variables is responsible for 80 percent of the result.

Performance measures   Indicators of the work performed and the results achieved in an activity, process, or organizational unit. Performance measures may be financial or nonfinancial.

Process   A series of linked activities that perform a specific objective. A process has a beginning, an end, and clearly identified inputs and outputs. Assembling a car or preparing a budget are examples of linked activities that constitute a process (see the process diagram).

Process Diagram

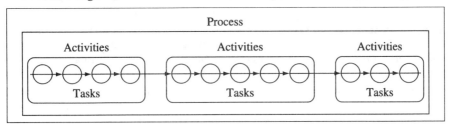

Quality   A customer's total experience with the product or service provided, including features and the performance dimensions of those features such as reliability, usability, safety, and repairability.

Quality function deployment (QFD)   A structured matrix approach to documenting and understanding customer requirements and translating them into technical design characteristics for each stage of product development and production.

Recurring cost   All costs associated with producing, distributing, and servicing a product that occur every period.

Required profit margin   The profit margin, expressed as a percent of sales, required by a firm. It is determined by careful consideration of available information on customers, competition, a firm's anticipated future product mix, sales volume, market share objectives, and the long-term financial returns required in that industry.

Research and development (R&D) cost   The sum of all costs resulting from applied research, engineering design, analysis, development, test, evaluation, and management development efforts.

Return on assets   A formula that divides total income by total assets. It is frequently used to evaluate the effectiveness of asset utilization.

Return on sales   A formula that divides operating profit by total sales revenue. It is frequently used to determine the rate of return from products.

Standard cost   Predetermined costs based on existing engineering specifications, production methods, and processes.

Strategic intent   An approach to formulating strategy that begins with a goal that exceeds a company's present grasp and resources and then attempts to achieve that goal by setting challenges that focus employees' efforts in the near to medium term.

Strategy   The way that an organization positions and distinguishes itself from its competitors. It is the basic business approach a firm follows to meet its goals. *Positioning* refers to the selection of target customers. A firm distinguishes itself from other organizations on the dimensions of quality, cost, and time.

Strategic supply chain management (SSCM)   A structured business approach to *balance, synchronize, and synergize* all internal and external resources and assets.

Target cost   The allowable amount of cost that can be incurred on a product and still earn the required profit from that product. It is a market driven costing system in which cost targets are set by considering customer requirements and competitive offerings. Cost targets are achieved by focusing on product and process design and making continuous improvements in all support processes.

Time   When used strategically, means rapid development of products with new features or innovative technologies and quick manufacture of those products. Time also means that existing products must be available when a customer needs them.

Total quality management (TQM)   An approach that focuses all organizational resources on achieving quality throughout the value chain. Emphasis is on quality from the customer's point of view. Cost should be reduced as product failures and follow-on customer service requirements are reduced.

Value added   An activity judged to contribute to customer value or satisfy an organizational need. The attribute "value-added" reflects a belief that the activity cannot be eliminated without reducing the quantity, responsiveness, or quality of output required by a customer or organization.

Value analysis   A planned, clean sheet approach to problem solving and cost reduction without sacrificing functional worth and quality. Generally used and employed to improve value after production has begun.

Value engineering   A systematic method of evaluating the functions of a product to determine whether they can be provided at a lower cost without sacrificing the features, performance, reliability, usability, and recyclability of the product. Generally used at the design stage of a product to improve customer value and reduce costs before production has begun.

Variable cost   A cost element that varies directly and proportionately with changes in cost drivers such as the volume of production.

Variance   The difference between an expected and actual result.

S E L E C T E D
B I B L I O G R A P H Y

ENGLISH

Ansari, S.; J. Bell; and J. Blumenthal. "Strategy Deployment." Research Report. Arlington, Texas: CAM-I, 1993.

Asanuma, B. "Interfirm Relationships in Japanese Manufacturing Industry." Working Paper, Kyoto University,x October 1991, pp. 1–25.

Asanuma, B. "Manufacturer-Supplier Relationships in Japan and the Concept of Relation-Specific Skill." *Journal of the Japanese and International Economies* 3 (1989), pp. 1–30.

Asanuma, B. "The Organization of Parts Purchases in the Japanese Automotive Industry." *Contemporary Economics* 58 (Summer 1984), pp. 38–48.

Cooper, R.; and W. B. Chew. "Control Tomorrow's Cost Through Today's Designs." *Harvard Business Review* (January–February 1996), pp. 88–97.

Cooper, R.; "How Japanese Manufacturing Firms Implement Target Costing Systems: A Field-Based Research Study." Draft Paper presented at Management Accounting Conference, Jan. 31, 1994.

Evers, R. "Value Engineering." *Cost Engineering* 28, no. 12 (December. 1986), pp. 32–36.

Faisal, J. H. *Practical Value Analysis Methods.,* New York: Hayden Book Company, 1972.

Freedman, J. M. "Target Costing." *Management Accounting* 75, no. 10 (April 1994), pp. 72–73.

Gagne, M. L.; and R. Discenza. "New Product Costing, Japanese Style." *The CPA Journal* 63, no. 5 (May 1993), pp. 68–71.

Hedberg, S. R. "Design of a Lifetime." *Byte,* October 1994, pp. 103–5.

Heller, E. D. *Value Management: Value Engineering and Cost Reduction.* Reading, Mass.: Addison-Wesley Publishing Company, 1971.

Hiromoto, T. "Another Hidden Edge—Japanese Management Accounting.," *Harvard Business Review,* July–August 1988, pp. 22–26.

Horvath, P. "Target Costing: State-of-the-Art Report." CAM-I Report Number R–93-CMS–03. Arlington, Texas: CAM-I, 1993.

Hronec, S., *Vital Signs: Using Quality, Cost and Time Performance Measures to Chart Your Company's Future.* Detroit: Arthur Andersen, 1993.

Kato, Y. "Target Costing Support Systems: Lessons from Leading Japanese Companies." *Management Accounting Research* 4 (March 1993), pp. 33–47.

Kato, Y.; G. Boer; and C. Chow. "Target Costing: An Integrative Management Process." *Journal of Cost Management,* Spring 1995.

Koons, F. J. "Cost Engineering in Microelectronics." *AACE Transactions* F9(1)–F9(4), 1991.

Lee, J. Y. "Use Target Costing to Improve Your Bottom Line." *CPA Journal,* 64, no. 1 (January 1994), pp. 68–70.

Matthyssens, P.; and C. Van den Bulte. "Getting Closer and Nicer: Partnerships in the Supply Chain." *Long Range Planning* 27, no. 1 (1994), pp. 72–83.

Miller, J. A. "Target Costing for the Chapter 11 Business." *Bankruptcy Law Review* 3, no. 4 (Winter 1992), pp. 51–3.

Monden, Y. *Cost Reduction Systems.* Portland, Ore.: Productivity Press, 1995.

Moden, Y.; and J. Lee. "How a Japanese Auto Maker Reduces Costs." *Management Accounting* 75, no. 2 (August 1993), pp. 22–26.

Moden, Y.; and K. Hamada. "Target Costing and Kaizen Costing in Japanese Automobile Companies." *Journal of Management Accounting Research* 3 (Fall 1991), pp. 16–34.

Morgan, M. J. "A Case Study in Target Costing: Accounting for Strategy." *Management Accounting* 71, no. 5 (May 1993), pp. 20–22.

Nadeau, M. "Not Lost in Space." *Byte,* June 1995, p. 50.

Okano, H. "Target Cost Management and Product Development at Toyota." Working Paper Series, no. 9502, February 1995.

Polakoff, J. C. "Hitting the Bull's Eye with Target Costing." *Corporate Controller* 5, no. 1 (September–October 1992), pp. 41–43.

Sakurai, M. "The Concept of Target Costing and its Effective Utilization. Cost Management Systems Phase 2 Research." CAM-I CMS Program Research Report Arlington Texas: CAM-I, 1987.

Sakurai, M. "Target Costing and How to Use It." *Journal of Cost Management* 3, no. 2 (Summer 1989), pp. 39–50.

Society of Management Accountants of Canada (SMAC). "Developing Comprehensive Competitive Intelligence Systems." Management Accounting Guideline #39, Hamilton, Ont.: SMAC, June 1995.

SMAC, IMA, and CAMI. "Implementing Target Costing," Management Accounting Guideline #28, Hamilton, Ont.: SMAC, Spring 1994.

Tanaka, T. "Target Costing at Toyota." *Journal of Cost Management* 7, no. 1 (Spring 1993), pp. 4–11.

Tanaka, M. "Cost Planning and Control Systems in the Design Phase of a New Product." In *Japanese Management Accounting: A World Class Approach to Profit Management,* pp. 49–71. Portland, Ore.: Productivity Press, 1989.

Tani, T.; O. Hiroshi; N. Shimizu; Y. Iwabuchi; J. Fukuda; and S. Cooray. "Target Cost Management in Japanese Companies: Current State of the Art." *Management Accounting Research* 5 (1994), pp. 67–81.

Van Hull, P. *Global Best Practices QCT Product Development.* Detroit: Arthur Andersen, 1993.

Van Hull, P., *Global Best Practices Cost Management,* Detroit: Arthur Andersen, 1993.

Worthy, F. S. "Japan's Smart Secret Weapon," *Fortune,* Aug. 12, 1991, Vol. 124, No. 4, pp. 72–75.

Yoshikawa, T., Innes, J., and Mitchell, F. "Cost Management Through Functional Analysis," *Journal of Cost Management 3,* Spring 1989, pp. 14–19.

JAPANESE

Aota, Eisuke. "Target Cost Management in Copier Industry" [Fukushaki Jigyo deno Genkakikaku Katsudo]. *JICPA Journal* no. 440 (March 1992), pp. 66–71.

Arai, Hideo. "Cost Control and VE Activities with Different Business Functions at Nippon Denki Corporation" [Tosha no Seisan keitai Betsu Genkakanri to VE katsudo]. *Management Practice [Keiei Jitsumu]* no. 426 (October 1989), pp.1–19.

Ebisaka, S. "Cost Control in the Development Stage of A New Automobile" [Shinsha kaihatsu Dankai niokeru Genka Kanri]. *Management Practice [Keiei Jitsumu]* no. 438 (October 1990), pp. 32–39.

Hasegawa, Takuzo. "A Study on the Characteristic and Function of Genka Kikkau—For Target Costing Deployment in the Overseas Market" [Genka kikaku no Tokucho to Hongenteki kino no Kousatsu—Global ka o zentei to shita Kigyo no Kanri katsudo tenkai no tameni]. *The Journal of Gifu College of Economics* 27, no. 2 (September 1993), pp. 79–100.

Inaba, Kiyoemon. "Target Cost Management and IE" [Genka Kikaku to IE]. *IE Review* 32, no. 2 (May 1991), pp. 2–3.

Inove, Shinichi. "Overlapping Style Development and Globalization of Target Costing—A Survey of Japanese Companies with Global Operations" [Overlap gata Kenkyu Kaihatsu to Genka Kikaku no Kokusai iten]. *Industrial Accounting [Sangyo Keiri]* 52, no. 4, 1993 pp. 52–65.

Iwabuchi, Yoshihide. "Target Costing as Japanese Style Cost Control" [Nippon teki genka kanri toshiteno Genka kiakku]. *Konan Management Study* 33, nos.3 and 4 (March 1993), pp. 169 and 188.

Iwahashi, Toshio. "Target Cost Management in Processing and Assembling Industries—A Case Study of Kubota and Its Analysis" [Kakou Kumitate Sangyo no Genka kikaku Katsudo—Kubota ni okeru Jirei to sono Kaisetsu]. *IE Review* 32, no. 2 (May 1991), pp. 21–28.

Iwahashi, Toshio. "Target Costing and a Cost Table in the Development Stage of Kubota Tekko" [Kaihatsu Sekkei Dankai ni okeru Genka kikaku Katsudo to Cost Table]. *Management Practice [Keiei Jitsumu]* no. 426 (October 1989), pp.10–19.

Kan, Yasuhito. "Target Cost Management in Office Equipments Industry" [Zimuki Jigyo ni okeru Genka Katsudo]. *IE Review* 32, no. 2 (May 1991), pp. 29–34.

Kato, Yutaka. *Target Cost Management—The Strategic Cost Management* [Genka kikaku—Senryaku teki Cost Management]. Nippon Keizai ShinbunSha, 1993.

Kimura, Katsutoshi. "Target Cost Management for a New Automobile Development" [Shinsha kaihatsu ni okeru Genka kikaku katsudo]. *IE Review* 32, no. 2 (May 1991), pp. 37–41.

Kimura, Katsutoshi. "Target Costing Activity Based on A Product" [Shohin o Jiku toshita Genka Kikaku katsudo]. *JICPA Journal* no. 440 (March 1992), pp. 61–65.

Masa, Shiro. "Purchasing Strategy in Manufacturing Department of an Air Conditioning Unit" [Kucho Seisan honbu no Kobai Senryaku ni Tsuite]. *Management Practice [Keiei Jitsumu]*, no. 442 (February 1991), pp. 20–36.

Miyamoto, Kuniaki. "Durability of Control Methodology in Management Accounting" [Kanri kaikei niokeru Kanrigiho no Jizokusei]. *Accounting [Kaikei]* 145, no. 1 (1994), pp. 1–13.

Monden, Yasuhiro. "Techniques of Target Costing and Cost Kaizen to Be Price Competitive" [Kakaku Kyosoryoku o Tsukeru Genkakikaku to Genka Kaizen no Giho]. *Toyo Keizai Shinpo Sha*, 1994.

Nishiguchi, Fumio. "The Process of Product Development VE—An Introduction of Matrix VE in the Development and the Manufacturing Stage of a Product" [Kaihatsu VE no Susumekata—Seihin no Kaihatsu Seizo Process ni Taioshite Susumeru Matrix VE no Shokai]. *Management Practice [Keiei Jitsumu]* no. 429 (January 1990), pp. 33–43.

Nishiguchi, Fumio. "Target Cost Deployment at Nippon Denso Corporation" [Tosha ni okeru Genka kikaku no Tenkai]. *Management Practice [Keiei Jitsumu]* no. 426 (October 1989), pp. 20–43.

Ogawa, Masao. "A Study on the Functional Performance Level and Product Price for Setting VE Targets" [VE Mokuhyo no tameno Kino tassei do to Kakaku no Kenkyu]. *Management Practice [Keiei Jitsumu]* no. 421 (May 1989), pp. 32–42.

Okano, Hiroshi. "Invisibility in Management Accounting" [Kanrikaikei ni okeru Fukashisei]. *Journal of Cost Accounting Research* 17, no. 2 (1992), pp. 56–64.

Okano, Hiroshi. "Possibility of Japanese Management Accounting Theory—'Visibility' and 'Invisibility' of Accounting" [Nippon teki Kanri kaikei ron no Kanosei —Kaike ni okeru 'kashisei' to 'Fukashisei']. *Accounting* 143, nos. 1 and 2 (February 1993), pp.200–14.

Okano, Hiroshi. *Target Cost Management and Product Development at Toyota.* Working Paper No. 9502, Osaka City University, Graduate School of Business Administration, 1995.

Sakurai, Mihciharu. "New Developments of FMS and Management Accounting" [FMS to Kanri kaikei no Shintenkai]. *Corporate Accounting [Kigyo kaikei]* 37, no. 2 (1985), pp. 25–35.

Sato, Yoshihiko. "Purchasing (Cost Reduction) Activities for Industry Depends on Outside Order" [Gaiseihin izon gata sangyo no Kobai Katsudo]. *Management Practice [Keiei Jitsumu],* no. 442 (February 1991), pp. 48–57.

Shigeno, Katsumi. "Resource Planning Strategy at Sumitomo Jyukikai Kogyo" [Tosha no Shizai senryaku to sono Tenkai ni tsuite]. *Management Practice [Keiei Jitsumu]* no. 442 (February 1991), pp. 10–19.

Suzuki, Nagao. "VE Activity to Manufacture a Value Product" [Kachi-aru Seihin Zukuri o Mezasu VE katsudo]. *Management Practice [Keiei Jitsumu]* no. 426 (October 1989), pp. 34–46.

Suzuki, Teruo. "A Suggestion for Strategic Cost Management System—Basic Concepts of ICM System and Key Performance Indicators." *Management Practice [Keiei Jitsumu]* no. 415 (November 1988), pp. 39–57.

Takubo, Takayuki. "Cost Engineering Activities in the Development of a Home Appliances" [Kaden seihin kaihatsu ni okeru Cost Engineering katsudo]. *IE Review* 32, no. 2 (May 1991), pp. 13–18.

Tanaka, Masayasu. "Cost Control in the Development and Design Stage of a Product—(1) Its Concepts and Detailed Implementation" [Seihin no Kaihatsu Sekkei Dankai ni okeru Genka Kanri—Sono Kangae Kata to Gutaitekina Susume Kata]. *Management Practice [Keiei Jitsumu]* no. 409 (May 1988), pp. 26–37.

Tanaka, Masayasu. "Cost Control in the Development and Design Stage of a Product—(2) Its Concepts and Detailed Implementation" [Seihin no Kaihatsu Sekkei Dankai ni okeru Genka Kanri—Sono Kangae Kata to Gutaitekina Susume Kata]. *Management Practice [Keiei Jitsumu]* no. 410 (June 1988), pp. 34–51.

Tanaka, Masayasu. "Cost Control in the Development and Design Stage of a Product—(3) Concept of Target Cost and The Way of Setting It" [Seihin no Kaihatsu Sekkei Dankai ni okeru Genka Kanri—Genka mokuhyo no Honshitsu to Sono Settei hoho]. *Management Practice [Keiei Jitsumu]* no. 411 (July 1988), pp. 34–51.

Tanaka, Masayasu. "Cost Control in the Development and Design Stage of a Product(4)"— Methods For Decomposing Target Costs"[Seihin no Kaihatsu sekkei dankai ni okeru Genka kanri]. *Management Practice [Keiei Jitsumu]* no. 414 (October 1988), pp. 37–51.

Tanaka, Masayasu. "Cost Control in the Development and Design Stage of a Product—(5) Development and Application of New Cost Control System" [Seihin no Kaihatsu Sekkei Dankai ni okeru Genka Kanri—Shin Genkakanri System no Tenkai to Tekiyo]. *Management Practice [Keiei Jitsumu]* no. 415 (November 1988), pp. 21–37.

Tanaka, Masayasu. "Cost Control in the Development and Design Stage of a Product—6) Concepts and Methodology of Cost Estimation(1)" [Seihin no Kaihatsu Sekkei Dankai ni okeru Genka Kanri—Genkamitsumori no Kangaekata to Sono Hoho (1)]. *Management Practice [Keiei Jitsumu]* no. 417 (January 1989), pp. 26–44.

Tanaka, Masayasu. "Cost Control in the Development and Design Stage of a Product—(7) Concepts and Methodology of Cost Estimation (2)" [Seihin no Kaihatsu Sekkei Dankai ni okeru Genka Kanri—Genkamitsumori no Kangaekata to Sono Hoho (2)]. *Management Practice [Keiei Jitsumu]* no. 421 (May 1989), pp. 17–31.

Tanaka, Masayasu. "Cost Control in the Development and Design Stage of a Product—(8) Strategy to Achieve a Target Cost (2)" [Seihin no Kaihatsu Sekkei Dankai ni okeru Genka Kanri—Genka Mokuhyo no Tassei Hoho (2)]. *Management Practice [Keiei Jitsumu]* no. 423 (July 1989), pp. 42–58.

Tanaka, Masayasu. "Cost Control in the Development and Design Stage of a Product—(9) Japan's Current Situation and Issues" [Seihin no Kaihatsu Sekkei Dankai ni okeru Genka Kanri—Nippon no Genjyo to Kadai]. *Management Practice [Keiei Jitsumu]* no. 425 (September 1989), pp. 31–37.

Tanaka, Masayasu. "Cost Control in the Development and Design Stage of a Product —(10) Conditions and Issues For Successful Target Costing" [Seihin no Kaihatsu Dankai ni okeru Genka Kanri—Seiko saseru Tame no Jyoken to Kadai]., *Management Practice [Keiei Jitsumu]* no. 428 (December 1989), pp. 31–44.

Tanaka, Masayasu. "Cost Engineering Deployment in Product Development." *Corporate Accounting [Kigyo Kaikei]* 39, no. 2 (1987), pp. 21–30.

Tanaka, Masayasu. "Cost Estimations by 'Product' and 'Function'—A Report on Cost Estimation Reflected by Design Specifications" ['Mono' no Genkamitsumori to 'Kino-level' no Genkamitsumori to 'Kino-level' no Genka Mitsumori]. *Cost Accounting,* special issue no. 24, no. 288 (1988), pp. 41–72.

Tanake, Masayasu. "Cost Estimation System in the Computer Integrated Manufacturing" [CIM jifai no mitsumori genka keisan system]. *Accounting [Kaikei]*. 139, no. 2 (February 1991), pp. 202–22.

Tanaka, Masayasu. "Current Situation and Issues of Target Cost Management" [Genkakikaku no Genjyo to Kadai]. *JICPA Journal* no. 440 (March 1992), pp. 53–60.

Tanaka, Masayasu. "Developments of Cost Engineering in Japan—Based on Results of a Survey of Cost Engineering for a Product" [Nippon ni okeru Cost Engineering—Seihin ni Kansuru Cost Engineering no Jittai o Fumaete]. *Cost Accounting [Genka Keisan],* special issue no. 18, no. 278 (1987), pp. 37–66.

Tanaka, Masayasu. "Development from Target Cost Management to Profit Engineering" [Genkakikaku kara Riekikikaku eno Hatten]. *Management Practice [Keiei Jitsumu].* no. 439 (November 1990), pp. 36–39.

Tanaka, Masayasu. "Fundamentals and Use of Cost Tables" [Cost Table no Honshitsu to Katsuyo]. *Cost Accounting [Genka Keisan],* special issue no. 20, no. 281 (1986), pp. 35–53.

Tanaka, Masayasu. "How to Estimate a Product's Cost in the Development and Design Stage" [Seihin no Kaihatsu Sekkei Dankai ni okeru Genkamitsumori no Hoho]. *Cost Accounting [Genka Keisan],* special issue no. 22, no. 285 (1987), pp. 58–88.

Tanaka, Masayasu. "New Product Development and Target Cost Management" [Shin seihin kaihatsu to Genka kikaku]. *Corporate Accounting [Kigyo Kaikei]* 37, no. 2 (1985), pp. 51–58.

Tanaka, Masayasu. "Progress of Target Cost Management and IE" [Genkakikaku no Suishin to IE]. *IE Review* 32, no. 2 (May 1991), pp. 4–12.

Tanaka, Masayasu. "A Recommendation for Profit Engineering— (1) The Concepts and Implementation" [Profit Engineering no Susume (Jyo)—Rieki Sozo Kogaku no Kangae kata to Susume kata]. *Management Practice [Keiei Jitsumu]* no. 398 (June 1987), pp. 19–34.

Tanaka, Masayasu. "A Recommendation for Profit Engineering—(2) The Concepts and Implementation" [Profit Engineering no Susume (Ge)—Rieki Sozo Kogaku no Kangae kata to susume kata]., *Management Practice [Keiei Jitsumu]* no. 404 (December 1987), pp. 36–54.

Tani, T.; N. Shimizu; Y. Iwabuchi; and J. Fukuda. "Reciprocal Actions of Project Meetings for Target Costing" [Genkakikaku to Kaigitai deno Sogo sayo]. *Accouting [Kaikei]* 144, no. 3 (September 1993), pp. 380–92.

Teshima, Naoaki. "Cost Control in the Development Stage of a Product—Application of VE" [Seihin Kaihatsu no Cost Kanri—Kaihatsu Dankai e no VE Tekiyo]. *IE Review* 32, no. 2 (May 1991), pp. 42–51.

Teshima, Naoaki. "A Suggestion for Target Cost Management—Application of VE Method in the Development Stage of a Product" [Genka kikaku ni kansuru Ichi teigen—Seihin kaihatsu dankai e no VE Shuho no Tekiyo]. *Corporate Accounting [Kigyo Kaikei]* 44, no. 8 (1992), pp. 55–62.

Yagi, Kimitoshi. "Deployment of Resource Efficiency Activities at Fuji Denki Corporation" [Tosha ni okeru Shizai gorika katsudo no Tenkai]. *Management Practice [Keiei Jitsumu]* no. 442 (February 1991), pp. 1–19.

Yamamoto, Koji. "Activities Based Costing as Indirect Costs Control" [Kansetushi no Genda kikaku to shite no ABC]. *Economy Study [Keizai Kenkyo]* 39, no. 1 (December 1993), pp. 41–67.

Yoshikawa, Yutaka. "Cost Improvement Activities and Purchasing Strategies at Zexel" [Tosha no Genka kaizen katsudo to Kobai Senryaku]. *Management Practice [Keiei Jitsumu] no. 442 (February 1991), pp. 37–47.*

INDEX